Web Channel Develo[...] For Dummies®

D0985305

What is a web channel?

Just in case you need some good webcasting reference material before you head out to that cocktail party. Here are the major characteristics of all web channels, no matter what platform they happen to be:

- ✔ With web channels, content gets pushed to you from the Internet — instead of you having to go out and continually pull it from the Internet.

- ✔ You subscribe to web channels, the same way you subscribe to a magazine.

- ✔ With web channels, you get to decide when the channel gets updated. Channel updates can occur even when you're not around!

- ✔ Web channels can be just like web sites, but most web channels use new technologies like Dynamic HTML and JavaScript to create really glitzy front pages.

What is CDF?

CDF stands for the *Channel Definition Format,* a joint web channel standard that has been proposed to the World Wide Web Consortium (W3) by Microsoft and PointCast. CDF is a lot like HTML in that it uses tags to signify key components of a web channel. CDF files are used to control both the look and feel of a web channel, as well as to tell Internet Explorer 4.0 and PointCast when to update channel content.

CDF tags for creating an Internet Explorer 4.0 channel

The following table gives you the basic tag syntax needed to create a CDF file, in order to create an Internet Explorer 4.0 web channel:

CDF Tag	What It Means
`<?XML version="1.0"?>`	Sets XML as the language that the Explorer is reading in the CDF file
`<CHANNEL>...</CHANNEL>`	Defines the channel object
`<ABSTRACT>...</ABSTRACT>`	Tells subscribers what the channel or a channel item is all about
`<SCHEDULE>...</SCHEDULE>`	Sets the default schedule times for updating a channel
`<LOGO../>`	Specifies the logos and icons used in the Microsoft Active Channel Guide, as well as within Internet Explorer 4.0
`<ITEM>...</ITEM>`	Specifies a part of the channel that shows up in the Explorer Active Channel Menu.
`<TITLE>...</TITLE>`	Describes the name of a channel item.

...For Dummies: #1 Computer Book Series for Beginners

Web Channel Development For Dummies®

Cheat Sheet

JavaScript for creating Netscaster channels

You think making a Netcaster channel is tough? No way! The following JavaScript commands are used to specify a Netcaster web channel:

JavaScript	What It Does
nc.activate	Activates Netcaster
import nc.getChannelObject	Tells the browser to get all Netcaster channel information
import nc.addChannel	Tells Netcaster to get ready to add a channel
channel = getChannelObject()	Channel parameters can be found with anything that has the word channel in front of it, and is seperated by parentheses or a period
channel.url	Specifies the channel front page
channel.name	Sets the name of the channel
channel.desc	A brief description of the channel
channel.intervalTime	How often the channel is updated
channel.absoluteTime	The default update time of the channel
channel.estCacheSize	Estimated size of the cache necessary to load the channel
channel.maxCacheSize	The largest cache the channel can have
channel.depth	How many layers deep that should be read when the channel is updated
channel.mode	Specifies whether the channel is a full screen Webtop or runs in a Navigator window

In addition to these commands, you'll also need a link that actives the channel and calls the JavaScript commands just specified. Here's what that link may look like:

```
<A HREF="" onCLick="addMyChannel(); return false;">…</A>
```

...For Dummies: #1 Computer Book Series for Beginners

WEB CHANNEL DEVELOPMENT FOR DUMMIES®

WEB CHANNEL DEVELOPMENT FOR DUMMIES®

by Damon Dean

IDG Books Worldwide, Inc.
An International Data Group Company

Foster City, CA ♦ Chicago, IL ♦ Indianapolis, IN ♦ Southlake, TX

Web Channel Development For Dummies®

Published by
IDG Books Worldwide, Inc.
An International Data Group Company
919 E. Hillsdale Blvd.
Suite 400
Foster City, CA 94404
www.idgbooks.com (IDG Books Worldwide Web site)
www.dummies.com (Dummies Press Web site)

Library of Congress Catalog Card No.: 97-80867

ISBN: 0-7645-0309-X

Printed in the United States of America

10 9 8 7 6 5 4 3 2 1

1DD/RQ/RS/ZX/IN

Distributed in the United States by IDG Books Worldwide, Inc.

Distributed by Macmillan Canada for Canada; by Transworld Publishers Limited in the United Kingdom; by IDG Norge Books for Norway; by IDG Sweden Books for Sweden; by Woodslane Pty. Ltd. for Australia; by Woodslane Enterprises Ltd. for New Zealand; by Longman Singapore Publishers Ltd. for Singapore, Malaysia, Thailand, and Indonesia; by Simron Pty. Ltd. for South Africa; by Toppan Company Ltd. for Japan; by Distribuidora Cuspide for Argentina; by Livraria Cultura for Brazil; by Ediciencia S.A. for Ecuador; by Addison-Wesley Publishing Company for Korea; by Ediciones ZETA S.C.R. Ltda. for Peru; by WS Computer Publishing Corporation, Inc., for the Philippines; by Unalis Corporation for Taiwan; by Contemporanea de Ediciones for Venezuela; by Computer Book & Magazine Store for Puerto Rico; by Express Computer Distributors for the Caribbean and West Indies. Authorized Sales Agent: Anthony Rudkin Associates for the Middle East and North Africa.

For general information on IDG Books Worldwide's books in the U.S., please call our Consumer Customer Service department at 800-762-2974. For reseller information, including discounts and premium sales, please call our Reseller Customer Service department at 800-434-3422.

For information on where to purchase IDG Books Worldwide's books outside the U.S., please contact our International Sales department at 415-655-3200 or fax 415-655-3295.

For information on foreign language translations, please contact our Foreign & Subsidiary Rights department at 415-655-3021 or fax 415-655-3281.

For sales inquiries and special prices for bulk quantities, please contact our Sales department at 415-655-3200 or write to the address above.

For information on using IDG Books Worldwide's books in the classroom or for ordering examination copies, please contact our Educational Sales department at 800-434-2086 or fax 817-251-8174.

For press review copies, author interviews, or other publicity information, please contact our Public Relations department at 415-655-3000 or fax 415-655-3299.

For authorization to photocopy items for corporate, personal, or educational use, please contact Copyright Clearance Center, 222 Rosewood Drive, Danvers, MA 01923, or fax 508-750-4470.

is a trademark under exclusive license to IDG Books Worldwide, Inc., from International Data Group, Inc.

About the Author

Damon Dean

I'm just a regular guy who loves to write and who loves technology. This is my second book, and my first ...*For Dummies* book. Hopefully, I lived up to the reputation. During the day, I get paid to make games for a living. Life is good. By night, I write. I do what I love, and people pay me for it.

And yes, I do happen to believe that web channels are the wave of the future. You heard it here . . . though probably not first.

ABOUT IDG BOOKS WORLDWIDE

Welcome to the world of IDG Books Worldwide.

IDG Books Worldwide, Inc., is a subsidiary of International Data Group, the world's largest publisher of computer-related information and the leading global provider of information services on information technology. IDG was founded more than 25 years ago and now employs more than 8,500 people worldwide. IDG publishes more than 275 computer publications in over 75 countries (see listing below). More than 60 million people read one or more IDG publications each month.

Launched in 1990, IDG Books Worldwide is today the #1 publisher of best-selling computer books in the United States. We are proud to have received eight awards from the Computer Press Association in recognition of editorial excellence and three from *Computer Currents'* First Annual Readers' Choice Awards. Our best-selling *...For Dummies®* series has more than 30 million copies in print with translations in 30 languages. IDG Books Worldwide, through a joint venture with IDG's Hi-Tech Beijing, became the first U.S. publisher to publish a computer book in the People's Republic of China. In record time, IDG Books Worldwide has become the first choice for millions of readers around the world who want to learn how to better manage their businesses.

Our mission is simple: Every one of our books is designed to bring extra value and skill-building instructions to the reader. Our books are written by experts who understand and care about our readers. The knowledge base of our editorial staff comes from years of experience in publishing, education, and journalism — experience we use to produce books for the '90s. In short, we care about books, so we attract the best people. We devote special attention to details such as audience, interior design, use of icons, and illustrations. And because we use an efficient process of authoring, editing, and desktop publishing our books electronically, we can spend more time ensuring superior content and spend less time on the technicalities of making books.

You can count on our commitment to deliver high-quality books at competitive prices on topics you want to read about. At IDG Books Worldwide, we continue in the IDG tradition of delivering quality for more than 25 years. You'll find no better book on a subject than one from IDG Books Worldwide.

John Kilcullen
CEO
IDG Books Worldwide, Inc.

Steven Berkowitz
President and Publisher
IDG Books Worldwide, Inc.

Eighth Annual Computer Press Awards ≥1992

Ninth Annual Computer Press Awards ≥1993

Tenth Annual Computer Press Awards ≥1994

Eleventh Annual Computer Press Awards ≥1995

IDG Books Worldwide, Inc., is a subsidiary of International Data Group, the world's largest publisher of computer-related information and the leading global provider of information services on information technology. International Data Group publishes over 275 computer publications in over 75 countries. Sixty million people read one or more International Data Group publications each month. International Data Group's publications include: **ARGENTINA:** Buyer's Guide, Computerworld Argentina, PC World Argentina; **AUSTRALIA:** Australian Macworld, Australian PC World, Australian Reseller News, Computerworld, IT Casebook, Network World, Publish, Webmaster; **AUSTRIA:** Computerwelt Osterreich, Networks Austria, PC Tip Austria; **BANGLADESH:** PC World Bangladesh; **BELARUS:** PC World Belarus; **BELGIUM:** Data News; **BRAZIL:** Annuário de Informática, Computerworld, Connections, Macworld, PC Player, PC World, Publish, Reseller News, Supergamepower; **BULGARIA:** Computerworld Bulgaria, Network World Bulgaria, PC & MacWorld Bulgaria; **CANADA:** CIO Canada, Client/Server World, ComputerWorld Canada, InfoWorld Canada, NetworkWorld Canada, WebWorld; **CHILE:** Computerworld Chile, PC World Chile; **COLOMBIA:** Computerworld Colombia, PC World Colombia; **COSTA RICA:** PC World Centro America; **THE CZECH AND SLOVAK REPUBLICS:** Computerworld Czechoslovakia, Macworld Czech Republic, PC World Czechoslovakia; **DENMARK:** Communications World Danmark, Computerworld Danmark, Macworld Danmark, PC World Danmark, Techworld Denmark; **DOMINICAN REPUBLIC:** PC World Republica Dominicana; **ECUADOR:** PC World Ecuador; **EGYPT:** Computerworld Middle East, PC World Middle East; **EL SALVADOR:** PC World Centro America; **FINLAND:** MikroPC, Tietoverkko, Tietoviikko; **FRANCE:** Distributique, Hebdo, Info PC, Le Monde Informatique, Macworld, Reseaux & Telecoms, WebMaster France; **GERMANY:** Computer Partner, Computerwoche, Computerwoche Extra, Computerwoche FOCUS, Global Online, Macwelt, PC Welt; **GREECE:** Amiga Computing, GamePro Greece, Multimedia World; **GUATEMALA:** PC World Centro America; **HONDURAS:** PC World Centro America; **HONG KONG:** Computerworld Hong Kong, PC World Hong Kong, Publish in Asia; **HUNGARY:** ABCD CD-ROM, Computerworld Szamitastechnika, Internetto online Magazine, PC World Hungary, PC-X Magazin Hungary; **ICELAND:** Tolvuheimur PC World Island; **INDIA:** Information Communications World, Information Systems Computerworld, PC World India, Publish in Asia; **INDONESIA:** InfoKomputer PC World, Komputek Computerworld, Publish in Asia; **IRELAND:** ComputerScope, PC Live!; **ISRAEL:** Macworld Israel, People & Computers/Computerworld; **ITALY:** Computerworld Italia, Macworld Italia, Networking Italia, PC World Italia; **JAPAN:** DTP World, Macworld Japan, Nikkei Personal Computing, OS/2 World Japan, SunWorld Japan, Windows NT World, Windows World Japan; **KENYA:** PC World East African; **KOREA:** Hi-Tech Information, Macworld Korea, PC World Korea; **MACEDONIA:** PC World Macedonia; **MALAYSIA:** Computerworld Malaysia, PC World Malaysia, Publish in Asia; **MALTA:** PC World Malta; **MEXICO:** Computerworld Mexico, PC World Mexico; **MYANMAR:** PC World Myanmar; **NETHERLANDS:** Computer! Totaal, LAN Internetworking Magazine, LAN World Buyers Guide, Macworld Netherlands, Net, WebWereld; **NEW ZEALAND:** Absolute Beginners Guide and Plain & Simple Series, Computer Buyer, Computer Industry Directory, Computerworld New Zealand, MTB, Network World, PC World New Zealand; **NICARAGUA:** PC World Centro America; **NORWAY:** Computerworld Norge, CW Rapport, Datamagasinet, Financial Rapport, Kursguide Norge, Macworld Norge, Multimediaworld Norge, PC World Ekspress Norge, PC World Nettverk, PC World Norge, PC World ProduktGuide Norge; **PAKISTAN:** Computerworld Pakistan; **PANAMA:** PC World Panama; **PEOPLE'S REPUBLIC OF CHINA:** China Computer Users, China Computerworld, China InfoWorld, China Telecom World Weekly, Computer & Communication, Electronic Design China, Electronics Today, Electronics Weekly, Game Software, PC World China, Popular Computer Week, Software Weekly, Software World, Telecom World; **PERU:** Computerworld Peru, PC World Profesional Peru, PC World SoHo Peru; **PHILIPPINES:** Click!, Computerworld Philippines, PC World Philippines, Publish in Asia; **POLAND:** Computerworld Poland, Computerworld Special Report Poland, Cyber, Macworld Poland, Networld Poland, PC World Komputer; **PORTUGAL:** Cerebro/PC World, Computerworld/Correio Informático, Dealer World Portugal, Mac*In/PC*In Portugal, Multimedia World; **PUERTO RICO:** PC World Puerto Rico; **ROMANIA:** Computerworld Romania, PC World Romania, Telecom Romania; **RUSSIA:** Computerworld Russia, Mir PK, Publish, Seti; **SINGAPORE:** Computerworld Singapore, PC World Singapore, Publish in Asia; **SLOVENIA:** Monitor; **SOUTH AFRICA:** Computing SA, Network World SA, Software World SA; **SPAIN:** Communicaciones World España, Computerworld España, Dealer World España, Macworld España, PC World España; **SRI LANKA:** Infolink PC World; **SWEDEN:** CAP&Design, Computer Sweden, Corporate Computing Sweden, Internetworld Sweden, it.branschen, Macworld Sweden, MaxiData Sweden, MikroDatorn, Natverk & Kommunikation, PC World Sweden, PCaktiv, Windows World Sweden; **SWITZERLAND:** Computerworld Schweiz, Macworld Schweiz, PCtip; **TAIWAN:** Computerworld Taiwan, Macworld Taiwan, NEW ViSiON/Publish, PC World Taiwan, Windows World Taiwan; **THAILAND:** Publish in Asia, Thai Computerworld; **TURKEY:** Computerworld Turkiye, Macworld Turkiye, Network World Turkiye, PC World Turkiye; **UKRAINE:** Computerworld Kiev, Multimedia World Ukraine, PC World Ukraine; **UNITED KINGDOM:** Acorn User UK, Amiga Action UK, Amiga Computing UK, Apple Talk UK, Computing, Macworld, Parents and Computers UK, PC Advisor, PC Home, PSX Pro, The WEB; **UNITED STATES:** Cable in the Classroom, CIO Magazine, Computerworld, DOS World, Federal Computer Week, GamePro Magazine, InfoWorld, I-Way, Macworld, Network World, PC Games, PC World, Publish, Video Event, THE WEB Magazine, and WebMaster; online webzines: JavaWorld, NetscapeWorld, and SunWorld Online; **URUGUAY:** InfoWorld Uruguay; **VENEZUELA:** Computerworld Venezuela, PC World Venezuela; and **VIETNAM:** PC World Vietnam. 3/24/97

Dedication

For my parents. The first time, it was purely out of love. This time, it's because they let me crash at home for a few months while I wrote this book and didn't even ask me once for a rent check.

Author's Acknowledgments

No man is an island. There's no "I" in team. If you're not part of the solution, then you're part of the problem. The clichés go on and on and on. The bottom line is that a book is not the work of one person, but the result of endless work by many people. First and foremost, my heart-felt thanks go out to Bill Helling, my editor, whose quiet and soft-spoken demeanor never ceased to scare me into submitting chapters. Thanks also to Peter Bitar, Paul Kuzmic, and everyone else at IDG Books who made this book happen and supported me when it looked like I was going to be late. Oh, wait. I was late.

I'd also like to thank my family, in particular, my parents, who let me stay at home once again when my landlord decided to sell the apartment I was living in. Thanks to everyone at PostLinear Entertainment, who graciously let me finish this book while I was also trying to finish and ship my first software product. Finally, thanks to all my friends who I haven't seen and who cursed me when I fell off the face of the Earth for three months to write this book.

Publisher's Acknowledgments

We're proud of this book; please register your comments through our IDG Books Worldwide Online Registration Form located at http://my2cents.dummies.com.

Some of the people who helped bring this book to market include the following:

Acquisitions, Development, and Editorial

Project Editor: Bill Helling

Acquisitions Editor: Pete Bitar

Media Development Manager: Joyce Pepple

Associate Permissions Editor: Heather H. Dismore

Copy Editor: William A. Barton

Technical Editor: Jamey Marcum

Editorial Manager: Elaine Brush

Editorial Assistant: Paul E. Kuzmic

Production

Project Coordinator: E. Shawn Aylsworth

Layout and Graphics: Steve Arany, Cameron Booker, Lou Boudreau, M. Anne Sipahimalani, Michael A. Sullivan

Proofreaders: Kelli Botta, Michelle Croninger, Joel K. Draper, Rebecca Senninger, Robert Springer, Janet M. Withers

Indexer: Infodex Indexing Services, Inc.

Special Help

Joell Smith, Associate Technical Editor

General and Administrative

IDG Books Worldwide, Inc.: John Kilcullen, CEO; Steven Berkowitz, President and Publisher

IDG Books Technology Publishing: Brenda McLaughlin, Senior Vice President and Group Publisher

Dummies Technology Press and Dummies Editorial: Diane Graves Steele, Vice President and Associate Publisher; Mary Bednarek, Acquisitions and Product Development Director; Kristin A. Cocks, Editorial Director

Dummies Trade Press: Kathleen A. Welton, Vice President and Publisher; Kevin Thornton, Acquisitions Manager

IDG Books Production for Dummies Press: Beth Jenkins, Production Director; Cindy L. Phipps, Manager of Project Coordination, Production Proofreading, and Indexing; Kathie S. Schutte, Supervisor of Page Layout; Shelley Lea, Supervisor of Graphics and Design; Debbie J. Gates, Production Systems Specialist; Robert Springer, Supervisor of Proofreading; Debbie Stailey, Special Projects Coordinator; Tony Augsburger, Supervisor of Reprints and Bluelines; Leslie Popplewell, Media Archive Coordinator

Dummies Packaging and Book Design: Patti Crane, Packaging Specialist; Lance Kayser, Packaging Assistant; Kavish + Kavish, Cover Design

◆

The publisher would like to give special thanks to Patrick J. McGovern, without whom this book would not have been possible.

◆

Contents at a Glance

Cartoons at a Glance

By Rich Tennant

page 131

"HOLD YOUR HORSES. IT TAKES TIME TO BUILD A WEB CHANNEL FOR SOMEONE YOUR SIZE."

page 295

page 193

"HOW'S THAT FOR PUSH TECHNOLOGY?"

page 7

"QUICK KIDS! YOUR MOTHER'S EMBEDDING JAVA APPLETS IN HTML."

page 221

"WHAT CONCERNS ME ABOUT WEB CHANNELS IS THAT THEY ALL APPEAR TO BE CHANNELING THROUGH BRENT'S BEDROOM."

page 57

Fax: 508-546-7747 • E-mail: the5wave@tiac.net

Table of Contents

Chapter 6: Making Connections with The PointCast Business Network 101

Chapter 7: Other Cool Things to Do with Channel Definition Format (CDF) 117

Introduction

· ·

From the cockpit, I'd like to welcome you to the friendly pages of *Web Channel Development For Dummies!* My name's Damon, and I'll be your Captain today. We've reached our cruising altitude of approximately four feet above the ground. Our estimated flight time to Web Channel Nirvana is approximately 400 pages. There's a slight tail wind, so we may just get there a bit ahead of schedule.

The weather up here at the front of the books is fantastic, and we're expecting clear skies all the way to the Appendixes today. I've switched off the *fasten seat belt* sign. At this time, you're free to maneuver throughout the book, but as a precaution we ask that when you are engaged in a chapter to please keep your Internet Tools fastened. Pockets of unpleasant circumstances and the occasional standards conflict are common on the way to Web Channel Nirvana.

As always, we realize you have a choice in book publishers, and we'd like thank you for your patronage.

About This Book

And now, a word from our sponsor.

"Hi, I'm Fred, the sponsor of *Web Channel Development For Dummies.* Damon asked me to take a few moments to explain this book in television terms, because that's what web channels are really all about — making the Web seem more like television.

"If you read this book start to finish, you'll find everything you need to know about getting your first web channel up and running. But, come on, who watches the same channel for three hours straight? No one! Unless, of course, you count PBS subscribers. So feel free to channel surf here in *Web Channel Development For Dummies.* If you get lost, that's no problem. Just consult your TV Guide . . . er . . . Index to look up whatever seems appealing to you.

"There's even a glossary to help you out with definitions of key terms in web channel development. Think of it as the Prevue Channel — with definitions.

Let me bottom line it for you. This book is utterly hip and will be massively appealing across demographics. You've got your Internet Explorer Active Channel types covered. Netcaster channels — they're in there. PointCast, you bet it's covered! Personally, I loved the Marimba scene with the Castanet Channels. Now that was steamy."

Uh . . . thanks Fred. I'll get that script to you next week.

How This Book Is Organized

Say, just for argument's sake, that you decide to read this book from front to back. If you were to read the book that way, you'd read the parts in the following order. Nevertheless, you don't have to read the book that way. It's entirely up to you! We're flexible! But, no matter how you decide to read the book, the information in each of the parts can stand on its own, and it'll look something like this.

Part I: An Introduction to Webcasting

Seems like a good place to start? Get the lowdown on all the different types of webcasting, along with profiles of the players that make up the web-channel landscape. If you've never heard of webcasting or web channels, this is the place to get a first class primer on the topic.

Part II: Webcasting the Microsoft Way

Microsoft is a player in everything they touch, and web channels are no exception. In this part, you find out everything you ever wanted to know about building channels for the Microsoft Internet Explorer 4.0, and their web-channel standard, the Channel Definition Format (CDF). The PointCast Business Network, which also uses CDF, is covered in this part as well.

Part III: Webcasting the Netscape Way

Microsoft and Netscape have become bitter rivals on the web-channel front. As a result, Netscape has developed their own standards for web-channel development, not to mention their own web-channel viewer: Netcaster. In this part, discover how to build channels for Netcaster, as well as for Marimba Castanet, which is supported within Netcaster.

Part IV: Maintaining and Upgrading Your Channel

After you go through all the work to create a channel, you want to make sure that people come back again and again. Consider this part to be your handy guide to figuring out when it's time to change the channel. Whether it's a little spring cleaning or a full-fledged upgrade, this part covers all the components of keeping your channel running in tip-top shape.

Part V: The Part of Tens

I like David Letterman just as much as every other ...*For Dummies* author, so I, too, have included a series of top ten lists. Actually, it's required, but shhhh! You didn't hear it from me. Here you get — among other things — the top ten web channels, ten great JavaScript tricks, and ten development mistakes you should never make!

Part VI: Appendixes

In this part, you can find a handy glossary as well as contact information on web-channel companies. I even have an appendix on everything that you need to know about the CD-ROM included with this book.

Stuff You Don't Need to Read

Ack! Stuff you don't need to read? That's blasphemy — isn't it? Well, not really. The book is organized according to technology and topic. If you already know that you want to develop web channels only for Netcaster, by all means, skip the Microsoft stuff. I won't hold it against you.

This book is completely modular, meaning each of the sections is pretty well self-contained. If you already know about Netcaster, but don't know diddly about the CDF format, go there and read that section. I promise I won't tell if you won't!

Icons Used in This Book

On our chartered course to Web Channel Nirvana, you'll find some of the following icons pop up along the way. You may want to stop and smell the roses when you see one. Generally, these icons represent the really important tidbits that I want you to know about. So, if you've already learned to trust me, check them out. They're defined as follows:

Yes! A quick way through the woods. When you see this icon, it means you may not need to read what's about to follow. If you've got a good idea of what's going on, skip to where I tell you to go and you save yourself some time.

Even if you ignore everything I say in this book, when you see this icon, stop and take notice. This is where all the really good stuff ends up! Here, I show you how to save time and energy by navigating you around the tricky stuff.

Things that make you go hmmm . . . like road signs along the way that provide interesting bits of information that may, or may not, save you some time in the long run.

Danger, Will Robinson! Danger! Sometimes the road often traveled can be, well, pretty darn bumpy. Just ask New Yorkers. When you see this icon, trouble may be ahead, so take a good look for instructions on navigating around potential disaster.

I'm a big fan of technology, and every now and then, I just can't help myself. If you too are a technophile, look out for this icon. We'll share some good quality geek moments.

If a product that is covered in the book is on the CD-ROM, it's denoted with this icon.

About the CD-ROM

Speaking of the CD-ROM, this book has one, which means, yep, you guessed it: Goodies! On the CD-ROM are several programs that can help you create your first web channel, including HTML editors, graphics tools, and even Internet Explorer 4.0. To use the CD-ROM that comes with this book, you need the following:

- A PC or a Macintosh with a CD-ROM drive.
- A sound card — after all, sound editing tools are on this disk. For the Mac fans, sound support is built in, so you don't need to worry about it.
- At least 8MB of RAM (preferably 16MB, but 8MB will do) and at least a 486/66 processor. For Mac users, that translates to any Power PC processor.

See Appendix C for all the details on the CD's contents and how to start using them.

Where to Go from Here

Are you still here? Well, stop reading here, and get to it. People are waiting to see your content pushed to their desktop. What's that? What does push mean? Now I know for sure. It's time to turn the page and open up a new world. The world of webcasting — ahhhhhh!!!!

Part I
An Introduction to Webcasting

The 5th Wave   By Rich Tennant

"HOW'S THAT FOR PUSH TECHNOLOGY?"

In this part . . .

People often say that you must crawl before you can walk. Frankly, I think it's a conspiracy. But I'm not "the man," so I just play by the rules. What was I talking about? Oh, yeah, *webcasting*. A lot of definitions are circulating about web channels and webcasting. I don't know about you, but I was totally confused the first time I tried to define webcasting. That was before I decided to write a book on the topic (in case you were curious).

This first part I designed as a primer on webcasting. If what you really want is for someone to tell you what the heck webcasting is, this part is the place for you. If you're already an expert and just want to get my take on webcasting, this part is also a good place to start. This part covers the basic definitions of web channels, the different kinds of web channels out there, the tools necessary to create a web channel, and the fundamentals of designing your first web channel. It's good times, so read on!

Chapter 1

The Wild, Wild World
of Webcasting

● ●

● ●

*A*s a public service, I thought I'd get the hype out the way first. So, just for a second, imagine that lots of beautiful people are scampering around, raising their drinks around their computers, wearing next to nothing, playing Frisbee with a Golden Retriever. Try to picture the guy who does the Visa commercials reading the following text:

Web browsing is for wimps. Why browse if you can have the Internet come to you? Forget loading pages. Forget waiting for a decent connection speed. Forget all the things you hate about the Internet.

After you hit the computer in the morning, you get the news, the sports, and the stocks right alongside of your cereal. You find out what new CDs are to be released that day and why al dente is better than alfresco. And by the time you're off to work, you're tellin' all your friends on the subway the difference between a Manhattan and a Rob Roy!

The technology's called webcasting, *and it's the newest thing on the Net. Webcasting is the give-me-what-I-want-and-get-out-of-my-way version of the Internet. That's why they also call it* push technology. *It's the Internet . . . but with a New York state of mind. So grab your web viewer and get ready to push, because webcasting is here to stay, and it doesn't take to pulling anymore.*

Okay, I feel better. Now for the sobering truth: Webcasting can't take ten years off your life, three inches off your waist, or get you that tax refund you've been trying to find. It can't make you a sports hero or a movie star, and, I'm sad to report, it can't make your hair grow back.

Despite all these drawbacks, however, you *can* find some good in webcasting. Webcasting can bring the Internet to you without you so much as touching your PC, which gives you all sorts of chances to say, "Look, Ma — no hands!" Webcasting can provide a new and — dare I say? — efficient way for you to communicate with your customers. If you're nice and whisper gently in its ear, webcasting can provide you with a better way of reaching millions of people on the Internet. And, really, who doesn't need a million new friends?

Webcasting Brings the Internet to You

How is webcasting going to revolutionize the Internet? Who knows? But I *can* tell you that webcasting changes the way that people use the Internet, and that's pretty big news. The main focus of webcasting is to bring content from the Internet to the end-user rather than vice-versa, which is the way the Net works right now.

Developers throw around the word *content* all the time, and the term can mean just about anything. For the purposes of this book, however, I loosely define content as *text, graphics, sound,* and *video,* as well as *applications.*

Well, all right! You may have noticed a big push lately to increase the interactivity and the appeal of web sites. Everybody wants to be *the* "destination site" or "bookmark site" on the Internet. That's because everyone and his mother has a web site. The joke around Silicon Valley is that, inside the city limits, the police ask you to provide proof of a URL along with proof of insurance if they pull you over.

More web sites mean more traffic and more people online. More people online means that the Internet is getting slower and information is getting harder to find. The slower the Internet gets and the harder the information is to find, the more likely people are to just go and do something else. Given all the money that's been invested on the Net infrastructure and on its content, an Internet with no foot traffic is likely to make a lot of venture capitalists more than a little uneasy. So you can understand why the search for new ways of delivering content to users has become such a big deal.

That said, you need to understand that webcasting isn't rocket science. In fact, it's not even science. Webcasting simply begins with the assumption that people would rather have some kinds of information come to them instead of needing to go out on the Web to get it themselves all the time. The philosophy behind this concept is pretty much the same as that behind television — but without all the commercials.

What is webcasting exactly?

Although webcasting sounds like something you'd see on the Fly Fishing Channel ("Watch carefully as Bob webcasts onto the mouth of the river in search of the ever-elusive big-mouthed bass"), it's really all about the process of delivering content directly to your PC, without you ever needing to touch a button.

I know that may sound a lot like hype, but it's true. A not-so-small company (not anymore, at least) named PointCast provides a great example. PointCast developed an ingenious product, the PointCast Business Network, which works as a screen saver on your PC. Whenever you aren't doing anything at your PC, the PointCast Businees Network kicks in and uses the Internet to deliver up-to-the-minute news, sports, and business headlines right to your PC (see Figure 1-1). It's simple, efficient, and requires virtually no effort on the part of the user. Just set it to the PointCast Business Network and wait for the content to come to you. With more than a million users, PointCast has staked its claim as the first bonafide webcasting success story.

A good way to conceptualize webcasting is to think of the whole thing as the Web in reverse. The basics are essentially the same. On your PC, you have a piece of software, which displays content. (Lots of kinds of software are available, and I discuss those later.) On the Internet, a *server* houses the content that it subsequently transfers to your PC on request. So far so good. Instead of using your web browser to go out and search for that content on the Web, however, you subscribe to a *channel,* and then, on a regular basis, the content from that channel downloads to your PC. Your biggest investment is finding the right channels to fit your interests, but you need to find each one only once!

A channel is very loosely defined as content that is delivered to your PC. For a more complete definition, see the section entitled "Can you explain that whole channel thing?", later in this chapter.

Figure 1-1:
The
PointCast
Business
Network
was the
first
practical
example of
webcasting.

Webcasting works because of a technique called *push*. Push simply means that the channel content gets sent from the Internet to your PC, without you specifically needing to request it. You may be wondering just how content is going to magically appear on your desktop, particularly if you didn't do anything! Push happens because you set up a subscription to a channel, indicating when you want the content to come to you. After that subscription is set, all of the big-time negotiation between my computer and the server goes on without me even knowing about it.

What's even better about push is that you don't need to be online to take advantage of it. Most webcasting products enable you to set up your software so that it goes out and gets updates while you're asleep, away from home, or even out to lunch. All that you need is an Internet connection and, of course, to leave the computer turned on.

The "other" definition of webcasting

Webcasting wasn't always about channels, subscriptions, and Internet transmissions while you sleep. Originally, the term *webcasting* referred to a "live" broadcast event that happened at a Web site. With the advent of Java applets, Cool Talk, and Real Audio, delivering constantly updated content to a site became much easier, with sites such as ESPNET.Sportszone and IBM's Olympic sites leading the way.

A very good recent example of this trend is the Gary Kasparov versus Big Blue chess competition. Every day during the competition, IBM broadcast the match, move by move, on one of its Web sites by using a Java applet. The company also provided commentary via live chat. The result was that you could watch the match unfold as it unfolded — not that it was unfolding all that swiftly, of course.

How successful these types of ventures may be in the future remains to be seen. A number of web channel viewers now support Java (and other technologies, as well). So you're likely to see similar types of broadcasts come directly to web channels in the very near future.

A brief word about desire

The concept may seem obvious — so obvious, in fact, that I forgot to put it in here the first time that I wrote this chapter — but the whole idea behind webcasting is to take advantage of people's need to remain constantly informed. The most advanced pagers deliver news headlines and stock quotes directly to you, no matter where you are in the world. Personal communication is a multibillion dollar industry and is based very simply on people's desire to constantly keep informed.

Webcasting is the Internet's version of this desire. The difference is that to broadcast something obscure, such as the latest in spring fashion, over a pager is totally cost prohibitive, not to mention unfocused. But on the Internet, you may have thousands of people who'd gladly pay to have that kind of information sent to them every morning. And if thousands of people want that kind of information, at least a dozen or so companies are going to want to get their message to those people. Most of those people have money, too. Ah, commerce!

Can you explain that whole channel thing?

Web channels are, for the most part, very similar to television channels but with some key differences that are worth exploring. The biggest difference involves signals. TV stations broadcast a signal through a transmitter out to the world. If the signal is strong enough, and I have an antenna, I can receive the signal and see what's on the channel by firing up the old television.

That's not quite how web channels work. A web channel doesn't really use a transmitter, per se. All the channel content sits on another computer on the Internet, called a *server*. When I subscribe to a channel, my computer sends a signal to the server on the Internet telling it to send me the content.

Now here's the tricky part: Rather than send me everything on the server, which would be redundant, the server and my computer carry on a small discussion about what channel content I already have on my computer. After they figure out the differences between what I have and what the server has, they send me all the stuff I don't have, as well as updates to the information I already have on my computer. These differences between TV channel transmission and web channel transmission are shown in Figure 1-2.

This leads to the second big difference between TV channels and web channels, which is their content. Television channels send big, fat video signals that people can just suck right up and enjoy. On the Internet, having that kind of bandwidth is a pipe dream. So, at least for now, most web channel content consists of the same basic materials as Web pages, meaning small graphics, small audio, small applications, and a whole lot of text. On average, you can expect these files to range anywhere from 1K to 1MB in size.

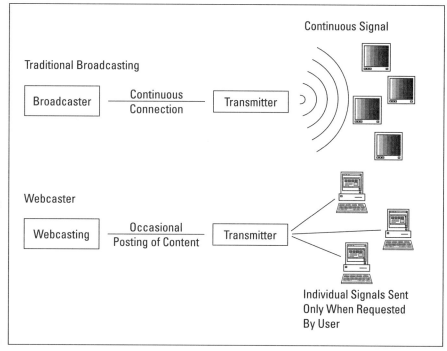

Figure 1-2: Television channels broadcast a continuous signal. Web channels don't.

What's the difference between a really good web site and a web channel?

That's a sensational question! Thanks for keeping me honest. If you were just comparing a basic web site and a simple web channel, the differences would be pretty dramatic. Channels update their content continuously and push that content to the user (as I mention earlier in this chapter in "What is webcasting exactly?"), while on the average web site, content gets updated far less frequently and you must go to the site to get that information.

As you get to the higher end of the web site world, however, considering sites such as ESPNET.Sportszone.com, ABCNews.com, and CNET.com, the differences seem a lot less clear. Take ESPN as an example. Figure 1-3 shows the new Game Log feature at the SportsZone site. Game Log is a feature built into Game Cast — a Java applet that constantly updates the status of a baseball game, right down to each and every pitch. Game Cast updates the site, on average, every 30 or 40 seconds, providing game statistics as well as player profiles. Game Tracker runs on your desktop in its own window, so you can shut down Netscape and Game Cast still keeps the connection to ESPN active.

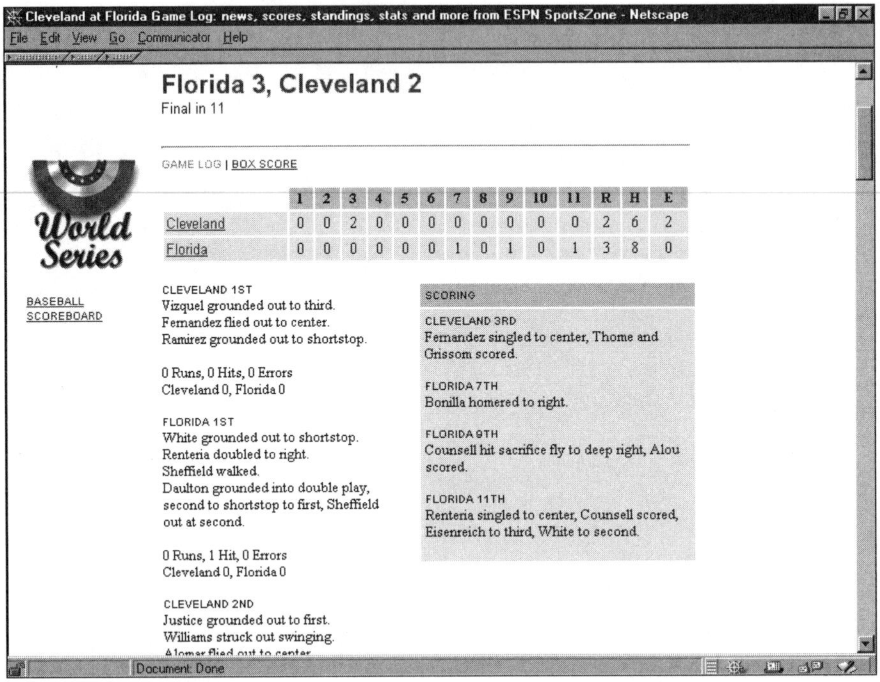

Figure 1-3:
The Game Cast on ESPNET. SportsZone updates itself after every pitch!

If that's not the essence of webcasting, I don't know what is! I still, however, needed to go to the ESPN site, search for the right game, launch the application, and then shut down the other windows after Game Cast was running. If the ESPN Game Cast were a web channel, I'd already have configured it for the game. Activating the web channel would have brought the game up automatically.

Another example that highlights the difference between advanced web sites and web channels is ABCNews.com. ABC news has both a web site and a web channel on the Internet. As Figure 1-4 shows, the physical distinctions between the two are pretty slight. The content on the site and the channel are nearly identical, and both are available through Netscape Communicator.

The primary difference between the two is that, with the web channel, you choose up front how you want the interface to appear. You also get to select how often you want the channel to update. On the site, you don't have these options.

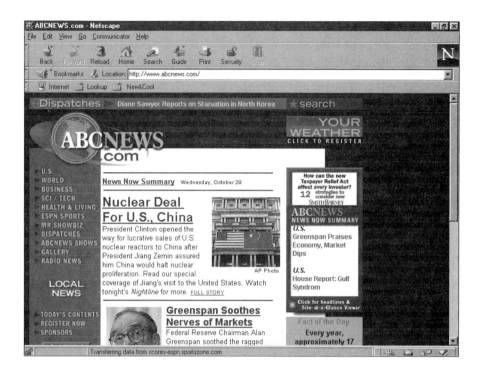

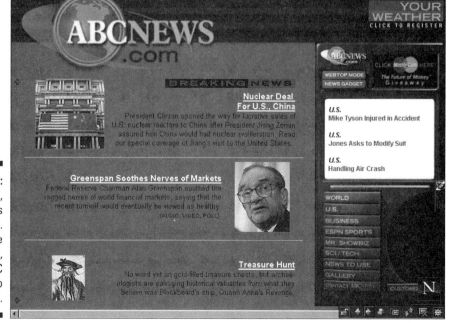

Figure 1-4:
On top,
ABC News
web site.
On the
bottom,
the ABC
news web
channel.

What these examples demonstrate, more than anything, is that webcasting is an evolution of the Web, not a revolution to replace it. The Game Cast is an example of a push technology that's in use at a web site. It's a great piece of technology and better than any number of web channels, but again, the whole idea behind web channels is to eliminate steps and bring you the content you want without you needing to spend time finding it.

Tuning in to Webcasting

Perhaps you've noticed, but I've been euphemistically throwing around the words *desktop, computer,* and *software,* without really touching on what you actually use to view web channels. That's because I'm sneaky. (And also because I wanted to wait until this section to lay everything out on the line.)

Actually, you have quite a few options for viewing web channels — in large part because of the number of formats that currently exist for web channels. That's the part that no one ever tells you about in the hype. There is no such thing as a single, all-encompassing web-channel format. Instead, a number of formats are all vying for market share and for the collective mind share of the Internet user.

Maestro, one more time, for way too much emphasis! There is no one all-encompassing web-channel format. You must choose between the competing formats in developing a web channel.

If you're looking to blame someone, as I was, you're just going to be frustrated, because no one company has dominated this market. Push technology and webcasting caught a lot of people off guard, most notably Netscape and Microsoft. Nobody expected PointCast to do as well as it did, except for maybe the people at PointCast.

Webcasting suffers from what I call the cockroach syndrome. If you've got a room full of cockroaches in the dark, and you turn on the light, they all scurry off in different directions. The development of webcasting was as if someone saw PointCast, yelled "Push!" — and software companies all ran off in different directions to develop webcasting tools.

The result, unfortunately, is that web channels don't share a common standard, leaving you and me with the unenviable task of having to choose among competing standards. This situation involves both good news and bad news. The good news is that, over the past year, webcasting has consolidated down to two basic types of web-channel viewers — those that use a web browser and those that don't. De facto standards are beginning to emerge, with several of the companies that make web channels partnering with either Netscape or Microsoft to support their web-channel viewers in the latest versions of Communicator and Explorer.

Which leads us to the bad news, I'm afraid. Even now, Netscape and Microsoft haven't learned to play nice yet and work with the same standards for the browsers! So developing a web channel for Internet Explorer is different than developing one for Communicator. Make no mistake — as a developer, your biggest challenge is in choosing between these two different standards.

Webcasting without the web browser

Why forget about the web browser entirely? Zillions of people are out there with web browsers, and they're probably not all that interested in trashing them just because some yahoo writing a *...For Dummies* book thinks that doing so is a good idea. Nevertheless, this yahoo thinks that the following list offers some very good reasons to step up and leave the web browser behind:

- **Web browsers can be slower than many web non-browser channel viewers.** Web browsers do a lot of stuff these days. They're e-mail clients, HTML editors, news readers — and I hear that the new Internet Explorer even reminds you to take out the trash on Tuesdays. (*Memo to myself:* Patent that idea before Bill Gates sees this book.) They also employ a lot of new technology, all of which affects the connection time and the burden on your processor.

- **Proprietary web-channel tools are better for big companies.** One of the growing sub-segments of webcasting is in corporate environments. Specifically, many companies are looking to communicate more effectively with their sales staffs and other employees who work off-site. Many of the proprietary web-channel tools are geared towards creating large-scale communications tools for these types of companies.

- **Web-channel viewers are simpler.** Web-channel viewers do only two things: get content and display it. They're designed to get information whenever they're told to, and that's all they really do. Web browsers try to be your one-stop shop for the Internet by throwing in everything but the kitchen sink.

The tools of choice

If webcasting in the face of steep competition from Microsoft and Netscape sounds like a tough sell, that's because it is. Nevertheless, some companies have been successful in this area. Two companies, PointCast and Marimba, stand out above the rest, in part because they've developed great tools but also because they represent the current trend in web-channel development. Both companies are deeply involved with one of the big browser companies in supporting a set of standards for webcasting.

Be sure to check out the PointCast and the Marimba software on the CD! See Appendix C for details.

The aforementioned PointCast has been at this task longer than anyone. With more than a million users, they've got the largest installed base of web-channel viewers around. Their new tool, PointCast Connections, enables you to create a web channel that's accessible through the PointCast Network (see Figure 1-5). Together with Microsoft, they've developed a set of standards known as the *Channel Definition Format,* which can enable you to turn any web page into a web channel.

On the opposite side of the fence is Marimba and its Java-based suite of products. The products include the Castanet Tuner, a web-channel viewer, Bongo (a development tool for the tuner), and the Castanet Transmitter, which manages data going to and from the server. Unlike PointCast, Marimba has partnered with Netscape and made the Castanet Tuner accessible from within Netscape Communicator 4.0.

What's the downside?

Just about everything involves a catch of some type, and these web-channel tools are no different. Like it or not, after you start using these tools, it'll be some time before you finally get used to the development environment. Some of the other webcasting tools that I don't mention in the preceding sections, such as BackWeb and Intermind, use completely different languages to create web-channel content. Before jumping on board one of these tools, you need to weigh the costs associated with the ramp.

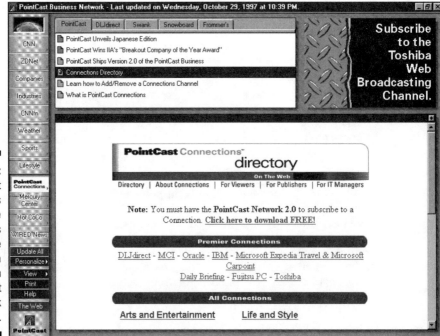

Figure 1-5: PointCast Connections can give you access to more than a million PointCast Network users.

The other thing to consider is the strength of the companies that offer these other tools. The Internet is notorious for its here-today-and-gone-tomorrow companies. Although both Marimba and PointCast are about as solid as such companies come, they're now squarely in the middle of the browser war. And, relatively speaking, their installed bases are low, in comparison to Netscape and Microsoft. Granted, PointCast has been exceptionally successful, and Marimba is getting a lot of mileage out of being in the Netscape corner, but neither company can boast the same kinds of installed base figures as can either of the browsers. For developers of web channels, this fact simply means that you should look at these companies and their products with a very keen eye.

How do the web browsers fit into webcasting?

Not to put too fine a point on things, but the browsers seem to have been caught with their virtual pants down. Just how true this statement is no one really knows, but you get the feeling that neither Netscape nor Microsoft saw webcasting coming. They were just moving along, spending their time and money trying to bury each other with new features in their browsers. and then — whamo! Webcasting came along and clipped them from behind.

I have this feeling not because I think that these companies are slow but because of the ways in which their webcasting strategies have emerged. Usually, big-time advances in web development go past the *World Wide Web Consortium* (or, if you're into shortcut terms, *W3*). The W3 was formed to facilitate the creation and management of standards for the Internet. As such, they've helped to set the standards for HTML, JavaScript, Dynamic HTML, and a host of other web technologies over the past five years. The big boys developed their HTML and Java standards with the blessing of this organization, and concerning webcasting, you'd think the W3 Consortium would have exercised the same kind of oversight. Microsoft, to its credit, has filed a standards paper with the consortium on webcasting but did so only after its release of the feature in the latest version of Internet Explorer.

For more information on the W3 consortium, point your (gasp!) web browser to www.w3.org, the leading web site for information on developing technologies on the Internet. And who knows? The organization may even develop a web channel someday.

Without a formal definition of webcasting from the W3 consortium, Netscape and Microsoft have been left to battle one another for the title of de facto webcasting standard. Neither side has blinked yet, and now both

Communicator 4.0 and Explorer 4.0 offer webcasting features built into the browsers themselves, even though these features aren't compatible with each other.

Internet Explorer's webcasting basics

Microsoft loves to create new jargon. They probably have a department for it. With Internet Explorer, you'll be introduced to Active Channels, the Microsoft term for webcasting. Active Channels take advantage of some pretty cool new technology that, in effect, can turn even the most mundane of web sites into a web channel. In fact, you can subscribe to both channels and web sites in Internet Explorer 4.0, simply by using the Subscribe feature.

I know it sounds a bit odd to subscribe to both channels and web sites, but trust me, it works pretty well. Active Channels nearly always come with an identifying icon, so picking them out is usually pretty easy. But you're definitely not beholden to the Active Channels. If you visit a site and decide "Hey, I'd like to have that site come to me every day," you can subscribe to that page. (The Subscription Wizard is shown in Figure 1-6.) Whenever you fire up the browser after that, it goes directly to that site and brings back the updated content.

Figure 1-6:
By using the Subscription Wizard, I can get notification if my favorite Web page has changed.

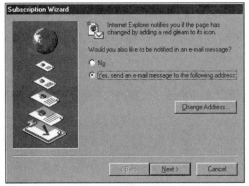

Now that's simple! So simple, in fact, that I think I can just pack up and go home and forget about all this web channel stuff . . . Uh . . . not quite. It turns out there's a new language you'll need to learn, and oh yeah, did I mention the part about having to time code everything you create so that Explorer knows to bring it down to the user's PC. No? Hmm . . . well, I'll come back to that in Chapter 5.

Okay, so maybe webcasting isn't that simple after all. In trying to make the webcasting architecture as open as possible, Microsoft made it a little too open and have made the use of some fairly common web-publishing conventions more complicated. Does that particular problem mean that you should skip the technology entirely? Absolutely not. It does mean, however, that using Microsoft isn't as easy as the company would like you to believe.

Don't forget that this book's CD has a copy of Internet Explorer 4.0 for you.

Netcaster, Netscape's built-in web channel viewer

Netcaster isn't all that different from the webcasting features in Internet Explorer 4.0. You're still pushing content to the user. The end-user still subscribes to a channel and then specifies when to download the information. The difference between the two tools boils down to implementation. Netcaster uses proprietary JavaScript to create an entirely different look and feel than you find in Explorer 4.0.

If Internet Explorer was going for the Hyundai approach, Netcaster is more like a Cadillac. Netcaster is big, cushy, and filled with lots of web-channel features right in the middle of your web browser. Dubbed a "Webtop" by the marketing folks at Netscape (the Channel Properties dialogue box is shown in Figure 1-7), Netcaster runs in the background on your desktop and downloads content while you work on other things. On closer inspection, you find that Netcaster feels much like PointCast in that content is constantly coming at you and appearing on a full desktop.

Figure 1-7:
You can set up Netcaster to take over your entire desktop window.

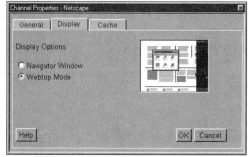

The downside to Netcaster is that's it's a boatload of JavaScript. Everything from the interface design to the delivery of content, right down to the channel options utilize JavaScript. JavaScript is great, don't get me wrong, but when delivered *en masse* like this, it can bring an entire PC to a halt over time, and that's exactly what Netcaster does.

In addition to its Netcaster feature, Netscape has also partnered with Marimba to build the Castanet Tuner into Communicator 4.0. The Tuner can run both as part of Communicator 4.0 or as a stand-alone application. Sure, this feature amounts to a glorified plug-in, but this relationship shows the commitment of both companies to developing a set of standards for webcasting based around Java and JavaScript.

Get Ready to Webcast!

All right — I'm done with Chapter 1. How about you? Now, before you run off to that cocktail party and start musing about the ways of the webcaster, here are some key tips to keep in mind:

- ✔ Webcasting is all about *pushing* content from the Internet to the end-user.

- ✔ Web channels come in lots of shapes and sizes, and as a developer, choosing the right size channel for your purposes is very important.

- ✔ Netscape and Microsoft don't like each other. More important, however, they don't like sharing webcasting standards.

Beyond the hype, some valuable reasons exist for delivering content directly to users, which I explore in-depth in Chapter 3. As a developer, however, you need to keep in mind the following points as you begin to look at developing web channels:

- ✔ You probably want to develop web channels geared toward people who have a web browser first, because such a strategy increases your audience size and because, generally, developing for the browsers is easier. That said, you're certain to wind up making some compromises in quality and experience, but in the end, such flexibility is sure to prove worth the effort.

- ✔ As you get more experienced, you can branch out into the webcasting tools that don't involve a web browser. These tools are more flexible than their browser-based relatives but usually have a greater ramp-up time because the development environment is new.

Web channels are not a fad. It's a better way to deliver targeted information to your customers, your friends, and the millions of people you don't know on the Internet. Now that you've got an overview (providing you've read through this entire chapter), you can start getting down to the business of building channels!

Chapter 2

Web Channels and the Tools to Build Them

• •

In This Chapter

▶ The different types of web channels

▶ The tools you always need to develop web channels

▶ Different tools for different web channels

• •

*I*n Chapter 1, I pose the question: "What is a web channel?" This chapter poses a much different but equally important question: "What do you use to create a web channel?" The answer depends a lot on what kind of web channel you're making. Nevertheless, you may be pleasantly surprised to find that most of the tools you currently use to build your web site aren't about to become obsolete. In fact, you're probably going to need them to get your first web channel up and running. You may need a few other tools as well, so I hope you have some extra space on ye olde hard drive!

The Hierarchy of Web Channels

As you may have already guessed, not all web channels are created equal. You may even go so far as to say that many web channels don't even seem to come from the same planet, given how different they appear! But assuming that they do all come from Earth, web channels do share certain similar underpinnings, no matter how complex they may appear to be.

You can split up web channels into the following four basic categories:

✔ **HTML channels:** Web channels that use good, old-fashioned HTML to deliver pushable content from a web server to a user. Internet Explorer, PointCast, and the Netscape Netcaster support these web channels almost exclusively.

There's a new fangled kind of HTML running about town. Perhaps you've heard of it. It's called Dynamic HTML, and it's being touted as the best thing to ever happen to HTML. Dynamic HTML is showing up on both Mircosoft and Netcaster channels all over the Internet now. It's definitely not your father's HTML, so check out The Part of Tens for some tips on how to get it into your channel today!

✔ **JavaScript channels:** JavaScript provides a lot of the underpinnings for Netcaster and Explorer channels. Although JavaScript is implicit in the Netcaster design, it's more of an add-on for Explorer to increase a developer's flexibility in channel design.

✔ **Java channels:** Both Netcaster and Explorer support Java in their web-channel viewers. And products such as the Marimba Castanet Tuner are built with Java and can support almost any Java applet.

✔ **Proprietary channels:** Many of the "enterprise" (meaning corporate) web-channel companies such as BackWeb use a proprietary scripting language, meaning a language specific to their channel viewer, to create channels.

These categories aren't exactly mutually exclusive. Explorer, Netcaster, and PointCast all provide a common HTML interface for their web-channel viewers, but they all support Java or JavaScript as well. The same holds true for some of the proprietary channels. What this categorization provides, however, is an easy way of showing how web channels can grow from being the kissing cousin of a web site to a fully developed Internet and customer service information system. Not surprisingly, as you move to a more complex channel, the tools that you use to create the channels become more complex.

Now that all that hierarchy stuff is in your head, forget about it for just a second. I say that because, as you start out with web-channel development, you don't need to stray that far from your current web-page nest. You can build web channels with the tools you're using right now. The web channel is simpler that way, but it's also easier to maintain and update. To me, ease of creation is the most important part of web-channel development. After all, if you must give up everything you already know about the Internet, why try webcasting at all?

Even as you get farther into web-channel development, you can take solace in knowing that you aren't giving up many of the tools you're currently using. Most of the more advanced web-channel formats still use the basic file and graphics formats for the rest of the web. If you want to add animation or sound to your channel, you can definitely use the same tools that you already use for these elements.

If you want to download shareware or freeware versions of some of these web-development tools, a number of great web sites can help you out. Try `www.download.com` and `www.developer.com` for all your Internet tool needs. They've yet to fail me!

You Always Need Graphics

You can't have a channel without graphics. Well, you could, but nobody would look at it. Well, they may look, but they probably wouldn't enjoy themselves very much. Graphics are the very heart of any web channel, no matter whether it's in Explorer or part of the Castanet Tuner. People like to be "wowed" — and you can wow them by using graphics.

So if you just dropped some cash to pick up the latest upgrade to your favorite graphics editing tool, you can breath a big sigh of relief, because no matter how complex your web channel may be, it's always going to need graphics. In fact, if you haven't picked up a professional tool such as Adobe PhotoShop, Fractal Painter, or CorelDraw, you really should. It makes your life a whole lot easier in the long run, and your graphics look much better.

Be sure to examine the demo version of PhotoShop on the CD.

A great graphics tool is one of the keys to success with web-channel development, no matter how complex the site. Not that the same isn't true of a web site, but with a web site, your interface and your restrictions are pretty much set for you. Web sites force you to be smart and spartan about your graphics load if you want people to continually visit your site. On the web, long load times are the kiss of death, and graphics are the usual suspects.

On a web channel, however, you can build a much more rich and interesting graphical interface. You're probably wondering how that's possible? It's still the same old Internet with the same slow modems. All true, but this area is where web channels differ from a traditional web site (see Figure 2-1). Because a web channel updates only new information from the channel server, everything that's already downloaded stays on your hard drive. That makes designing a graphically intensive interface easier to swallow, because the viewer downloads it only once, after they subscribe to the channel.

I come back to this topic in Chapter 3, but for now, just understand that you have more options for web-channel design than with a web page. To support that increased graphics capability, you need to have a good graphics editor.

Figure 2-1:
Web
channels
can use
more
graphics
than your
average
web page.

Don't Give Up the Spinning Icons Just Yet

From advertising banners to photo galleries to annoying flashing icons, GIF animations are everywhere on the web. And why not? They're relatively light on bandwidth; they attract your eye; and they bring otherwise dead web pages to life.

For the beginning web-channel developer, GIF animations may become your best friend for delivering effectiveness in your first channel. Explorer, Netcaster, and PointCast Connections all support animated GIFS. A number of web-channel developers, however, have given up on GIF animations and use JavaScripted layers to develop similar animations. Although doing so is a good way to save space (the average layered JavaScript animation being about 30 percent smaller than a similar GIF animation), JavaScript takes more time to code and, more important, requires that your web-channel viewer support JavaScript. Nevertheless, GIF animations remain a compelling option for adding impressive effects to a web channel.

Whatever happened to image maps?

The *digerati* (pronounced "web snobs") don't seem to like image maps very much anymore. Fewer and fewer web sites use them these days. Mostly, this falling out of favor of image maps is because, by using JavaScript, you can create animated icons that are both more compelling and smaller.

Whatever the reasons, just because they're not popping up on web sites much anymore

doesn't mean that you can't use image maps in web channels. Explorer, Netcaster, and the PointCast Network all support image maps in web channels. So if you've got them in your site, you can use them in your channel, too. And just to prove that you can have them and still look cool, check out the following figure. If CNN can use image maps in PointCast, certainly you can have them in your web channel.

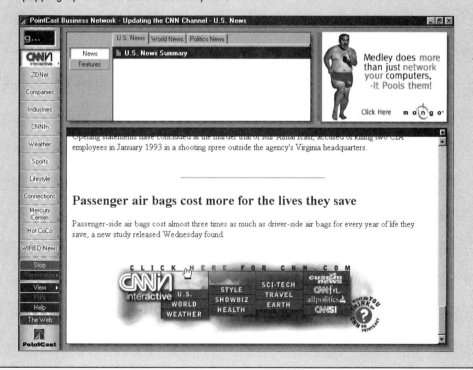

As you move into the high end of channel development, GIF animations become much less common. Some of the tools support them, but others use Java, JavaScript, or a proprietary animation tool to do the same animating. Whatever the method you use to create them, animations aren't going away, so having a GIF animation tool at the outset can greatly simplify your life and help you to communicate with authority.

HTML Gets You Your First Web Channel

One of the great things about webcasting is that you don't need to go out and get a whole new wardrobe to get a channel up on the Internet. Both Internet Explorer and Netscape Communicator have basically bolted their web-channel viewers onto their web browsers. You shouldn't be shocked, therefore, to find out that HTML is the backbone of the webcasting features in both the big browsers. The two companies have set up their browsers to go out on the Internet and look at a site to see whether the HTML source files have changed. If these files have changed, the browsers grab the content of those pages and bring it back to the user.

In theory, you can turn any web site into a web channel by adding a few tags to your HTML source files. Notice that I said "in theory." That's because, in practice, it's actually harder to do. But I'm getting ahead of myself. The fact remains that you can use HTML to create a web channel if you know the right tags to put into your web pages.

Take a look at Figure 2-2. It shows a web channel developed for the PointCast Network. As you can see, the channel looks a lot like a web page embedded inside the PointCast Network viewer. That's because it *is* a web page embedded inside the PointCast viewer. Yet, it's being pushed, so it qualifies as a web channel. You can see the same web page in Internet Explorer, unpushed, as shown in Figure 2-3.

HTML is a solid architecture for building a basic web channel. After you get into channels that don't use the web browsers, however, the HTML usually gets left behind. Even though HTML is pretty straight-forward and you can scale it to include CGI, Perl, Java, and JavaScript, it's also fairly limiting. HTML is basic in that it's a set of standards for page layout, not an application-development environment. After you get to the Java channels and proprietary channels, HTML is no longer necessary because the web browsers are no longer involved. Communication goes directly from the viewer to the server, as is the case with the Castanet Tuner, as shown in Figure 2-4.

Figure 2-2:
This web channel is embedded inside of the PointCast Network.

Figure 2-3:
This example is the same site as viewed through Internet Explorer 4.0.

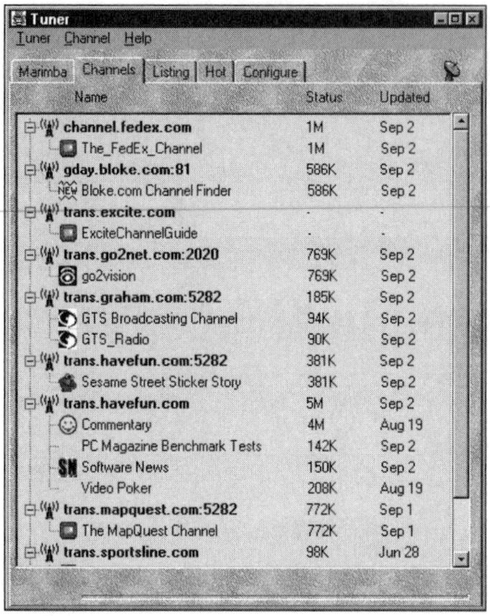

Figure 2-4:
Tuner, the
web-
channel
viewer for
Castanet
channels.

JavaScript Brings Your First Web Channel Alive

Okay, so JavaScript isn't a tool per se. It's a language. But if you want to create a web channel that has both functionality and flair, JavaScript becomes one of your most valuable commodities. That's because JavaScript has become the language of choice for the vast majority of web channels popping up on the Internet. To give you an idea of just how prevalent JavaScript is, here's a brief list of companies that have web channels using JavaScript:

- CNN

- Disney

- ABC News

- NBC News

- Wired

- The Wall Street Journal

- ESPNET.Sportszone

- Warner Brothers

Why is JavaScript so prevalent in web-channel design and why are these big companies using it? The answers have more to do with the Web itself than with web channels (see Figure 2-5). Certainly you have other ways to add functionality through the Netscape and Microsoft web-channel viewers, but JavaScript is the easiest entry point for anyone who wants to get a web channel up quickly. Plus Javascript has become the predominate way that companies and personal developers extend the functionality of their web sites, so having a simple crossover from site to channel means that more people are likely to make the conversion.

You can use JavaScript to do a number of things that immediately adds life to your web channel, and they all work as an extension of an HTML page. You can, for example, accomplish the following tasks:

- ✔ Add icons that animate or change state as you scroll over them.
- ✔ Add layers of text and graphics that appear or disappear based on the user's selection.
- ✔ Embed sounds in a channel.
- ✔ Create pop-up menus that appear after your mouse rolls over a picture or a link.
- ✔ Create animations and slide shows with text and graphics that fade in and out.

Figure 2-5:
The Wired channel uses JavaScript to show text when your mouse rolls over the Pause button.

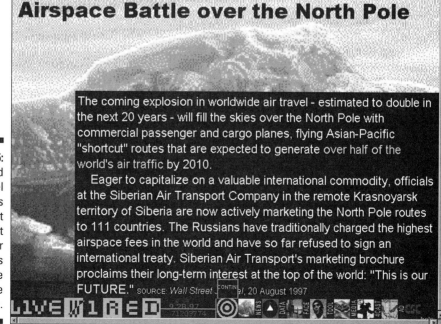

Airspace Battle over the North Pole

The coming explosion in worldwide air travel - estimated to double in the next 20 years - will fill the skies over the North Pole with commercial passenger and cargo planes, flying Asian-Pacific "shortcut" routes that are expected to generate over half of the world's air traffic by 2010.

Eager to capitalize on a valuable international commodity, officials at the Siberian Air Transport Company in the remote Krasnoyarsk territory of Siberia are now actively marketing the North Pole routes to 111 countries. The Russians have traditionally charged the highest airspace fees in the world and have so far refused to sign an international treaty. Siberian Air Transport's marketing brochure proclaims their long-term interest at the top of the world: "This is our FUTURE." SOURCE: *Wall Street Journal*, 20 August 1997

I'm not going into the details of how and why JavaScript works, because, well, I don't have that many pages to work with in this book. But if you want more in-depth information on what you can do by using JavaScript, check out *JavaScript For Dummies,* by Emily A. Vander Veer (IDG Books Worldwide, Inc.). I don't expect you to learn JavaScript overnight, but later in the book, I show you some JavaScript tricks for your Netcaster, Explorer, and PointCast web channels, even if you've never used JavaScript before. All of that good fun begins in Chapter 14.

What about JScript and VBScript in channels?

Good ol' Microsoft just has to make things more difficult than they really should be. If you haven't heard of JScript or VBScript, that's okay. A lot of people are in the same boat with you. Visually, virtually no difference exists between these scripting languages — to the point where only an expert could probably tell the difference among pages enabled with VBScript, JScript, or JavaScript.

So why bother mentioning these other scripts? Well, because of compatibility questions. Neither JScript or VBScript is completely compatible with the Netscape Communicator. JScript is the Microsoft flavor of JavaScript. It's pretty much the same thing as JavaScript, except that it came from Microsoft, which means that a few things don't quite work the same. It's supported by both browsers at this point, but for channel development, I can't really recommend JScript for implementation on a Netscape Netcaster channel. For an Explorer or a PointCast channel, JScript is fine. Still, I'd opt for JavaScript, simply because, if you use JavaScript, you're covered no matter which browser or web-channel viewer you go with.

VBScript, as are JavaScript and JScript, is a scripting tool that enables you to create various applications and effects inside a web page. Although you may find VBScript in a number of web channels specific to the Microsoft Internet Explorer or the PointCast Network (as shown in Figure 2-6), using it to build a channel in Netcaster is a futile effort.

Figure 2-6:
The CMP
TechWeb
web
channel for
Explorer is
built with
VBScript.

The Java Channel Machine

So maybe you're tired of the entire HTML and JavaScript web-channel concept. Maybe that's simply too easy, and you want to jump to the head of the class and get right into Java instead. Well, that's fine, but after you start working with Java and web channels, you really have only two courses of action open to you: Either you embed a Java applet into a web channel that uses HTML or you create a Java channel that runs on its own, usually through the Marimba Castanet. Either way, you're talking about taking a big step in web-channel development.

The Java applet inside . . . HTML

Embedding a Java applet inside a web channel that you create for either Explorer or Netcaster works exactly the same as in a web browser — just like using HTML and JavaScript together. The nice thing about using Java, however, is that doing so maintains the entire architecture that exists in a web site, which makes porting even the more complex web sites to a channel that much easier.

In addition to supporting applets through HTML, Netcaster also supports nearly any Java application through its channel viewer. This feature is a direct result of Netcaster's ability to support Castanet channels from Marimba. The result is that if you find a unique Java applet, like the MapQuest interactive location finder, shown in Figure 2-7, then you can subscribe to that applet with Netcaster.

Java sans HTML

The folks at Marimba probably jumped right to this section first after they got their complimentary copy of the book. And rightfully so, because this section covers their corner of the webcasting world. Marimba has created a complete webcasting solution, called *Castanet,* that uses Java for its core components but doesn't need a web browser to deliver the content to users.

The Marimba webcasting product line includes a Java client viewer (called the *Tuner*), a Java development tool *(Bongo)*, and a server application that manages web-channel traffic *(Transmitter)*. Together, these products provide a closed web-channel loop. You create channels by using the development tool and manage them by using the server application — and the end-user views them by using the channel viewer.

Figure 2-7: MapQuest, a Java applet you can subscribe to in Netcaster.

The Castanet Tuner can view almost any Java application that you create in Bongo or another development tool. If I want to create a simple poker game in Java and call it a channel, I can, as shown in Figure 2-8. The advantage to using Bongo, however, is that it's designed to help you create interfaces and channel content without doing much in the line of Java programming. This capability saves you time, for one thing, and makes the learning ramp associated with this kind of technology a bit easier to climb.

Figure 2-8:
You can turn even a poker game into a channel by using the Marimba Castanet Tuner.

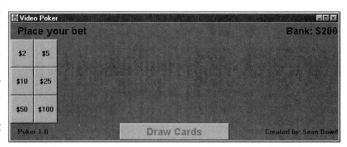

Proprietary Channels for the High End

At the company for which I used to make games was a guy (me, actually) whose job was to create HTML pages and post them to our internal network. You could open up your web browser and view the files, which included project status, developer notes, and other quasi-useful information. I brazenly called an it *intranet,* but it certainly didn't have the sophistication or the flair of the intranets created for large corporations today.

Corporate intranets are becoming more and more common, as are *extranets,* which essentially are intranets for customers. These large scale, highly secure networked environments are ideal for web-channel development, and some companies have developed technologies designed specifically to meet this growing demand. The most notable of these companies is BackWeb.

BackWeb, and their recently acquired subsidiary, Lanacom, have developed proprietary tools for pushing content over the Internet (see Figure 2-9). BackWeb developed their own *API (application programming interface)* for creating BackWeb servers on the Internet. As does Marimba, BackWeb also has a client application that enables these servers to push content on to the desktop; it doesn't, however, use Java as a development environment.

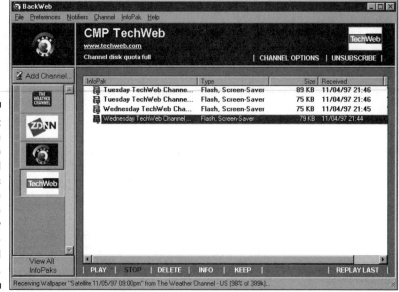

Figure 2-9:
The
BackWeb
channel
interface is
much more
intricate
than any
other web-
channel
tool.

Even though BackWeb is set up to push content to just about anyone, with its acquisition of Lanacom, BackWeb is poised to dominate the corporate intranet and extranet market. Although the company's tools are exceptionally complicated, no other company is competing against them for this growing market. As a result, the BackWeb interface is likely to become the de facto standard for developing large-scale intranet and extranet web channels.

Ack! It Seems Like a Lot!

Is someone in the back having a brief panic attack? I know that I describe a lot of tools in this chapter, and how can anyone possibly expect you to get everything right the first time, particularly considering that you're probably working on your first-ever web channel? I'm dying over here!

You don't need to worry, really. This part of the book is all about figuring out how the playing field looks, and the farther you get into webcasting, the more similar these channels are all going to seem. The following list describes some things that I posted up on the wall as I started writing this chapter. Just keep them in mind as you go along.

✔ Webcasting is fun.

✔ Creating web channels is easy.

✔ I can make one channel that works for lots of web-channel viewers.

✔ I get to show this channel off to people after I'm done.

✔ I'm going to unload a "world of hurt" on my competitors.

✔ Your shoe's untied. (Made ya look!)

Now, on to the design!

Chapter 3

Designing Your First Channel

• •

In This Chapter

▶ Deciding if you are ready for a web channel

▶ Setting your web-channel goals

▶ Evaluating your web-site content

▶ Reaching the right audience

▶ Interface design made easy

• •

*I*n this chapter comes the fun part. I can recall one of the first times I put up a web site. The company I was working for was in the process of developing three games, none of which had been announced to the press. The president of the company came to me and asked if I'd build the web site. I said sure, but then I asked what he wanted me to put on it. He replied, and I'm quoting here, "I don't care. Just as long as it gets people to the site and tells them who we are."

Ah, the second rule of web-site development rears it's ugly head: If in doubt, err on the side of too much content, even if the content doesn't have anything to do with your company. By the way, the first rule (in case you didn't know) is that if you don't know how to build something, steal it from the site of someone who does. So, together with another producer, I made up as much stuff as I could and got it on the site . . . where it sat, and sat, and then sat some more.

Even with nothing to speak of on our site, we had an average of 12,000 page impressions per month, a modest figure. We did some research and found that fewer than one quarter of the people who came to the site were repeat viewers. They came, they got bored, and then they left, never to be heard from again. In the end, we scrapped the whole site and started over again after we finally had something worth talking about.

We had the option to start over. With web *channels,* however, you may not get that second chance. People subscribe and expect to be paid off immediately for their trouble. If you can't deliver the goods, why would they think of coming back? Web channels require persistent content — content that's regularly updated and is fresh. And you must deliver that content consistently, and — oh, yeah — it had better be *good,* too.

Should You Have a Web Channel?

If you've read this far, I'm pretty sure that you're convinced that the answer is yes — and, trust me, I don't want to dissuade you at all. The decision to create a web channel, however, is a big one. It requires a commitment of time and resources that may . . . or may not . . . justify the cost.

A web channel is kind of like a boat. You buy a boat; say that it's a nice boat, so it costs you $100,000. What you never see in the sales brochures, however, is that after you buy the boat, it costs another $30,000 a year for maintenance, docking fees, and gas. Ouch! Better to go in prepared for the worst and be pleasantly surprised. Web channels are a lot of work, and before you decide that talking to your potential customers is the way of the future, you may want to understand all the costs involved.

Pop Quiz: Are You Ready for Webcasting?

So, now that I've scared the bejezus out of you (and convinced you not to buy a boat anytime soon), here's a quick five-question quiz to help you figure out whether you should create a web channel. This quiz is by no means definitive, but if you answer *No* to more than half of these questions, I'd seriously think twice about the investment you're about to make.

As an aside, this quiz applies equally to those of you who don't currently have a web site and are thinking of doing a channel in lieu of a site. The same rules apply, but consider how much time you're willing to spend — and remember: No cheating!

Pick up your pencils. You may begin:

✔ **Do you have content that people want on a regular basis?** First and foremost, do you have content that people are going to want on a fairly regular basis. Whatever your goals are, you need to think of yourself as a programming director. You need to offer something that people want — and want more than every so often. A lot of media companies use web channels, simply because their content is always changing (see Figure 3-1).

Figure 3-1:
Media companies have it easy. Their content is always changing.

✔ **Do you update your web site more than twice a week?** This question is about your commitment. Imagine that you write a weekly column for a newspaper. The deadline is always there, and if you miss it, you leave the paper out on a limb. Your commitment is the only thing between that column being written and the paper scrambling to fill a slot. Web channels require a similar commitment. Otherwise, your audience fades away as your content goes stagnant.

✔ **Can you make your content small?** One of the keys to success with web channels is minimizing the amount of data you try to push to the end-user. If you use a lot of graphics as part of your business (employing a stock photo house, for example), you need to get creative to get your packet size down. Users get tired of waiting, and they can blame the delays on their Internet service provider for only so long.

✔ **Are you ready to listen to feedback?** As is true of so many things on the Internet, web channels are at their best if you use them to promote two-way communication — which means that you need to get feedback from the people who use your channel and then adapt its content to their specified needs as well as to your own. That's what keeps people coming back.

✔ **Are you willing to constantly promote your site?** Web channels, unlike web sites, are not easy to notice. The concept is still catching on, which means that getting your channel noticed requires a more concerted effort. People can all too easily get lost in a new technology. With the amount of effort you need to put into your channel, you'll want to make sure that it's seen by as many people as possible within the developer community. That means getting to know the others within the webcasting community and promoting your channel to them as well.

Goals Made for Achieving

An old adage about mountain climbing says that the best reason to climb a mountain is because it's there. Some of you out there are pure technophiles, as I am. I love playing with technology and tinkering until I come up with something that I like. For those people, "because it's there" is perhaps a good enough reason to create a web channel. For the average corporate webmaster or project manager, however, that logic probably isn't going to hold up very well under management scrutiny.

So before you get ready to start ripping apart your web content, you'd better have some idea as to why a web channel is a good thing for your business. In some cases, such as those of CNN or ABC, the goal is obvious. For a florist or a nightclub or even a high-tech company, however, the goals may be less obvious.

To make a web channel work for you, you may need to change the way in which you think about your business and your current web site. (Again, if you don't have a web site, just pretend that you do.) The first step in figuring out why a web channel is a good idea is to review your business and ask yourself the following questions:

✔ **Does my business do anything that's continually changing?** This one really can be just about anything. If you own a restaurant, your specials are always changing. For a nightclub, the musicians are always changing. For the intrepid software company, ship dates are always changing. (Mine did, at least.) If you're creating a web channel just for the heck of it, try to find that one area of your current site that lends itself to recurrence (see Figure 3-2). As long as you know that something needs to change, you've got something that you can develop your channel around, which becomes extremely important as we get to the channel's design. If your business requires that content is always changing, then you open yourself up to creating an information gap between you and your customers. A web channel can help to shrink this gap.

✔ **Do my customers need to talk to me on a regular basis?** Sure, this question applies much more concretely if you have customers, but regardless, you should ask yourself whether the service you provide is conducive to feedback. Are people happier with their flowers if they can recommend new arrangements to you? What if your customers don't understand the new improvements in client/server application? Creating a channel will help to facilitate communication — and ultimately can help keep your customers informed.

If you're having trouble figuring out what your customers may want to talk to you about, take a poll. They're sure to tell you what their needs are if you give them the opportunity, and a poll can help you to decide what's the right type of feedback to look for in the channel.

Figure 3-2:
This snowboarding channel keeps channel viewers continually abreast of events and swap meets for owners.

✔ **What can I provide my customers that's of value to them?** Again, this one comes down to looking very closely at the services you provide. Some of them may not even lend themselves to constant updates but may still be useful to people. Find the value in the things that your company (or your site) provides. That's probably what users care the most about. Find a way to make your content interesting and recurring. If you do, your users stay interested.

✔ **What's cool that I can do?** Not that I think you should be all flash and no substance, but if you find something cool and you're interested in giving it a try, go for it (see Figure 3-3). You may be drawing on something that's on the periphery of your business or even partnering with another company. You may become involved with some sort of a charity. The idea is to find some kind of content that you can use as a hook to get people involved in your channel.

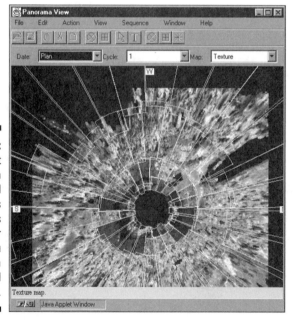

Figure 3-3: At this Jet Propulsion Lab channel that tracks the Mars Pathfinder probe, you can pilot a virtual Pathfinder.

All the list making and hard thinking about goals can't begin to compare to a few good hours on the Internet looking at what other people are doing with their web channels. You don't need to copy what others are doing, but the best way to find out whether your web-channel goals may be a bit on the ambitious side is to look at the other web channels out there. You see a lot of similarity between channels, even those from widely different companies or disciplines. You may also find things that you want to avoid, such as Java or Dynamic HTML, either because they're too complex or they're already being done by a number of other people.

A Surprise Web-Site Inspection!

I have this recurring nightmare about my mom showing up at my apartment to check and see whether my laundry is still lying around on my bedroom floor. (It is, by the way, so please don't tell her.) Whenever she saw that my desk was getting too cluttered or that my floor was becoming buried underneath my toys, I inevitably got the "This room had better be cleaned up before I get back" treatment. So I did what any self-respecting teenager would have done: I threw everything in my drawers and closets and went right back to whatever I was doing. Oh, the room looked clean enough on first inspection, but below the surface, it was a jumbled mess.

The lesson I learned, eventually, was to keep around only the stuff that I really wanted. That way, my room never got too messy. Wise words — and they apply equally well to web channels. Before you can start programming your web channel, you need to figure out what's usable and what isn't on your current web site. Even if you go for the most basic of web channels — the kind in which you turn your web site into a web channel — you still must chose which pages to push and which to leave on the server for users to find, if they so desire.

Web-site firestorms

Quick, your web site is on fire! You've got ten seconds to grab the most important part of the site and take it with you. After that, all the information is lost. If you don't have a web site, pretend that you do and that it has the kind of information that you want on your web channel. What section do you keep? What's expendable?

Time's up. The site is gone. What did you remember to take with you? The things that you decided to take are the things that are the best candidates for your web channel. They're the most valuable to you; they were the easiest to remember; and they were the lightest. (Okay, that's stretching the virtual metaphor, I know, but it works.)

This degree of scrutiny is what you need to give to your web-site content as you're preparing to create a channel. You can afford to be frugal. Think headlines rather than articles. People can always click for more, but what you're trying to do is capture the areas that are of most interest to them and then provide just enough information to hook them. Make sure that you keep the following concepts in mind as you review your site:

- Content needs updating often.
- Graphics are more expensive than text.

✔ Too much text is a turn-off.

✔ Animations are eye-catching and work well.

✔ You can always link back to more content.

Take small bites, not huge portions

Things get a little sticky here. I just told you that you should pare down your web site content so that delivering a message to your audience is easier. How, then, do you deal with the channel viewers built into Netcaster and Explorer? By using either of those products, you can turn your web site into a channel without a tremendous amount of work. Should you still, therefore, keep the web site mentality that says more is better?

Absolutely not, and here's why: What you're seeing now are companies experimenting with webcasting. They're essentially porting their content from one environment to another and hoping to do so with as little work as possible. The result is a number of web channels that look surprisingly similar to their corresponding web sites. Although this approach works for news companies such as NBC News it doesn't work for other kinds of companies. People catch on and eventually ask a very simple question: "How is this different from a bookmarked web site?" If that kind of questioning becomes prevalent among users, they're likely to turn off to the idea of web channels entirely.

One way around this problem with web channels in the browsers is to create what amounts to a *front page* (see Figure 3-4). You push the front page to the user, showing the channel headlines and containing links that point back to the site, where the user can find more information. This approach is a mild form of web-channel cheating, because it crosses the line of what's a channel and what's a web site, but it does serve both to provide the initial headlines and enable users to go deeper if they choose. Using a front page also minimizes the amount of content refitting that you need to do to get a channel up and running. By the way, both Explorer and Netcaster have "Channel Wizards" — tools that automatically generate web channel front pages — that accomplish this very task!

Figure 3-4:
The NBC
News
channel
pushes its
front end to
the user,
and the
links on the
page take
you back to
its web site.

Preaching to the Choir

Perhaps you've already decided that a web channel is right for you; you've set your goals; and you've got a list of the content you want to turn into a channel. Now, you have just one thing left to consider: your audience. Certain designs and styles appeal to certain people, while a particular tone or word choice may turn off others. All these factors play into your site design.

News media, for example, must portray a sense of journalistic integrity in their word choice and style. (I hate to keep using the media, by the way, but they were the first ones to latch onto webcasting.) Their channels are conservative but very well produced. By contrast, the channels belonging to movie companies such as Disney usually have a much more entertaining style. The word choice is more colloquial, and the graphical style appeals more toward the family and kids. Based on their perceived demographics, such companies create sites to reinforce this image to their web audience.

In this area, as in all things, perception does not always match reality. You don't see a lot of profanity mixed with skulls and crossbones at the Vintage Motorcycle channel. Nor do you see a lot of dry and stuffy financial data clogging up the Quicken (Intuit) channel, as shown in Figure 3-5. Many web channels have adopted a journalistic sense in their tone and style, hoping to appeal to the broadest cross-section of users possible.

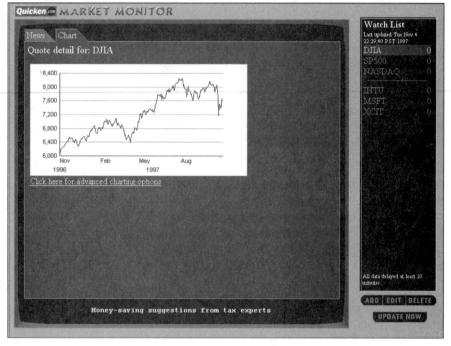

Figure 3-5:
The
Quicken
channel
posts a lot
of financial
information
but tries
hard not to
make it
seem too
dull.

Ultimately, the decision of tone comes down to identifying your target audience. Having a take on your potential audience is a good thing, particularly if you're a small company trying to make your presence known via your web channel. The following list describes some considerations you may want to make concerning your audience while designing your content:

✔ **The average age of the audience matters.** Are you playing to a younger crowd, as in the case of a game company or a nightclub, or are you after a more conservative and older audience, as in the case of a health-care company or a stock brokerage?

✔ **Don't sacrifice your audience for reach.** In the grand scheme, diluting your message to try to pick up more people doesn't work in your favor. If you know your audience, talk to them — and if other people like your style, they come around. If not, you probably didn't want them there anyway.

✔ **Get a head check whenever you can.** The second you think you know your audience, you find that they aren't who you thought they were. This is why web channel feedback is so important. Be sure that you take a poll every so often just to make sure that you're really talking to the people to whom you think you're talking.

The best approach, I think, is to be accessible to your audience. If you're not sure who your users are, find out. And after you know, make sure that you reinforce the message they're sending you. The message is simple. Poll and poll often.

The Five Immutable Laws of Web Channel Design

You really have only two kinds of channels for any given subject matter in this world. The channel that gets out there first and the channel that does it the best. So I'm ripping off the *21 Immutable Laws of Marketing!* If the shoe fits . . . ah, you know the rest. I certainly can't guarantee that your channel is the first one out there. For that matter, I can't even guarantee that it's the best. I can, however, promise to show you the really important stuff that can help you design the best channel possible. The rest, as the proverbial "they" say, is up to you!

I certainly don't want to go overboard here, but a channel is a lot like a work of art. You must nurture it and mold it into something you're happy with. You undoubtedly aren't going to get it right the first time, and even after you do finally come up with something that's acceptable to you, you're probably still not satisfied.

Hence, the five laws. They're here to guide you through the process of designing your channel. They're not the line in the sand of web channels. Think of them as a road map to good channel making. Follow these rules and you save yourself time and energy in the long run. Okay, enough pitching of the rules. Here you go!

Rule #1: Pick a viewer and stick with it

Until web channels mature in, say, a couple years, you're stuck picking your poison. Again, for the record, your choices of web-channel viewers fall roughly into the following categories:

✔ **Web-channel viewers embedded in browsers.** These are the simplest push-content viewers in that they use the existing web browsers. The upside is that they're a known quantity and everybody has one. The downside is that, well, web channels made for the browsers look a lot like web sites rather than web channels.

> ✔ **Java-enabled web viewer.** If you're into strict Java, this group is the one for you. It includes the Marimba Castanet and the BackWeb channel viewer. The upside is that these viewers involve real push without the browser. The downside is that not a lot of people have heard of Marimba or BackWeb yet.
>
> ✔ **Everyone else.** You've got companies such as PointCast and Intermind in this group. PointCast and Intermind use mostly HTML, but each has its own tool for creating web-channel content. The upside is that their viewers are easy to use, and that the tools are pretty easy to master. The downside is that there aren't a whole lot people using these viewers compared to the browsers.

The bottom line on this one for me is to first go with the one with which you feel the most comfortable. You can always support other channel viewers later. At the beginning, ease of use and a simple implementation makes your life a lot easier. Go with what you know and move out to more elaborate web-channel types after you're ready.

Rule #2: Always make the sauce first (and don't forget the measuring cup)

One year, for Mother's day, my dad decided to surprise my mom and make dinner for her. He went to the computer, looked up the recipe, printed it out, and started assembling his ingredients. The first line on the instructions read "Make the sauce." My mom had used the recipe so many times that she didn't need to note the quantities of each ingredient. She just kept fiddling until it tasted right.

You don't want to make this mistake on your first web channel. If you begin by fiddling, you end up designing your interface over and over again until you settle on the content you want in the channel. Do yourself a big favor and get all your content together first. That way, you have everything in front of you before you devise the interface. After you settle on the big ticket items, you can then start fiddling.

You may have seen your web-site content (that is if you have a web site that you want to convert to a channel) a thousand times over, but pushing is not the same as waiting for someone else to pull it. Take an inventory of your content by category. See how many graphics, animations, and sound files you think you're going to use. And take a look at all the text you plan on using to get your message across. Then ask yourself the following questions:

> ✔ What's my message here?
>
> ✔ Is this amount of content too much to convey that message?
>
> ✔ How can I make a bigger statement by using less content?

After you ask yourself those questions, see whether you can take something out. See, too, whether you can change anything to make it more focused. Should you scrap a graphic for some text? Should you create new graphics instead of text? Get all these issues on the table at the beginning and resolve them. That way, as you get to the design of the overall interface, you know exactly what you're broadcasting.

Rule #3: Make your interface big . . . once

Check out Figure 3-6. It shows a pretty appealing web channel with a lot of graphics. The channel took a good 20 minutes to download the first time that I subscribed. That's okay, however, because I needed to download it only once, and after that, all the content that came through was in small packets.

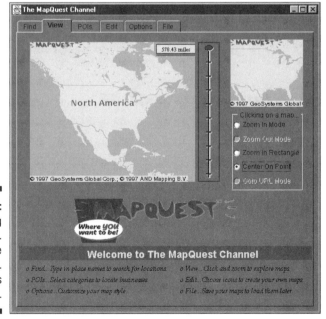

Figure 3-6:
Big
interface.
One
download.
So says
Rule #3.

Here's where you get to have your fun. Your interface is your chance to set a style and tone for your channel that tells people exactly what kind of content they can expect to come from you. How your interface appears is the most important aesthetic decision you make in this entire process, because your interface is the one thing that you must live with for a while.

You can't just go out and change your interface everyday. You could, but people may get angry if it was always graphically intensive — and besides, most people are creatures of familiarity. If they get used to something, it becomes familiar and they tend not to like it changing. Magazines and newspapers are the prime examples. They change their designs once every few years or so. To do so any more often than that would make people question their commitment to a style and to their audience.

Both Netcaster and Explorer encourage you to take the front page of your channel and make it the most graphically appealing part of the channel. The only downside to this is that it's really hard not to end up pushing the entire front page over and over again with these browsers, without using a lot of JavaScript. Be careful with going too far overboard with your first channel on these platforms. It could come back to haunt you!

The great thing about designing your interface is that you can put a lot into it. You've got a chance to really set your channel apart, and unlike with a web site, you don't need to reload a channel every time you go to it. So add the graphics, incorporate the sounds, and get as creative as you want. You get this sort of chance only once in a while, so take advantage of it.

Rule #4: You're a magazine; so act like one

Okay, really, you're a web channel, but magazines provide a great metaphor for web-channel design. I keep saying how important fresh and new content is on your channel. Now, however, I'm going to tell you that your content doesn't always need to be that way. Not every web channel needs to read like CNN Headline News.

Generally, magazines have three basic components. They begin with a front of the book section that includes news, previews, and some letters. In the middle, they offer up the features and the cover story. In the back (or, in some cases, the front, too), recurring columns or sections round out the content of the magazine. People design magazines this way simply because such a design offers a great way to mix news with opinions and articles that speak to the heart of whatever the magazine is about.

Successful web channels work in much the same way, as shown in Figure 3-7. If all you need is headlines, you may as well give up, because you can't beat NBC and ABC at what they do best. You must strive to find the right mix of quick-hit headlines to capture the audience and get them interested in your subject matter. You also need some recurring sections on your channel that can become familiar to your audience. Familiarity is your best friend, because it keeps people coming back.

Take the example of a sewing web channel. Every day or two, the broadcaster puts up a new tip or two on sewing techniques. The broadcaster also keeps a current calendar of events of interest to the audience (for example, sewing trade shows!). These items are the "newsy" elements of the channel that make up its persistent content. In addition, however, every couple weeks, the broadcaster adds an opinion piece on, say, new fabric types available. This piece isn't news but is probably of interest to viewers.

The great thing about this kind of style is that you can mix content that needs continual updates with content that you can update as time permits and still have a robust web channel.

Figure 3-7: The combination of news and features in this channel make it more fun to view and entices you to look further at the content.

Rule #5: Always have the feedback button

The last and perhaps the most crucial element of the web-channel design is the feedback mechanism. I'm know I'm making it sound so serious, but really — if you want people to come back over and over and over, you need a way for them to tell you what they like and dislike about your channel.

Many of you probably have feedback e-mail for your web sites. For some, this kind of feedback is successful, but others don't get one word. On web channels, however, you want to make a conscious effort to entice feedback. Why? Well, look at it this way: You're the one charged with creating content on a fairly regular basis. At some point, the well's going to get a little dry. Why not set up a mechanism whereby your audience can help you out with some of the work? Let them take a shot at recommending something for the channel. Doing so certainly can't hurt.

By the way, this situation applies equally to businesses as well as to personal channels. Suppose that I'm the president of Coke and I want to make the Coke web channel. Well, I can say only so much about the product, the merchandise, and the history of the company. At some point, I need something else to talk about. If you, as a channel viewer, have a communication link to me, you can make all kinds of requests, and if others have the same requests, I can use that feedback to design some new content. The bottom line is that, if you frame it in the content of being part of a community, you can develop a strong link that can help you find new sources of content for your audience.

Are You Ready to Push Yourself?

Well, guess what? That's the end of Part I. I laughed. I cried. I didn't sleep much while I wrote it. That's what *I* got out of it. For you, here's a look back at what I covered:

- ✔ Web channels are just your everyday, throw-the-content-in-the-face-of-the-guy-who-asked-for-it kind of technology.

- ✔ Many people have webcasting solutions, tools, and plans for Internet broadcasting. The lesson, as always, is to start with what you know and then get cocky and try new stuff.

- ✔ Yahoo! No, not the web site, just the word, meaning "Thank goodness that I don't need to throw out everything I know to make a channel."

- ✔ Goals. You must have them.

- ✔ Content. Create it first. Make it simple. Make it small.

- ✔ Rules. Live by 'em.

Part II
Webcasting the Microsoft Way

In this part . . .

All righty then! Enough of this who's-who stuff. Now comes the fun part . . . building your first web channel. We've established that Microsoft and Netscape don't much care for each other, and their products are on different paths these days. As I started putting this book together, I had the Netscape channels in Part II and the Microsoft channels in Part III. I'd put them that way because I really believed that the Netcaster channels would be easier to create.

Turns out that things work just the opposite way. Ooops! Microsoft channels are pretty much a snap after you get all the lingo down. In fact, that's pretty much what you can expect to find in this part: Everything you wanted to know about creating web channels by using CDF (or by going the Microsoft way — take your pick): a little Internet Explorer 4.0, a little PointCast, and a *whole lot* of stuff on CDF. What is CDF, you ask? I'm glad you did! Just turn the page. . . .

Chapter 4

Exploring the New Internet Explorer

*T*hat everyone loves to hate Microsoft is a forgone conclusion. Microsoft owns the operating system and mastered the word processor. And you can't make much of a Windows 95 program without Microsoft Visual C++. In short, Microsoft's kicked butt, taken names, and still had time left over to buy out a few hundred companies and spawn a few thousand millionaires with their stock options. But I'm not bitter — really!

All joking about monopolies aside, Microsoft managed to develop a very good web browser in Internet Explorer. Two years ago, Explorer owned less than 5 percent of the total web-browser market. Today, that number has grown to more than 35 percent. Granted, the installed base is buoyed by the fact that the company ships Internet Explorer with every copy of Windows 95, which is a great gig if you can get it. Microsoft also gives it away free to corporations and consumers alike, unlike Netscape, which is still trying to find a way to make money with its web browser.

Still, despite the perks one gets by being a Microsoft product, Internet Explorer 3.0 has the reputation of being a solid web browser with a clean interface design. Some say that it's faster than Navigator, and it should be, because it can talk directly with the operating system (another perk to being a Microsoft product). Sure, Explorer works better if you use JScript, Microsoft's own brand of JavaScript. And, sure, no other browser supports VBScript except Explorer. But shoot — the industry's sure to come around someday. Do they have a choice?

Now comes Internet Explorer 4.0, and perhaps the best way to describe it is as a really good attempt at trying to fix something that wasn't broken. Explorer 4.0 contains a load of new features and supports a number of new standards (including some that Microsoft made up themselves). That's the good news. Sort of. The bad news is that Microsoft rushed the "beta" version of the software out to the Internet community loaded with bugs that make it crash. On top of that, the company developed at least one standard — the one for webcasting — that the other big browser (yep, the one that still owns 65 percent of the market) doesn't support. Guuugh!

Now seems like just as good a time as any to point out that there is a good newsgroup for venting that frustration against Microsoft. And better yet, Microsoft supports it, so have at it! Several newsgroups can be found at www.microsoft.com/ie/resources.

Grabbin' a Copy of That New Internet Explorer

Actually, you have a couple ways to get a copy of Internet Explorer and its components. Your poison, so to speak, depends on how fat your modem line happens to be and whether you like paying a small fee for your browser.

As always, Internet Explorer 4.0 is free, which means that, at any time, you can hop on over to www.microsoft.com/ie/ie40/ and grab a copy. The only drawback to this method, however, is size. The basic types of installations for Explorer 4.0 are as described in the following list:

- ✔ **Big Install (14MB):** This "minimum" install includes Internet Explorer 4.0, support for Java, and the Microsoft tools for connecting to the Internet.

- ✔ **Really Big Install (15MB):** In addition to Explorer, the "standard" installation also includes Microsoft Outlook Express (an e-mail client) and Microsoft Wallet, a secure extension to Explorer 4.0. Wallet secures important information such as credit-card numbers and other stuff that hackers would love to steal from your PC.

- ✔ **Mondo-Huge Install (22MB):** Laughably called the "full" install, this version adds a host of other Microsoft products to the suite, including NetMeeting (a networked conferencing tool), NetShow (a network multimedia tool), FrontPage Express (a web publishing tool), the Microsoft Web Publishing Wizard, and Microsoft Chat 2.0.

Alternatively, you could bypass the entire downloading process, which could take weeks, and purchase the Internet Explorer CD-ROM. For about $5, you get the Mondo-Huge install sent to you, along with enough online coupons to keep you going for Christmases to come. You can order the CD-ROM from the Microsoft web site, located conveniently at www.microsoft.com

Note: If you bought your PC or your company's PCs on or around Christmas 1997, you may not need to worry about any of this stuff, because, well, Explorer 4.0 may already be installed on your PC. Microsoft has deals in place with nine of the major PC manufacturers, including Apple Computer, to distribute Internet Explorer 4.0 on PCs, beginning in the late fall. So before you jump on the web, you may want to check your browser.

Ya! We've got Internet Explorer 4.0 on the CD ready for your downloading pleasure. So, you can just go there and get it right now!

Breaking Down the New Internet Explorer 4.0

Internet Explorer 4.0 is a complete revision from Internet Explorer 3.0, and by that, I mean that Explorer 4.0 now includes a whole suite of add-on products in addition to a number of new features added to the browser. As is Netscape, Microsoft is trying to build a product that's your one-stop shop for Internet connectivity (Easy Connect), browsing and webcasting (Explorer), e-mail and newsgroups (Outlook), online transactions (Wallet), and, finally, chat (Net Meeting).

Although this philosophy is strikingly similar to, say, Microsoft Office, as a web channel creator, you simply don't even need to bother with most of these add-ons. All you really need to care about is Explorer and what it supports. So, without any further adieu, here's what Internet Explorer 4.0 supports:

> ✔ Active Channels and the Channel Definition Format. Active Channels are the Microsoft version of webcasting and the Channel Definition Format is the language that drives the Active Channels.

> ✔ Support for Dynamic HTML (and things such as Cascading Style Sheets), the latest version of HTML that supports animation and layering.

> ✔ Integration of the Visual Basic scripting tool, VBScript.

> ✔ The Active Desktop and Active Screensavers. Each of these items add functionality to your PC by integrating HTML with your desktop.

Anyone else notice the influx of really energetic adjectives in those bullets? Not just a channel, but an *Active* channel. HTML itself is boring, but if it's *Dynamic,* look out! And what's really the point in having a Basic scripting tool, if you can have a *Visual* one? Some of these things you may never have heard of before. That's really okay, because the adjectives don't actually mean much. What's important are the features, and I cover each of those in the following sections!

Internet Explorer 4.0 boasts a number of other additions that can be useful in developing advanced applications for the browser. Explorer 4.0 includes support for Direct Animation, for example, which is an application-programming interface for using Java or C++ to create multimedia applications through web sites. Explorer 4.0 also includes a new version of the Active Script Debugging Interface, which Microsoft introduced in Version 3.0. Finally, Explorer 4.0 supports Internet Security Zones, which enable you to segment a URL into specific areas with different "security" levels. These levels allow you to limit access to web sites, as well as individual areas within a web site.

Push me the content!

At long last, a screen shot! Figure 4-1 shows a channel in Internet Explorer 4.0. Now, if you hold the book away from your eyes and look away and then look at the screen shot and then look away and look at the screen shot again, you may start to get nauseous. But you may also get the sneaking sensation that, at a quick glance, a web channel looks a lot like a web page.

The simple reality is that web channels in Explorer 4.0 are pretty much glorified web pages. The Microsoft strategy is to extend the concept of a web site to include the pushing of content from the site to the user, through the everyday use of the browser. This strategy gives the user a new way of viewing information and the developer a new way of presenting content to the user, although the underlying technology remains the same.

Microsoft used two basic underlying technologies to build their web channel system — namely the Microsoft Active Channel technology and the Channel Definition Format, the joint Microsoft and PointCast web-channel standard. Together, these two technologies enable developers to create a wide array of pushable content by using JScript, Dynamic HTML, and other web standards. Users can, therefore, view this content through the web browser, on their desktop, or as a screensaver.

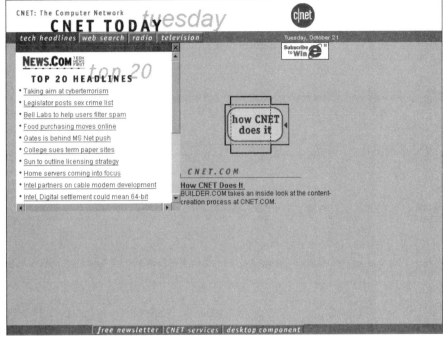

Figure 4-1:
The CNET
channel's
content is
getting sent
to you every
time you
fire up
Internet
Explorer 4.0.

By using these tools, you can create web channels that users can access in a variety of ways. These tools do come with a catch, however, and is it ever a big one! Both these technologies are Microsoft specific, so users who have Netscape Communicator 4.0 (or just Navigator) can't take advantage of any of what you're about to read! To get an idea of what this situation may feel like to a user, get a copy of Communicator 4.0 (which I talk about more in Chapter 8) and take a look at the Microsoft web site. Then try the same thing using Internet Explorer 4.0. Viewed in Explorer 4.0, the site has all sorts of additional animations, menu controls, and Windows 95 interfaces that the browser calls for. Viewed in Communicator, however, it's just another web page without the fancy interface.

On your desktop, all channels are Active Channels

Internet Explorer 4.0 connects the traditional web browser with the operating system. My first impression as I first read about Microsoft wanting to take this course was "Yikes!" But indeed, if you use Explorer 4.0, you're no longer limiting HTML to the web browser. Although Microsoft would never tell it to you this way, what they essentially did with Explorer 4.0 was to slip in some changes to Windows 95 by creating support for basic HTML in other places in Windows, including the Control Panel and the Display settings. These changes enable developers to do two very new things:

✔ **Deliver content to users directly through their desktop, instead of through the browser.** Figure 4-2 shows how this feature looks. By creating a tab that sits on your desktop, you can choose to have web content, in channel form, delivered actively right to your desktop.

Figure 4-2:
The Active
Desktop.

✔ **Deliver content to users through the standard Windows screen saver.** Installing Internet Explorer 4.0 adds a new folder tab to your Display properties in the Control Panel, as shown in Figure 4-3. By setting your web channels here and then specifying the HTML version of the screensaver, you can have channel content pushed to the desktop by using plain HTML and the standard Windows 95 screen saver.

How did this happen? How did Microsoft suddenly jump in there and change Windows 95 without really telling anyone? For about two years now, Microsoft has been pitching ActiveX as the answer to the desktop. ActiveX is a set of new tools that enables programmers — and now web developers — to integrate their programs with Windows 95 itself.

Whenever the folks at Microsoft refer to Active Channels as a key component of Internet Explorer 4.0, what they're really saying to you, the developer, is "Hey, see all the cool places your content can be seen?" And it's true. ActiveX enables you to extend your web channel to more places on the desktop than just the browser. But first things first. About those web channels and the format they use. . . .

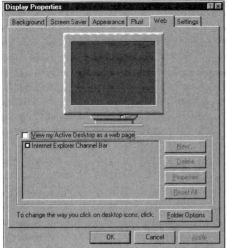

Figure 4-3:
After
installing
Internet
Explorer 4.0,
you find
that some
new tabs
have
crawled
into your
Control
Panels.

CDF does not have Mob ties

Microsoft doesn't like to go at things alone. Doing so makes the company look a little bit like a bully. So, whenever Microsoft acquires a technology or proposes a new one as a standard, it tends to line up its partner companies with it to join in the cheer. The effect is kind of like the mob trying to look legitimate before Congress by bringing their accountants. In this particular case, Microsoft and PointCast teamed up to propose a unified way to pushing content to users.

The result of this collaboration is the *Channel Definition Format (CDF)*. Sounds impressive, doesn't it? But it's really very simple. CDF is not much more than some new tags that you need to learn. The tags look strikingly similar to HTML tags, and you can compose them by using the same HTML editing tools that you use to create your web pages. I cover the usage of these tags in Chapter 5, but as a preview, here are the four major CDF tags that you use to create channels:

- ✔ **The Channel tag.** You guessed it. It looks as follows: `<CHANNEL>`... `</CHANNEL>`. This tag defines a CDF web channel. It works the same as `<HTML>`...`</HTML>` tags work in an everyday web page. This tag also includes the primary startup URL for the channel.

- ✔ **The Logo tag.** The `<LOGO/>`...`<LOGO/>` tag specifies the icons that are used to represent your channel on the Active Desktop, as well as in Explorer. These graphics become the primary way that users recognize your channel. Choosing cool graphics may be one of the more important decisions you make! Channel graphics in the Explorer drop-down menus are shown in Figure 4-4.

✔ **The Item tag.** The `<ITEM>...</ITEM>` tag creates the links to channel pages that the user sees in the channel menu in Explorer or on the Active Desktop. The tag also includes the dynamic text that appears after you run the mouse over the link, as shown in Figure 4-5.

✔ **The LASTMOD command.** Okay, I lied. This one isn't a tag. It is, however, a command within the `<ITEM>` tag. But I wanted to introduce it here, because it's the essence of the web channel. This command determines whether a page is updated since the last time a user viewed it. If so, the page automatically gets pushed to the user.

Talking about new tags that aren't part of the HTML standard may seem a little strange, but that's all part of the Microsoft strategy to make CDF the standard for webcasting. Microsoft, along with PointCast, has submitted the CDF to the World Wide Web Consortium to become the webcasting standard. If the Consortium accepts CDF as such, CDF is very likely to be added to future versions of HTML. Having a familiar design and architecture makes the inclusion of CDF into HTML that much easier and likely. But such inclusion also puts a great burden back onto Netscape to accept CDF as the de facto web-channel standard, which Netscape has vehemently opposed, given that they're promoting a standard of their own.

What's the deal with the ?s in the CDF files?

Whenever you create a CDF file, you need to also put the following piece of code right at the top:

`<?XML version="1.0"?>`

XML stands for *Extensible Markup Language*, which may sound slightly familiar if you've ever heard of *SGML*, or *Standard Generalized Markup Language*. (By the way, shouldn't Standard Generalized be a double negative?) Essentially, XML is a language that enables developers to create their own tags for a particular application and then create an architecture to support the use of those tags in an application.

Consider the example of a site where lounge lizards could go to buy cocktail recipes and pipes and get the latest on lounge acts coming to town. Every person who enters gets a profile, which includes a series of very specific tags, such as `<cocktails>`, `<pipes>`, and `<concerts>`, plus some other control tags such as `<their_town>`. By using XML, I could set up an application that checked their control tag `<their_town>` after they logged on and then provide them with the latest cocktail recipes from other lounge types in their area, along with specials on their favorite cigars by local merchants and information on upcoming concert events.

CDF does exactly this sort of thing but on a small scale. As part of its standardization efforts, Microsoft has proposed to the W3 Consortium that XML become an addition to SGML. A side effect of approval would mean that CDF would become a de facto web-channel standard, because CDF is a subset of XML. You can find out more about XML at `www.microsoft.com/standards/xml/`.

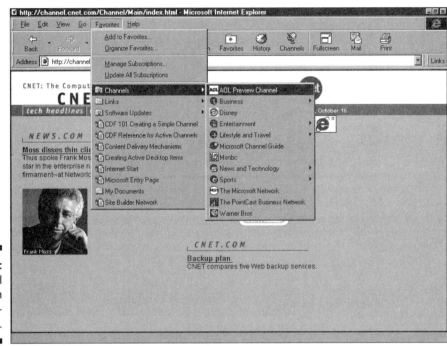

Figure 4-4:
Channel
graphics in
the drop-
down menu.

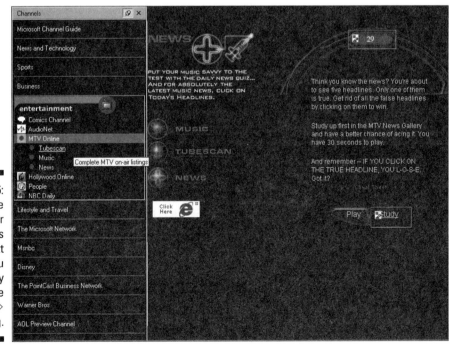

Figure 4-5:
Rolling the
mouse over
a link pops
up the text
that you
specify
in the
<ITEM>
tag.

Table 4-1 includes all the syntax for the CDF format, along with what the syntax means and what you can use it to accomplish. For your first few channels, you may use only a third of these commands, if not fewer! So, think of this as your working glossary to the CDF language. You can quickly tell that the syntax is nearly identical to HTML, with the exception that many of the tags are self contained. By self contained, I mean there's only one tag, instead of the open and close tags that are common in HTML. The self-contained tags in CDF subscribe to the following convention: `<TAG INFO="n" />`.

Table 4-1	Syntax for the Channel Definition Format	
Element	*Description*	*Syntax*
A	Describes a link.	`<A HREF="URL">...</A>`
Abstract	Text string used to describe a channel page.	`<ASTRACT>text </ABSTRACT>`
Channel	Describes the web channel, along with the BASE URL and cover page URL, as well as the number of links deep the site should be crawled.	`<CHANNEL BASE ="url"HREF="cover url" Level="n"> text </CHANNEL>`
Codebase	URL specifying code to install. Includes parameters for the size of the file, the type of setup, and the URL of the setup file.	`<Codebase SIZE="n" STYLE="Active Setup" VALUE="url"/>`
Config	Specifies the configuration needed for the desired software distribution type.	`<CONFIG>...<OSVALUE= "OS"/> </CONFIG>`
Dependency	Describes an element that must be present; otherwise, the distribution (install) can't be completed. Applies only when you're using CDF to update software.	`<DEPENDENCY>...</ DEPENDENCY>`
EarliestTime	The shortest period of time, in days, hours, or minutes, that an update can occur if an INTERVALTIME is set value.	`<EARLIESTTIME DAY="n" HOUR="n" MIN="n"/>`
HTTP-EQUIV	Used for sending or receiving files over the HTTP protocol.	`<HTTP-EQUIV NAME= "headerparam" VALUE="text"/>`
IntervalTime	Indicates the duration of time in which the channel will be checked once for an update, in days, hours, and minutes.	`<INTERVALTIME DAY="n" HOUR="n" MIN="n"/>`

Element	*Description*	*Syntax*
Item	Defines an item in a channel. Used to describe that item as a link within the Channel menu in Explorer.	`<ITEM HREF="url" LASTMOD="date" LEVEL= "n" PRECACHE="YES" | "NO">... text</ ITEM>`
Languages	The language used for the channel, in ISO 639 format.	`<LANGUAGES VALUE= "languages"/>`
LatestTime	The latest period of time, in days, hours, and minutes, that an update can occur if an INTERVALTIME value is set.	`<LATESTTIME DAY="n" HOUR="n"MIN ="n"/>`
Log	Specifies that the hit on a page should be recorded. Uses document:view as the syntax for this call.	`<LOGVALUE= "document:view"/>`
Login	Specifies a login that is used to authenticate a user after the site is crawled. If left empty, it prompts the user for the information.	`<LOGINDOMAIN= "domain"METHOD= "BASIC" | "DPA" | "MSN" | "NTLM" | "RPA"PASS="pass word"USER=" USERNAME"/>`
Logo	Specifies the logos to use in the Active Desktop (IMAGE) as well as in the Channel menu (ICON).	`<LOGO HREF="url" STYLE="ICON" | "IMAGE"/>`
LogTarget	Tells the browser where to send the log file, how to send the log file, and what information to send.	`<LOGTARGET HREF="url" METHOD="POST" | "PUT" SCOPE="ALL" | "OFFLINE" | "ONLINE">...</ LOGTARGET>`
OS	Specified Operating System.	`<OS VALUE="Mac" | "Win32" | "Win95" | "Winnt"/>`
OSVersion	Describes the OS version.	`<OSVERSION VALUE="n "/>`
Processor	Describes the processor type.	`<PROCESSOR VALUE= "Alpha" | "MIPS" | "PPC" | "x86"/>`

(continued)

Table 4-1 *(continued)*

Element	Description	Syntax
PurgeTime	After a log file is updated, any hits older than the time specified aren't logged.	`<PURGETIME DAY="n" HOUR="n"MIN="n"/>`
Schedule	Defines the start and end date when updates are to occur for channel. Date format is 8601:1988 date format (YYYY-MM-DD).	`<SCHEDULE STARTDATE= </SCHEDULE>`
SoftDist	The software distribution tag or the way in which content is installed on the user's PC. Includes parameters for install type, location, and version numbering.	`<SOFTDIST AUTOINSTALL="No"	"Yes" HREF="url" NAME="string" PRECACHE="No"	"Yes"STYLE= "ActiveSetup"	"MSICD"	"other" VERSION="n">`
Title	String that refers to the title of a channel.	`<TITLE>…</TITLE>`
Usage	Specifies how an element is used, as a channel, a screensaver, a desktop component, or an e-mail.	`<USAGE VALUE= "Channel"	"Email"	"DesktopComponent"	"NONE"	"ScreenSaver">`

Click! You're set up!

You can access the web channels through a button in the browser, through a button on the desktop, and even through a button next to the Start menu. In Internet Explorer 4.0, you're hard-pressed *not* to find the channels. Figure 4-6 shows all the locations within Explorer and Windows where you can access your favorite channels. The bigger question, however, is how do you subscribe to the channels in the first place?

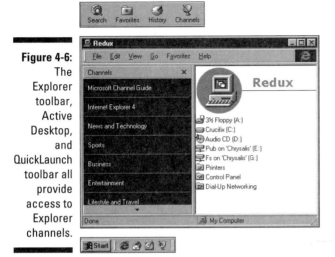

Figure 4-6:
The
Explorer
toolbar,
Active
Desktop,
and
QuickLaunch
toolbar all
provide
access to
Explorer
channels.

Come on! Everyone is subscribing . . . to anything

By using Internet Explorer 4.0, you can subscribe to both web channels and web pages. So, you may be wondering, what exactly is the difference then between the two? In the introduction to this chapter, I mention that web channels are just glorified web pages. I wasn't kidding. The only real differences between a subscription to a web page and a web channel are the following characteristics:

✔ Channels have their own interface that works in the background outside the Explorer interface.

✔ Channels have their own desktop interface and toolbar icon.

✔ Channels have hierarchical menus and graphics for emphasis.

✔ The subscription process is different between the web channels and web sites.

This statement, of course, begs another question. If the differences between web channels and web pages are so minute, how do you know if someone has an Explorer channel? To highlight Active Channels, Microsoft has created a de facto standard by creating an icon that you can put on your web site (similar to the one shown in Figure 4-7). If a user clicks the icon, that action launches the CDF file, sets the channel up in two areas within Explorer, as well as on the Active Desktop. Web sites that are bookmarked don't have this same kind of exposure in Explorer or on the desktop as channels.

Figure 4-7:
This icon
tells you
that an
Explorer
Channel is
available
for this site.

Add Active Channel

In contrast, if you want to subscribe to any old web site, you must use the Subscribe feature, which is located in Favorites⇨Subscriptions⇨Subscribe. If you find a page you like, choose Subscribe, and then you get the subscription menu. After you subscribe, the site can be added to any area of Explorer, including the Favorites menu, the Subscriptions menu or, gasp!, even the Channels menu.

You have options in the Subscription menu

Whether you decide to subscribe to a web channel or a web site, Explorer gives you the same set of options from which to choose. In a way, I'm glad they simplified the process by using the same menu for both, but come on — the differences between channels and sites are already sketchy enough. Using the same subscription interface doesn't do much for the cause!

The first thing you see after you subscribe to a channel is the Subscribe window, as shown in Figure 4-8. This window is the default window that you start and end with, no matter what happens in between. Mostly, you use it for setting your notification profile and scheduling your updates of content. You can also set your User ID and password in this window for channels that require them.

Figure 4-8:
The
Subscribe
window.
This is
where all
the magic
happens.

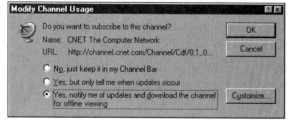

Modify Channel Usage

Do you want to subscribe to this channel?
Name: CNET The Computer Network
URL: http://channel.cnet.com/Channel/Cdf/0,1,,0...

○ No, just keep it in my Channel Bar
○ Yes, but only tell me when updates occur
● Yes, notify me of updates and download the channel for offline viewing

OK
Cancel
Customize...

Selecting the Customize button from the window opens a now familiar window for regular Windows 95 users: a Subscription Wizard! Who'dave guessed that? Briefly, here are the steps for you to follow to run through the Subscription Wizard:

1. **Decide whether you want just a notification or a notification and the pushing of pages by selecting one of the three buttons.**

   You have three choices. You can get no pages and just the notification; notification and the front page; or notification, the front page, and up to thousands of links deep, which is perhaps overkill.

2. **Click next, and select the an e-mail notification option.**

   If you want to be notified by e-mail, add an e-mail address and your mail server. If not, select No.

3. **Click next and specify your schedule by choosing a time to get updates.**

   If you chose Yes to getting pages pushed, you need to schedule when you want Explorer to check and see whether anything is new. You can autocheck, which is daily; set up your own parameters for checking; or you can simply do so manually whenever you fire up the browser.

Keeping itemized time

Earlier in this chapter, I describe some of the syntax that you use in defining a channel by using CDF. The key to ensuring that users receive their notifications that content is updated and is pushed to them lies in the following CDF parameter:

```
<ITEM HREF="URL" LASTMOD="date">...</ITEM>
```

The date, by the way, is in ISO 8601: 1988 date format. This line specifies the last time that a channel item was updated. The URL specified in the <ITEM> tag is checked according to the parameters set forth in the <SCHEDULE> tag. If the LASTMOD date has changed in the CDF file, the notification is sent to the user, as shown in Figure 4-9, and the new content is then pushed to the user (if, of course, the user specified it to do so).

This relationship is the essence of the how Explorer pushes content. Without the LASTMOD function, you have no channels. For web sites, Explorer uses a site crawler, or intelligent agent, to perform this same function so that users can subscribe to a site just as they would a channel.

The notification symbol indicates change.

Figure 4-9:
You've got new content! The notification symbol indicates that the LASTMOD date has changed.

Security

Security comes up time and time again in relation to the web browsers, mostly because I doubt that anyone thinks browsers are secure yet. In Explorer 4.0, Microsoft believes it's created the most secure web browser to date. Here are some of the features that Explorer 4.0 supports:

- ✓ **Security zones,** which provides different levels of security based on the assignments that the user specifies for a particular site.

- ✓ **Certificate management,** which enables network administrators to specify that various applications can (or can't) run on machines, based on who wrote the application. An extension of this concept is the Authenticode Certificate, which verifies that a piece of software hasn't been tampered with before being passed on to a user.

- ✓ **Permission-based Java security** enables you to specify which kinds of Java applets you want to pass through to your desktop.

- ✓ **Additional tools for transactions.** Explorer 4.0 provides a host of tools to ensure secure transactions, including the new Profile Assistant, support for Secure Sockets Layer (SSL), and Private Communications Technology (PCT), as well as the new Microsoft Wallet.

Where Do PointCast and BackWeb Fit in?

As you see in Chapter 6, PointCast has become an integral part of the Microsoft webcasting strategy. Together with BackWeb, the three companies have lobbied a lot of support for the CDF format. Both BackWeb and PointCast have built their software products by using the CDF format, so whenever you think about building a channel for Internet Explorer, you're also creating content that uses the same underpinnings for channels for both these companies.

In many ways, the Microsoft, PointCast, and BackWeb triumvirate is an odd marriage of convenience. PointCast builds Internet Explorer into the PointCast Network, so using CDF channels here wasn't much of a stretch. In the cast of BackWeb, which is using the Microsoft Active Setup technology with its own technology to create online installations that remain synched, even if the connection goes down, the match isn't quite so obvious. BackWeb, however, has become an integral part of the Microsoft plan because of its Internet expertise and sizeable installed base of proprietary web channels, which — until recently — did not support CDF.

Chapter 5

Channels the Quick and Painless Way — with Explorer

• •

In This Chapter

▶ Inside the CDF file

▶ Creating and testing your channel

▶ Promoting your channel

▶ Some advanced features of Internet Explorer 4.0

• •

*Y*ou've got a pretty nice web page, I'm willing to bet. No real need to change the way it looks or throw caution to the wind and dump the whole site for this crazy thing called webcasting. On the other hand, something about this webcasting thing has caught your fancy. You want a piece of the action. You've got your copy of Internet Explorer 4.0, and you're looking at a lot of the channels and thinkin', "Geez, *I* could do this!"

Well, my friends, that's exactly why this chapter is in the book. From here on out, you're getting no-holds-barred, hands-on, roll-up-the-sleeves-and-get-outta-my-way-'cause-I'm-buildin'-a-web-channel prose.

Rather than simply throw a whole bunch of HTML and JavaScript at you without any real context, which wouldn't be very nice, I thought I'd take a different approach. Just for fun, I created a web site devoted to all things Lounge, called Site Swank. The site covers music, cocktails, clubs, and other things that have become synonymous with the growing Lounge scene. For the purposes of example, I thought that taking Site Swank and converting it to Channel Swank, across the various channel platforms, would be cool. That way, I can show you how you can manipulate a common web site (or not, depending on the channel type) to create a web channel.

Note: According to Webster's, *Swank* means "dashing smartness, as in dress or appearance; pretentiousness; swagger." Personally, I'd just say, "see Frank Sinatra, circa 1950." That should cover it.

Site Swank is the basis for most of the web channel examples in the book. My hope is that, by using a real site, the "real world" examples in the book are that much more compelling and appropriate for the site conversions and channel building you're doing. Figure 5-1 shows the home page of Site Swank. The site is a mix and match of HTML, JavaScript, some CSS (Cascading Style Sheets), and the basics of animation. In short, it's much like a lot of other sites out there.

Just thought you'd want to know that everything in this book that relates to Site Swank (and its channel companion, Channel Swank), you can find on the book's accompanying CD-ROM, in the Swank file directory. (And don't forget that you can find Internet Explorer 4.0 on the CD, too.)

Now, about getting that Internet Explorer channel going. The process of converting your site to a channel in Internet Explorer 4.0 is pretty straight forward. You need to complete the following four basic tasks:

- ✔ Step One: Selecting the pages to push.
- ✔ Step Two: Creating a CDF file.
- ✔ Step Three: Getting on the Active Channel Guide.
- ✔ Step Four: Promoting your channel.

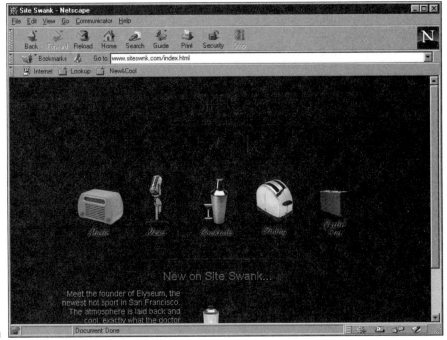

Figure 5-1:
Site Swank is the baseline for all the conversions to web channels in this book.

Step One: Selecting the Pages to Push

You could push every page in your web site to users, but they'd more than likely come to hate you for doing it. Imagine downloading all the graphics from a site to someone's hard drive every time that you updated the site. Ugh! Obviously, you don't want to set up your future subscribers that way, but you also want to communicate your message effectively. That's why you need to ask yourself the following two questions about your web channel before you get started:

- ✔ Do you want to keep your existing web front page as your web channel front page?
- ✔ How many other web pages from your site should you push?

This entire section is about making a good decision in choosing what content is important to your subscribers. If you've already got a web site front page that you're happy with and you have no intentions of changing it, you can skip right past the following sections and on to Step 2!

Can you push your web site front page as it is?

Check out Figures 5-2 and 5-3. In Figure 5-2, you have a web site front page with the news-style format that continues to be the rage among large-content web sites. The idea is to pack as much information in and enable the users to explore the site if they want. Figure 5-3 uses the more common icon-based approach to web-site design, mixing in a bit of text. Most Web sites fall into one of these two basic categories.

Both of these kinds of front pages work fine in an Internet Explorer 4.0 channel. The real question, however, is whether they deliver useful content to the user. The most basic idea for a channel is to get the important stuff to the subscribers and enable them to go farther for more if they want. Both of these examples violate that premise. The CNET site is too busy, and the SoftImage site doesn't provide enough information to be useful.

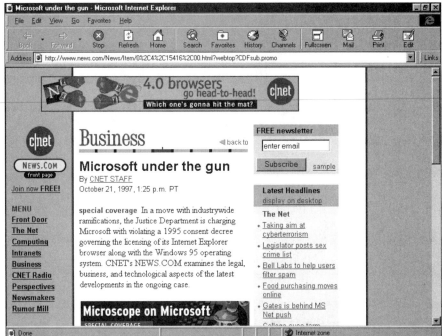

Figure 5-2:
The CNET
web site
uses the
common
news
format for
the design
of its
Web site.

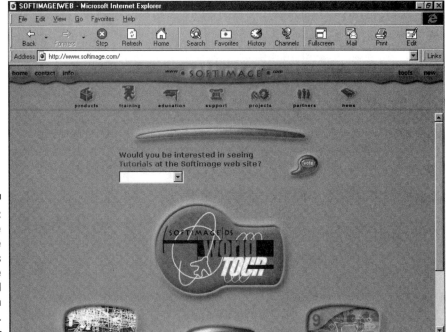

Figure 5-3:
The
SoftImage
Web site is
a more
traditional
icon-driven
Web site.

Your best bet is to create a new top-level channel page that combines the best elements of a news-style site and solid iconography to create a kind of "billboard-style" front page to your channel. By doing so, you have a method of delivering new content as well as maintaining a structure that enables easy access to other parts of your channel. For reference, you may want to go back and take another look at the Site Swank front page in Figure 5-1.

How many pages should you push?

Site Swank has six areas that users can access from the site, including those in the following list:

- ✔ The Home Page
- ✔ News
- ✔ Music
- ✔ Cocktails
- ✔ Clubs
- ✔ Travel

Each of these sections has cool and important information. I wouldn't want to have six pages in the Explorer Channel Bar, however, as users inevitably ask, "Why not just send me the important stuff?" And, of course, they'd be right. The trick is to condense your site to its most important features and then enable the users to go farther into your site if they want.

Remember, however, that your goal is to get a channel up quickly and easily. You shouldn't need to completely rework your web site just to accommodate channel users. Figure 5-4 shows the NBC news channel on Internet Explorer 4.0. You can see that the channel front page contains a lot of content that subscribers can access. Take a look, however, at Figure 5-5. You can see that the number of objects the Channel Bar lists is smaller in this figure.

In determining areas which are the best to promote, you need to consider the kind of foot traffic that your web site currently generates. Those areas that are the most popular are the ones to which you want to give an active link in the Explorer Channel Bar. To give you a general idea, however, the average number of links in the Channel Bar appears to be about four.

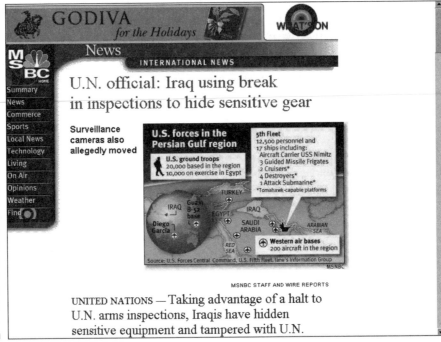

Figure 5-4:
The NBC news channel's front page accesses around ten areas within the channel.

Figure 5-5:
The area in the Channel Bar of the NBC news channel includes only five of the ten areas the page accesses.

Take Site Swank as an example. My ISP enables me to check my usage statistics by page. (Checking usage statistics is something that, if you don't already do, you should, just because doing so helps you figure out what works and what doesn't work about your web site.) I analyzed my foot traffic over the first month that it was up and found that the areas that were the most appealing were the news bits, the cocktail recipes, and the music section. Everything else tended to get about the same hit numbers per

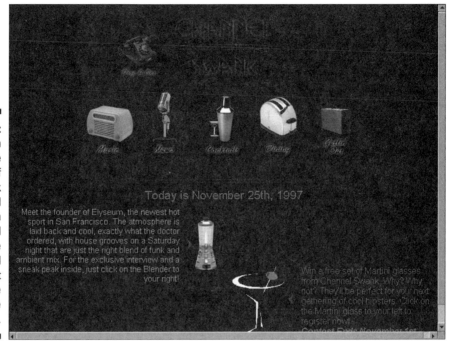

Figure 5-6:
Although only three areas of the Swank Channel appear in the Channel Bar, all the channel areas get exposure on the front page.

month. I concluded that the best way to go was to just go with those three pages in the Channel Bar and make sure that the front page of the channel called out all the others areas, with both icons and news-style flashes. Figure 5-6 shows how this setup looks.

Step Two: Creating a CDF File

After you decide how you want to present your web channel front page and determine the number of pages to include in the Channel Bar, you're pretty well ready to create your CDF file. The *CDF file* is the most important part of the Explorer 4.0 channel interface. This file controls the setup of all channels and then manages the content that the channel pushes to subscribers.

Any time that you create a channel, Explorer reads the CDF file to determine the web channel front page, as well as the other pages that are part of the channel. The CDF file enables you to set the graphics that appear in the Channel Bar, along with the accompanying channel-page links. After you update your channels, Explorer reads the CDF file to determine whether the content on any of the specified channel pages has changed. If so, Explorer pushes those pages. If not, they aren't pushed.

In Chapter 4, I include a table containing all the syntax for the CDF file. In this chapter, you begin to use some of that syntax. CDF is pretty robust in that you can do a lot with it. The good news, however, is that you can get your channel up and running by using only a very small amount of it.

Creating a CDF file is just like creating an HTML file. Whatever HTML editor you're using to create your web pages works just fine for creating CDF files, too.

This section goes point by point through the CDF file. If you've seen one before or just want to see the whole thing and paste in your own channel information, you can skip through the following few sections and go directly to the section "The whole enchilada," later in this chapter, which includes all the code together.

Naming your CDF

No, it's not a pet, and you don't need to take care of it like you do a Tamagachi (those nifty virtual pets that die every five minutes or so!), but you do need to choose a name for your CDF file. Explorer recognizes the CDF language through the CDF file extension. You can name your CDF file whatever you want as long as it has that .cdf at the end.

The CDF header

The CDF file uses the *Extensible Markup Language (XML),* which is a subset of the *Standard Generalized Markup Language (SGML),* as its primary language. Although different from HTML, the syntax is very similar, so it will no doubt begin to look familiar after you start using it. Because all browsers default to reading HTML, you need to tell the browser to read your CDF script in its correct language. The following identifying code, placed at the beginning of your CDF file, accomplishes just that purpose:

```
<?XML version="1.0"?>
```

Specifying the channel and the CDF

After you set the language, the next thing that Explorer needs is the location of the web channel's front page. To identify this location, you have a specific `<CHANNEL>` tag. Within the `<CHANNEL>` tag is an `HREF` function, which you use to specify the front page of the web channel.

In addition to specifying the location of the channel's top-level page, you also need to specify the location of the CDF file by using the BASE function. BASE tells Explorer where to look to read the CDF file as it updates the channel. In the end, the script for specifying Channel Swank is as shown in the following example:

```
<CHANNEL HREF="http://www.siteswank.com/channels/i
home.htm" BASE="http://www.siteswank.com/channels/ie/cdf/
swank.cdf>
```

Setting titles, logos, and abstracts

Not everything in the CDF file works the same as in HTML, as you're about to find out. As you probably noticed, the HREF function is a lift right out of HTML. In this brief section, you're going to find that the <TITLE> tag is just like the same tag in HTML, but the <LOGO> tag is not. The whole situation makes you feel like screaming, "Just pick one and stick with it, please!"

You have two basic ways to describe your channel. One involves text and the other involves graphics. The <TITLE> tag, which is just like the <HEAD> tag in HTML and basically does the same kind of thing, describes your channel by using text. It sets the title of the channel as it appears in the Explorer Active Channel Bar. To set your channel, just include the following code in your CDF file:

```
<TITLE> Channel Swank </TITLE>
```

The <LOGO> tags control how your channel appears in the more graphically oriented *Active Channel Bar,* which is shown in Figure 5-7. Actually, you have two graphics that you must specify. One is for the aforementioned Active Channel Bar. The other is for an icon that accompanies the title of your channel.

Note: You can see the Active Channel within the browser, as part of the full screen web channel viewer, or as a stand-alone floating window on the desktop.

The <LOGO> tag has two functions associated with it. One is the HREF function, which specifies the location of the graphics to use. The other is the STYLE function, which specifies whether the graphic is for the Active Channel Bar or for the icon that accompanies the <TITLE> tag. The icon is located in the channel file menu within Explorer.

Figure 5-7:
The Active
Channel
Bar.

Each of the graphics has a standardized size as well. The graphic that you use for the Channel Bar needs to be a GIF image that's 80 pixels wide by 32 pixels high. The ⟨TITLE⟩ tag icon can be either a GIF or an ICO image and must be a 16-pixel square. The following examples provide the final code for each of these graphics:

```
<LOGO HREF="http://www.siteswank.com/channels/ie/graphics/
icon.gif" STYLE="icon"/>
```

```
<LOGO HREF="http://www.siteswank.com/channels/ie/graphics
channel_menu.gif" STYLE="image"/>
```

The ⟨ABSTRACT⟩ tag, which you see again in a few paragraphs, specifies a pop-up dialog box that users see after they roll their mouse over the channel logo. The tag is versatile in that you can use it at the top level, as here, or within other tags, such as the ⟨ITEM⟩ tag, which I describe in the following section.

To describe Channel Swank to prospective subscribers, I use the following example. Figure 5-8 shows how this code line looks for the *Wall Street Journal Interactive* in the Channel Bar.

```
<ABSTRACT> The web channel for Swingers, Hipsters and other
Loungy types. Leave your coat at the door, grab yourself a
Bombay Tonic, slip into your chaise lounge, and set your
attitude to cool.</ABSTRACT>
```

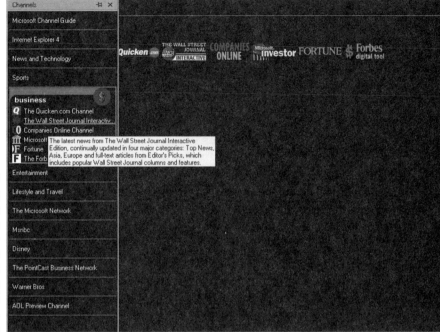

Setting your menu links

Earlier in Step One, I told you that you'd need to choose which pages on your site to include in your web channel. Here's where you specify those pages. The ⟨ITEM⟩ tag (which works like an HTML tag) enables you to specify the channel page links in both the Explorer Favorites menu as well as in the Channel Bar. Explorer checks each of the pages that you specify here for updates to your web channel and sends a notification to the users if those pages changed.

The ⟨ITEM⟩ tag handles two other tag types to create the entire menu link. The ⟨TITLE⟩ tag, which I mentioned briefly back in Chapter 4, sets the text that appears in the Favorites and Channel Bars. The ⟨ABSTRACT⟩ tag sets a small piece of text that describes what that part of the channel is about. Here is the code I used for the three areas of the Channel Swank that appears in those lists:

```
<ITEM HREF="http://www.siteswank.com/channels/ie/news.htm">
<TITLE> Swingin' News </TITLE>
<ABSTRACT> All the News that's fit to print </ABSTRACT>
</ITEM>
```

```
<ITEM HREF="http://www.siteswank.com/channels/ie/
cocktails.htm">
<TITLE> Smooth Cocktails </TITLE>
<ABSTRACT> Cocktail recipes for the ultra hip </ABSTRACT>
</ITEM>
```

```
<ITEM HREF="http://www.siteswank.com/channels/ie/
music.htm">
<TITLE> Sounds of Swank </TITLE>
<ABSTRACT> The classic toe tapping and finger snappin'
sounds </ABSTRACT>
</ITEM>
```

Default scheduling

In Internet Explorer, you can schedule the times that you want a web channel to be crawled. Crawling is the process by which Explorer goes out and checks the CDF file. If web pages have been changed since the previous time that Explorer looked at the CDF file, Explorer will go get those new pages and deliver them to the user. Figure 5-9 shows the dialog box that users use to schedule the updates of their channels. By using the CDF file, however, you can set the default scheduling right in Explorer.

Figure 5-9:
The Modify Channel Usage dialog box appears any time that you subscribe to a channel.

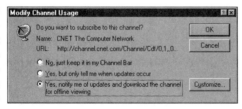

Scheduling is set within the ⟨SCHEDULE⟩ tag, which is handy. The ⟨SCHEDULE⟩ tag, as does the ⟨CHANNEL⟩ tag, must be at the top level of the CDF file if it's to work. In fact, a good practice is to put it right after the ⟨CHANNEL⟩ tag in your file.

The theory behind the ⟨SCHEDULE⟩ tag is that, by using it , you can better manage your server traffic. If, however, you're making your own personal channel and you don't spend much time consulting with your ISP, you may not even need this tag.

Now, what does the ⟨SCHEDULE⟩ tag do? Say, for example, that I want Channel Swank updated at least once a day for new content. I know that my greatest server traffic is late in the day, so I want the updates to occur before the end of the business day. The ⟨SCHEDULE⟩ tag, along with a few other tags that are subordinate to the ⟨SCHEDULE⟩ tag, enables me to accomplish this task.

The subordinate, or Child functions, are EarliestTime, LatestTime, and IntervalTime, all of which are defined briefly in Chapter 4. Together, you can use these functions to manage your channel updates down to literally the minute! While users ultimately have the choice of creating their own download schedule, you can help them out by following these steps to create the three tags that fit within the ⟨SCHEDULE⟩ tag.

1. **First, set the INTERVALTIME tag.**

   Interval time is how often I want the channel to update, which, in this case, is once a day. This tag look as follows:

   ```
   <INTERVALTIME DAY="1" />
   ```

You can take the IntervalTime down to the minute, if you so desire. Just change DAY to MIN, and keep the "1". Now, your channel would be updated every minute!

2. **Then set the EARLIESTTIME tag.**

   Earliest time is the earliest point within that day that I want the update to take place. In this case, I want the update to occur sometime in the morning, so I'd use a time such as 7 hours, to represent 7:00 AM. All times are clocked from midnight. The tag would look as follows:

   ```
   <EARLIESTTIME HOUR="7" />
   ```

3. **Finally, set the LATESTTIME tag.**

   Latest time is the last point within that day that the update can occur. In this case, I want the update to occur before 5 p.m. Keeping with the idea of a twenty-four-hour clock, I'd specify 17 hours accordingly.

   ```
   <LATESTTIME HOUR="17" />
   ```

Put it all together, and the schedule function in your CDF file looks like the following example:

```
<SCHEDULE>
<INTERVALTIME DAY="1" />
<EARLIESTTIME HOUR="7" />
<LATESTTIME HOUR="17" />
</SCHEDULE>
```

You can also set the interval of time with which the scheduling function begins and ends. If, for example, you have some special function going on for a day, and you want to increase the amount of times that the channel updates for that day, you can use the STARTDATE and ENDDATE functions in the <SCHEDULE> tag to increase this interval. For a special promotion in which you want the channel to update every 30 minutes all day for that day, the default scheduling function would look as follows:

```
<SCHEDULE STARTDATE="1997.12.01" ENDDATE="1997.12.02">
<INTERVALTIME MIN="30" />
<EARLIESTTIME MIN="1" />
<LATESTTIME MIN="29" />
</SCHEDULE>
```

Note: The more functions you add, the more things you must update and take care of, so I'd shy away from using start and end dates if you're just beginning to work on your first Explorer web channel.

Maintaining LASTMOD

You may have wondered just how your web channel was going to update. Well, that's what the LASTMOD function is all about. Although Explorer does have a *site crawler,* a tool that automatically goes out and brings the content from a site back to the user, Explorer can't figure out what's new on its own. It needs your help, and that's where the CDF file comes into play.

Every time an Active Channel updates, the CDF file is read by Explorer first. Every time the CDF file is read, Explorer looks for changes in the file. What kind of changes would Explorer expect to find? Here are some examples:

 ✔ The number of links in the Active Channel Bar changed.

 ✔ The schedule times for updating the channel have changed.

 ✔ New pages need to be pushed to the subscriber.

LASTMOD is the function that enables you to tell the Browser that something has changed on one of the channel pages. You place LASTMOD within the <ITEM> tag; LASTMOD includes the last date that you updated the channel page. If you change the content — yep, you guessed it — you also must change the CDF file. Using the cocktails <ITEM> tag from *Setting your menu links,* LASTMOD would look as follows:

```
<ITEM HREF="http://www.siteswank.com/channels/ie
cocktails.htm" LASTMOD="1997-12-0100:00">
<TITLE> Smooth Cocktails </TITLE>
<ABSTRACT> Cocktail recipes for the ultra hip </ABSTRACT>
</ITEM>
```

I've also include a small table here (Table 5-1) that highlights the Syntax for the date in LASTMOD. LASTMOD uses Greenwich Mean Time, or Universal Time Code (UTC). This is one of several time standards that are used for keeping time on the Internet. The format for time in UTC is yyyy-mm-ddThh:mm

Table 5-1	Keeping Time in **LASTMOD**
Code	*Time specification*
yyyy	Specifies the year
mm	Specifies the month (01–12)
dd	Specifies the day of the month (01–31)
hh	Specifies the hour of the day (00–23)
mm	Specifies the minutes (00–59)

The whole enchilada

Whew! Now, all that CDF wasn't so bad, was it? Seems strange, but really, after you put all of those elements together in a CDF file, you're ready to set up your Active Channel in Explorer. The following example puts all the items that I discussed into one CDF file, which you can use as a template to create your own CDF file. (I put in LASTMOD statements for all the ITEMs in this example.)

```
<?XML version="1.0"?>
<CHANNEL HREF="http://www.siteswank.com/channels/ie/
home.htm" BASE="http://www.siteswank.com/channels/ie/cdf/ " >
<ABSTRACT> The web channel for Swingers, Hipsters and other
Loungy types. Leave your coat at the door, grab yourself a
Bombay Tonic, slip into your chaise lounge, and set your
attitude to cool.
</ABSTRACT>
<SCHEDULE>
<INTERVALTIME DAY="1" />
<EARLIESTTIME HOUR="7" />
<LATESTTIME HOUR="17" />
</SCHEDULE>
<LOGO HREF="http://www.siteswank.com/channels/ie/graphics/
icon.gif" STYLE="icon"/>
<LOGO HREF="http://www.siteswank.com/channels/ie/graphics/
channel_menu.gif" STYLE="image"/>
<ITEM HREF="http://www.siteswank.com/channels/ie/news.htm"
LASTMOD="1997-12-0100:00">
<TITLE> Swingin' News </TITLE>
<ABSTRACT> All the News that's fit to print </ABSTRACT>
</ITEM>
<ITEM HREF="http://www.siteswank.com/channels/ie/
cocktails.htm" LASTMOD="1997-12-0100:00">
<TITLE> Smooth Cocktails </TITLE>
<ABSTRACT> Cocktail recipes for the ultra hip </ABSTRACT>
</ITEM>
<ITEM HREF="http://www.siteswank.com/channels/ie/music.htm"
LASTMOD="1997-12-0100:00">
<TITLE> Sounds of Swank </TITLE>
<ABSTRACT> The classic toe tapping and finger snappin'
sounds </ABSTRACT>
</ITEM>
</CHANNEL>
```

Posting the CDF file

You always have one more thing to do. After you finish creating the CDF file, you must put it on your web server. Now, you can't test your CDF file locally unless you're running an HTTP Proxy Server, but who wants to go through that hassle? Your best bet is to create a simple HTML page on your local machine that includes an HREF to the CDF file on your web server (or ISPs web server, whichever the case may be).

You can use the following HTML to create a page to test your CDF file. Figure 5-10 shows the Channel Swank test page in Explorer:

```
<HTML>
<HEAD>
<TITLE>(Type a title for your page here)</TITLE>
</HEAD>
<BODY>
<A HREF="Insert the URL of your CDF file here"> I want to
subscribe to my first channel</A>
</BODY>
</HTML>
```

Make sure that you test all your links and your functions. In fact, the first thing that you probably want to test is the LASTMOD date. After you run the CDF file, go back to the CDF file and change the LASTMOD date for one of the links. Then post the new version of the CDF file to your web server. From there, follow these steps to test your CDF file:

1. **Within Explorer, select Favorites⇨Manage Subscriptions.** From here, find your channel and right-click it.

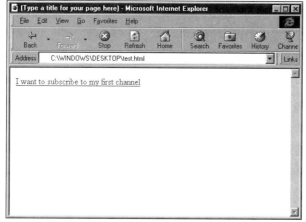

Figure 5-10:
Use this page to test your subscription.

2. **Select Properties to view your schedule properties.** You'll have to select the Schedule tab from the properties menu to actually see your channel schedule.

3. **Select New to change your schedule properties.** After you select New, you can then set your update time to be some very small interval, say five minutes. That way, you'll be able to see if Explorer is reading your CDF file changes when it tries to update the channel.

Using the Microsoft Channel Wizard: One man's tale

For all my talk about going through the CDF file-creation process, I do know a "simpler" way to create a CDF file. Microsoft, in trying to standardize all their products, including the ones using the web, created a Wizard for creating CDF files. If you've used any other Microsoft products lately, you're no doubt familiar with Wizards.

A Wizard is, essentially, a one-stop automated route to making a file, such as a Project document or a PowerPoint presentation. My experience with the Wizards is that they start off okay enough but that the final product is rarely ever what you had envisioned as you started. Such is the case with the Channel Wizard.

The Channel Wizard (shown here) is actually a web document, not a feature component of Explorer. You can access the Channel Wizard through the SiteBuilder Network at www.microsoft.com/sitebuilder/. The Wizard guides you through the basics of putting together the CDF file, including creating the <CHANNEL> tag and the <LOGO> information. The Wizard also enables you to set the basic scheduling information. But that's really all it does. You find nothing on the <ITEM> tags or on setting the Icon and Active Channel Menu text.

In short, although the idea was a good one, the execution is pretty underwhelming. I found myself just throwing out everything that came from the Wizard and just rolling my own CDF file. Funny — that's what I seem to do with all the Microsoft Wizards.

Step Three: Getting on the Active Channel Guide

Now that you're all ready to go to town on your channel, how are you going to get it up and running and tell people about it? Well, that's probably the most frustrating part of the entire Explorer web-channel experience. Right now, the only way in which having an Explorer web channel makes sense is if you're playing on the Microsoft Channel Guide team. Being on the Microsoft Active Channel Guide is the only way to guarantee exposure — at least until somebody develops a guide to Explorer channels, which depends, no doubt, on how successful the whole channel concept turns out to be. In the interim, get ready to jump through some hoops to become part of the Microsoft Active Channel Guide.

The big set up: The preview page

What happens after a potential subscriber decides to click your channel's image from the Channel Guide? The user gets to see the preview page, which is very much like the one shown in Figure 5-11. Every Active Channel page has a preview page because, well, Microsoft says so. You don't actually need to have one, but Microsoft requires that you have one to be part of its Channel Guide (more on that in the following section), so everyone has one if they want on the Active Channel Guide.

A preview page is really just a promotional page that tells potential subscribers what they get if they subscribe.

Figure 5-11:
A preview page for an Active Channel. Simple, isn't it?

According to Microsoft, web-channel developers must have a preview page, and the page must fit the following parameters:

- ✔ The preview page must be 460 pixels wide and 365 pixels high.
- ✔ The preview page must have its own URL.
- ✔ The preview page should not exceed 35K in size (although this requirement isn't enforced much).
- ✔ The standard "Add to Channels" icon should be used at the bottom of the preview page.

Now, I know this sounds awfully big brother-esque, but Microsoft does have a good reason to slap these requirements on channel developers. You see later on, in Chapter 9, I discuss Netcaster and how not having a standardized form for subscribing can create confusion among potential viewers. If you need proof, just fire up Internet Explorer 4.0 and look at the channel guide. All the channels are unique but share some common underpinnings. The result is that the channel environment looks clean and well thought out from a user's perspective.

The general rule is that web channel front pages should be functional but not overly splashy. Web channel preview pages, however, are an entirely different matter. If you've got a penchant for Dynamic HTML or heavy JavaScript animations, the preview page is your place to cut loose!

The big catch: SiteBuilder membership

Now, are you ready for a really big catch? To legally use its logo or to be a part of the Active Channel Guide, you must become a member of the Microsoft SiteBuilder Network. Perhaps many of you are already members, but I'm betting that the vast majority of people out there aren't.

The SiteBuilder Network, as shown in Figure 5-12, is the Microsoft online resource for Web professionals. For most people, becoming a member is free, but you really should jump on over to www.microsoft.com/ sitebuilder/default.htm to take a look for yourself. To become a member, you must sign an agreement, as well as submit your site for consideration, as Microsoft determines to what level of the network you're assigned.

Note: If you're not going to be part of the SiteBuilder Network, you don't need to do a preview page, because, well, you don't have any place to put it. In that case, you just want to put the link to your CDF file someplace on your web site's home page.

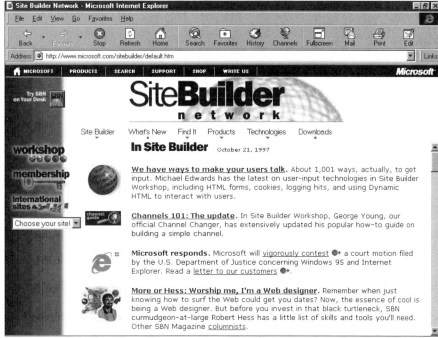

Figure 5-12:
The
SiteBuilder
Network,
the
Microsoft
online
resource
for Web
professionals.

Catch number two: Dynamic HTML

I can tell you one other good reason not to like Microsoft. Making channel developers become part of the SiteBuilder Network, a clear ploy to move people away from Netscape, is one reason. Another reason is that Microsoft requires you to use Dynamic HTML someplace in your channel if you want your channel on the Active Channel Guide. Dynamic HTML is the latest and greatest version of HTML that allows you to create layers within your HTML page, as well as create simple animations without needing JavaScript.

Now, why in the world would you want to tie a web channel to the use of Dynamic HTML? That's such a good question, and again, the answer boils down to Microsoft promoting their own standards in an effort to catch and surpass Netscape. Nobody ever (and I do mean ever) said that Microsoft was a benevolent company. Even though I happen to agree that Dynamic HTML is good for the industry, this move no doubt is going to leave a bad taste in every developer's mouth.

The Dynamic HTML can be in either your channel or in the preview page, just as long as you have it there somewhere. Certainly you can write your own Dynamic HTML, but if you want to make things easy on yourself, you can use one of two simple Dynamic HTML scripts that Microsoft provides on its Active Channel web site. (For fun, I include one of them.)

To use Dynamic HTML, you must place the following script in the <HEAD> tag of your HTML page, wherever you happen to be using the tag. This script is a simple one that checks to make sure that the browser can support the Microsoft Dynamic HTML:

```
<SCRIPT LANGUAGE="Javascript"><!— var bIsIE4 =
navigator.userAgent.indexOf("MSIE 4.0") != -1
&& navigator.userAgent.indexOf("b1") == -1//—>
</SCRIPT>
```

This script turns the text that you specify in your script from red to blue after the mouse runs over it. The script that makes it all happen is right here:

```
<SPAN ONMOUSEOVER="bIsIE4?this.style.color='red':null"
ONMOUSEOUT="bIsIE4?this.style.color='blue':
null">your text here</SPAN>
```

After you implement this simple script somewhere in your channel, you satisfy Microsoft's need to promote its own technology at your expense. But — hey! — at least your text looks kinda neat.

Note: If you're looking for a good book on Dynamic HTML, check out *Dynamic HTML For Dummies* by Michael Hyman (IDG Books Worldwide, Inc.).

Step Four: Promoting Your Channel

You really have no reason to create an Explorer Channel unless you're planning on being a part of the SiteBuilder Network, simply because no other major Active Channel Guides are out there. Of course, you don't need to be a member of the SiteBuilder Network to create a web channel. Promoting your channel, however, becomes much more difficult if you're not a member. As I mentioned in Step Three, though, the Active Channel Guide (as shown in Figure 5-13), is run exclusively by the SiteBuilder Network group at Microsoft.

Note: Even though only one channel guide is currently out there for Internet Explorer 4.0 channels, I don't expect that situation to last very long. Attempts at standardization inevitably leave some people on the outside and disenfranchised, so some other group is very likely to create an Explorer web channel guide before long.

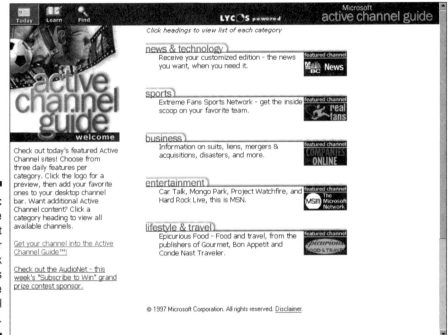

Figure 5-13:
The
Microsoft
SiteBuilder
Network
maintains
the Active
Channel
Guide.

The advantages to being part of the Active Channel Guide are pretty obvious. The Guide has a slot on the Active Channel Bar in Explorer, next to the Disneys and NBCs of the world, who no doubt have their prime real estate because they've entered into strategic agreements with Microsoft. Every channel that is part of the Channel Guide gets a preview page and receives the benefits of using the standardized icons. If you think that you don't need those things, just take a quick look at the PointCast Network. Expect its Add Active Channel icon to become synonymous with Internet Explorer 4.0 in a hurry.

Advanced Features of Internet Explorer 4.0

After you have your channel up and running, you may want to look at using some of the more advanced features of Internet Explorer 4.0 with your web channel. Be careful, however, because each of these items can add a lot of work to maintaining your channel, as they require that you either gather more information about your users up front or that you spend even more time maintaining your channel.

Accessing the Active Desktop

In addition to having an Active Channel, you can go even farther and put your channel directly on the users' desktops. After users install Internet Explorer 4.0, they have the option to install an Active Desktop Folder in the display. The Active Desktop is made up of an HTM file, and by making a small modification to a CDF file, you can place items in that HTM file. Active Desktop items are really designed for people who have a constant connection to the Internet, so unless that's your target demographic, I'd avoid the Active Desktop altogether.

If you do want to take a crack at persistent content on the Active Desktop, however, just a simple addition to the CDF file gets you going. Unfortunately, you can't integrate the Active Desktop with your CDF file for the Active Channel. You need a separate CDF file, even though the syntax is the same. To create an Active Desktop item, you need to modify the `<ITEM>` tag.

I go into more detail on the Active Desktop and CDF in Chapter 7.

Active e-mail and screen savers

You can do two other interesting little things with Internet Explorer 4.0. You can assign updates to come either via an e-mail notification or as part of a screen saver. Both use the `<USAGE>` tag within the `<ITEM>` tag in the same CDF file, and you can use them within your Active Channel CDF file. With screen savers, users are notified and asked whether they want to make the elements part of the Active Screen Saver. With e-mail, users are prompted for an e-mail address and an e-mail client if none exists. The only limitation on the e-mail notification is that it's limited to one example per CDF file. I go into more detail on the Active Desktop and CDF in Chapter 7.

Chapter 6

Making Connections with The PointCast Business Network

In This Chapter

▶ Defining The PointCast Business Network

▶ Building a channel for PointCast

▶ Promoting your PointCast Channel

*I*t's good to be the King. And, let's face it, when it comes to Push, PointCast is the King. They were the first, and to date they still do it the best. Call it good fortune, or karma, or just plain luck, but PointCast was the first company to think that people may actually like to have content sent to them passively, instead of having to look for it all the time.

The results of their efforts are most impressive. The PointCast Network, recently renamed The PointCast Business Network, has millions of users around the world. Granted, a great majority of them are corporate users, but I don't think anyone is complaining about getting the mindshare of corporate buyers. PointCast provides a great interface, utilizing a screen saver metaphor, and with partners like CNN and Ziff-Davis, they've become a key resource for business people on the go.

PointCast has been a close partner with Microsoft from the outset. Previous versions of PointCast have had Internet Explorer built right in, and this version is no different. In addition, though, PointCast co-authored the Channel Definition Format (CDF) standard with Microsoft. That's right! As crazy as it may seem, a couple of companies in the world of webcasting actually partnered and jointly developed a standard.

The result is that you won't have to do much of anything new to create a channel in PointCast. If you've made it through Chapters 4 and 5, you should be familiar with the CDF terminology, and the process is well automated, making the transition from an Explorer Channel to a PointCast channel an easy one. In fact, when it's all said and done, you may want to even do the PointCast Channel first, depending upon the business you're in.

The PointCast demographic may not apply to everyone's interests. As I mentioned, it is a predominantly business-oriented audience. Of course, this isn't to say that people in business don't want to read about where the coolest lounge clubs are. However, these people may not be as interested in lounge clubs as the general Explorer audience. Here are some figures, lifted directly from PointCast, highlighting their audience demographics:

- The average age of a PointCast viewer is 39.
- The average household income of a PointCast viewer is $80,000.
- 75 percent of viewers have graduated college or earned a higher degree.
- 77 percent of viewers use PointCast in a business environment.
- 95 percent of viewers are likely to recommend it to a colleague or friend.

Is this the audience you want to hit? Something to ponder as you're downloading PointCast 2.0 from the Internet — which is exactly what's coming next!

Getting The PointCast Business Network

Getting a product is always the easy part. But getting The PointCast Business Network is especially easy. The entire download is less than 4MB, and there's really just one version of the product. Compared to Explorer and Communicator, this is a dream! Figure 6-1 shows the download area of the PointCast web site.

The only knock against The PointCast Business Network is that once you've completed your download and install, you've got a large number of channels to update. This update can take up to 15 minutes even if you've got a modestly fast modem. The need to do this kind of update is understandable. PointCast can't just put six-month-old content into a new release version of the product. Nevertheless, be prepared to go get a beverage and check your voice mail while you're waiting for the first channel updates to occur.

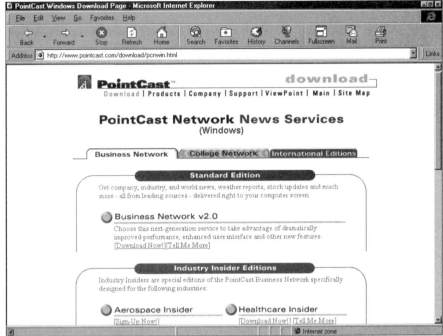

Figure 6-1:
What, just 4MB? Who knew!

A Brief Tour of the Push Leader

After you've installed The PointCast Business Network, you're going to find that this product has a lot to offer. Several web sites and channels are already installed for you. The list includes:

- ✔ CNN
- ✔ Ziff-Davis
- ✔ San Jose Mercury News (or the local newspaper in your area)
- ✔ ParentTime (an online parenting resource for professionals)
- ✔ Several PointCast channels that use the wire services (sports, business, lifestyle)
- ✔ A weather channel

In addition to the standard channels, PointCast also provides an area called PointCast Connections. Connections (shown in Figure 6-2) is the newest part to The PointCast Business Network and is the webcasting vehicle for the rest of us. Within the Connections area, you can subscribe to any PointCast channel that exists out there on the Internet. Connections also hosts the PointCast Channel, which provides the latest information on the company.

PointCast has two main ways in which you can view channel content. The more mundane way is to simply browse through the application. The second, and more interesting method, is to watch content roll by as a screen saver. Either way, the user has complete control of both the numbers of channels and the way in which they're updated.

Configuring channels in PointCast

Figure 6-3 shows the Add/Remove Channels function in PointCast. From this menu, you can configure the PointCast network any way you'd like, although there are some limitations. At any one time, you can have only nine channels active on The PointCast Business Network. Channels that are set up on install, such as the regional newspapers and PointCast Connections, do not count against the nine total. As a result, the channels that appear within the Connections area do not count against the nine channels, either.

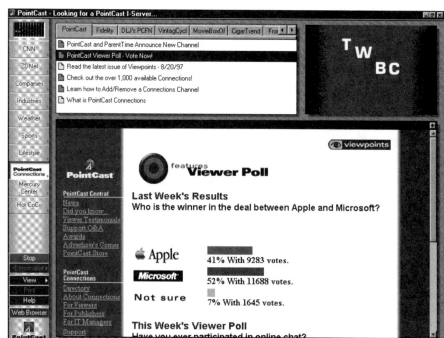

Figure 6-2:
Connections is the webcasting area for everyday users.

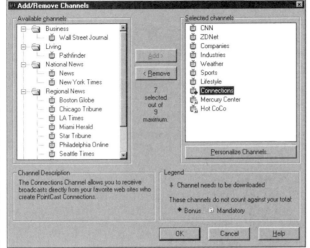

Figure 6-3:
From the
Add/Remove
menu,
you can
control the
number of
channels in
PointCast.

From within the Add/Remove channels menu, you can access the Personalize Channels function, shown in Figure 6-4. You can also get to this menu from the main screen. This menu allows you to set the preferences for each of the channels you have active on The PointCast Business Network. In addition, you're able to set the companies to track in the Companies Channel, as well as the industries to watch in the Industries Channel. You can even track the weather of your favorite cities in the Weather Channel. In other words, you've got options!

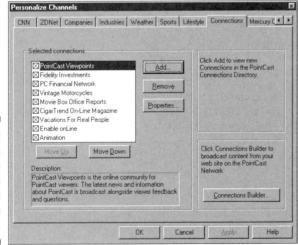

Figure 6-4:
The
Personalize
Channels
menu lets
you do
exactly that.

The Connections Channel area of the Personalize Channels menu is integral to setting up your web channel for PointCast. You can also access this menu directly from the Connections button on the left-hand side of the application. Simply right-click and select Personalize the Connections Channel. From this menu, you're able to:

- ✔ Add or remove Connections channels
- ✔ Set the properties for your Connections channels
- ✔ Use the Connections Builder to build your own PointCast Connections Channel

If you have both Explorer 4.0 and PointCast 2.0, when you select the PointCast icon to subscribe to a channel, Explorer may try to take over the subscribe process and put the channel in Explorer instead. To avoid this hang-up, subscribe manually using the Personalize Channels menu.

Browsing PointCast channels actively

Figure 6-5 shows the more active method of viewing channels in PointCast. With a few key exceptions, you'll find that its pretty much just like browsing the Web. Content on PointCast is organized along the same lines as it is in an Internet Explorer 4.0 Active channel. Items specified in a CDF file are shown in the program as headlines under a tab representing a channel.

Channels like CNN and Ziff-Davis have several sections within their channels. However, within PointCast Connections, there's only one section per channel where all the headlines reside. Each channel headline points to an HTML file on a web server. All the headlines are viewed within the PointCast interface. Interestingly enough, though, after you choose a link from those headline pages, PointCast spawns a web browser from within the application, as in Figure 6-6. Although you can specify the browser PointCast uses, Internet Explorer is built right in, making it the most appealing choice (not to mention that it is the default).

Updating your channels in PointCast can be an automated or manual experience, depending upon the kind of Internet connection that you have. To set your channel update preferences, you first have to select Personalize➪Application Settings from the left side toolbar inside PointCast. From there, simply select the Update tab and you're ready to configure your channels!

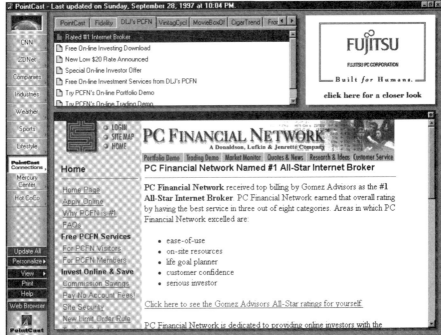

Figure 6-5:
Headlines
for
channels
are
specified
from a CDF
file just like
in Internet
Explorer 4.0.

Figure 6-6:
Choose a
link from a
headline,
and boom!
A web
browser,
inside
PointCast.

Updating channels in PointCast can be a frustrating venture. Although you can update any channel individually by right-clicking the channel button from the toolbar at the left side of the application, to automate the process means updating all the channels together. As you'll find on the install, this process can be cumbersome and time consuming. On the upside, however, your options for timing your updates are numerous. You can:

✔ Update channels continually all day

✔ Update channels only during non-business hours

✔ Update channels according to a custom schedule

✔ Update channels manually

Browsing PointCast channels passively

Of course, actively browsing channels isn't exactly what made PointCast famous. Plenty of other companies had a jump on them on that one. What garnered the attention of millions are the Smart Screens and the Ticker. Imagine getting up from your desk, going to make some copies, and coming back to your desk to find that the sports scores and the world news are scrolling by on your computer, as part of your screen saver. That's the Smart Screens doing their magic!

With the Ticker, headlines, the weather, and those same sports scores ramble on by in a ticker tape on your screen. Single-handedly these two features in PointCast brought corporate productivity to a screeching halt, right along with network connections to the Internet. Easily the most impressive part of PointCast, the Smart Screens were also the biggest gripe among network administrators — to the point where the product was banned by some companies. Oops!

Smart Screens and the Ticker work by taking over the Windows screen saver, as shown in Figure 6-7. After the Smart Screen is engaged, it simply scrolls through the active channel content. The Ticker works the same way. Headlines, weather forecasts, and sports scores go scrolling along the bottom or top of your screen in the form of a ticker tape. From the Personalize⇨Applications Settings menu, you can specify when the Smart Screen takes over the Windows screen saver — if ever.

Content from the base channels, meaning the ones that come with the product, is always visible on the Smart Screens. However, with the Connections Channel, you can personalize the content coming to you. You can select which Connections Channels you want to display on the Smart Screens and the Ticker by following these steps:

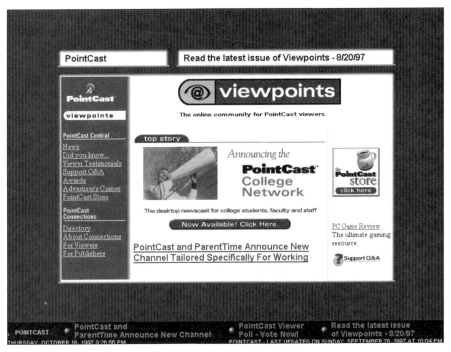

Figure 6-7:
Look at the content rolling by!

1. **Right-click the Connections Channel from the left toolbar.**
2. **From the active menu pop-up list, chose Personalize The Connections Channel.**
3. **Select a channel from the list.**
4. **Select the Display in Smart Screen or Display in Ticker check boxes.**

Creating Channels in The PointCast Business Network

I said this going in, and I'll say it again. Making channels with PointCast is easier than with any other webcasting tool. There's really just one thing you're going to need to create a channel for this product: a web site. If you've got that, plus some idea of the pages you'd like to push, you're ready.

Now, I'm not saying that you shouldn't go through the same process that you'd go through in designing a channel for any other product. The point here is that if you really are looking to get something up quickly, without using any other tools than PointCast itself, this is the way to go. Bad content is still bad content — and if you're making it, people are not going to subscribe to it.

That small warning aside, and assuming that you're ready to get your content up in a hurry, the next section has the steps that you need to follow.

Finding the Connections Builder

To get going, right-click the Connections Channel⇨Personalize The Connections Channel. This action brings up the Personalize Channels windows, which is where you find the Connection Builder. Then select the Connections Builder. Figure 6-8 shows the initial Connections Builder screen. From this menu, you can choose to start either a new Connection File, or open a previously created connection file.

Version 2.0 of The PointCast Business Network does not fully support the Internet Explorer CDF file format. So, although Explorer can read a PointCast CDF file, you cannot load an Explorer CDF file to be used in PointCast.

Figure 6-8:
From the initial screen, you can either create a new file or open an existing CDF file.

```
┌─ Welcome ──────────────────────────────────────────── ✕ ┐
│                                                          │
│  Welcome to the                                          │
│     PointCast Connections Builder                        │
│                                                          │
│  Select an option to begin.                              │
│                                                          │
│  ⦿ Open an existing PointCast Connection file:           │
│                                               ┌────────┐ │
│  [s:\Webcasting\Channel Swank\PCN\PCNcdf.cdl▼] │   OK   │ │
│                                  [ Browse... ] └────────┘ │
│                                               ┌────────┐ │
│  ○ Create a new PointCast Connection file     │ Cancel │ │
│    ☑ Using Connections Wizard                 └────────┘ │
│                                               ┌────────┐ │
│                                               │  Help  │ │
│                                               └────────┘ │
└──────────────────────────────────────────────────────────┘
```

Channel creation with the Wizard

Usually, I don't recommend using a Wizard, but in this case the PointCast Wizard is better than the alternative. The Wizard automates the CDF file creation process. In contrast, if you chose not to use the Wizard, you get the Connections Builder mini-application. Although this application is quite functional, you have to do everything manually, and who wants that! If you haven't seen the Connections Builder before, it's a whole lot easier to just go with the Wizard.

Step one: Introduction

The first thing you get when you start the Wizard is an introduction box. Just select Next, and you get the first window, as in Figure 6-9. You are asked to enter the name of your channel, a name for the tab in the application, a description of your channel, and the location of the page which tells more about what you're channel's all about.

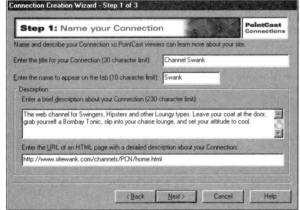

Figure 6-9:
This is the first step to creating a channel with PointCast!

Step two: Article properties

At this junction, you add all the HTML pages that you want to be a part of your channel. As with Explorer, you should be frugal here. If you add too many pages, the time to update your channel will be greater and could put off your subscribers. For each page, you have to assign a name and a corresponding URL. In addition, at this point, you have to decide whether you want the CDF file to be for the Smart Screen or for the actual Channel Viewer, as well as whether you want the file to be just HTML or an animation for the Smart Screen (see the following sidebar, "A brief look at PointCast Studio").

Step three: Configuration

This is the last part of the process, sort of. From this window, you enter the URL where the CDF file will sit, and you specify the update schedule for the channel. Additionally, you may choose to apply for a content rating, as shown in Figure 6-10. A content rating allows you to get updates from PointCast Connections about the latest updates in the software. A content rating also ensures that your channel won't be cut off by companies who filter their channels based on the ratings.

Note: Although you can set the schedule default here, it's likely that it will be reset by users of PointCast.

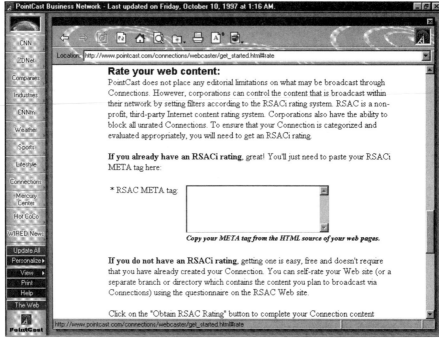

PointCast Business Network - Last updated on Friday, October 10, 1997 at 1:16 AM.

Location: http://www.pointcast.com/connections/webcaster/get_started.html#rate

Rate your web content:

PointCast does not place any editorial limitations on what may be broadcast through Connections. However, corporations can control the content that is broadcast within their network by setting filters according to the RSACi rating system. RSAC is a non-profit, third-party Internet content rating system. Corporations also have the ability to block all unrated Connections. To ensure that your Connection is categorized and evaluated appropriately, you will need to get an RSACi rating.

If you already have an RSACi rating, great! You'll just need to paste your RSACi META tag here:

* RSAC META tag:

Copy your META tag from the HTML source of your web pages.

If you do not have an RSACi rating, getting one is easy, free and doesn't require that you have already created your Connection. You can self-rate your Web site (or a separate branch or directory which contains the content you plan to broadcast via Connections) using the questionnaire on the RSAC Web site.

Click on the "Obtain RSAC Rating" button to complete your Connection content

http://www.pointcast.com/connections/webcaster/get_started.html#rate

Figure 6-10:
A content rating helps your channel avoid being filtered out by corporations.

A brief look at PointCast Studio

Unlike the . . . ahem . . . big two browsers, PointCast has created a tool that allows channel developers the opportunity to create their own animations for PointCast channels. The tool, called PointCast Studio, uses a very simple stage metaphor for creating these animations. The average animation is made up of actors (usually graphics), working on a stage (the screen), using a timeline and events to create the animations.

The animations are made up of web-friendly .gif and .jpg images, and are used with the Smart Screen feature. Of course, you don't have to use PointCast Studio. Any HTML page can be used with the Smart Screen, but part of the appeal of PointCast has been the active nature of the Smart Screen. This tool allows

you to take your content and present it in a more dynamic fashion.

When you create your CDF file, you can choose to add animation elements and specify them for the Smart Screen. That way, when the Smart Screen is enabled, the animations, rather than your static channel content, is put up on the screen. The only downside, as you may have figured out, is that you've got to create your content twice, once for the Channel Viewer and once for the Smart Screen. But, if you're looking for impact, there's no better way to do it than to do it with PointCast Studio.

You can find out more about PointCast Studio at pioneer.pointcast.com/products/studio/index.html.

The Connections Builder mini-app

After you've completed the Wizard, you're thrown into a mini-application that's built into the Connections Builder. From this application, the first thing you do is save your file. After saving your CDF file, you are able to review all your channel items and update any of the parameters by choosing them from the menu bar.

To complete your channel, you should first preview the channel, as shown in Figure 6-11. By using the Preview function in Connections Builder, you can see what your channel will look like in The PointCast Business Network — even if you haven't posted it to your web server. Of course, you'll need to unsubscribe before you post your channel for real. Thankfully, there's a button for that process, so just select the Remove this Channel icon from the preview page to get rid of your temporary channel.

When the CDF file was saved, PointCast included an icon and an .htm file with your CDF file that allows users to subscribe to your channel directly from your web site. This icon is a great way to let people know about your channel, and the .htm file includes all the script you need to show the icon. You should put the files on your web server and reference them in your subscriber page. Remember to put a link on the icon that jumps from the page to the CDF file you just created!

Figure 6-11:
Use the preview function to see your channel before you post it to your web server.

The last component of the channel creation process is, obviously, to post your channel to a web server. After you've done that, guess what — you're webcasting on PointCast.

Promoting Your PointCast Channel

A large number of PointCast channels exist. The Mining Company alone has a few hundred, so finding your little corner to carve out is going to require some promotional work. That said, there are a couple of very easy ways to promote your new PointCast web channel, and they won't even cost you a penny.

Without a doubt, the best way to promote your channel is through PointCast. PointCast has its own channel guide, called the Connections Directory, located on its web site. It's also shown in Figure 6-12. The channel guide includes the rating, a brief description of the channel (which is lifted right off your CDF file), and a button that directs the subscriber to your web site for more information. You can also subscribe right there by selecting the PointCast icon.

To add your channel to the Connections Directory, just follow these steps:

1. **Open the Connections Builder mini-application by right-clicking the Connections bar and selecting Personalize Channels.**

2. **From the Request menu, select Directory Listing.**

   When the menu pops up, you'll notice that all the fields have already been filled in for you. It's wise to double-check all your URL entries though, because they get checked when you submit the request.

3. **Chose Submit — and see where it gets you!**

Another easy way to promote your channel is by linking your web site to the PointCast 2.0 download. While this process is a bit like doing PointCast's bidding, if you're going to make a channel for their viewer, you may as well support the viewer, too. Plus, PointCast added the line to your subscriber page anyway when you created the CDF file, so there's really no work in it for you!

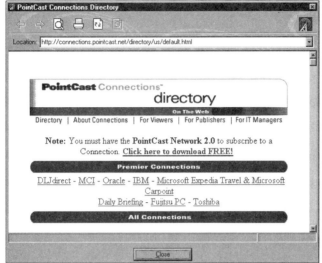

Figure 6-12:
The
Connections
Directory
on Excite!

Chapter 7

Other Cool Things to Do with Channel Definition Format (CDF)

. . . .

. . . .

*I*f you go through the entire install of Internet Explorer 4.0 and decide to risk having Microsoft mess with your Windows 95 configuration, things are going to look a little different after you click that restart button. How different? Well, just take a look at Figure 7-1. Until now, you've probably never seen anything that looked like an HTML document on your computer. Get ready, because here comes the future of the desktop, and it's got Internet written all over it.

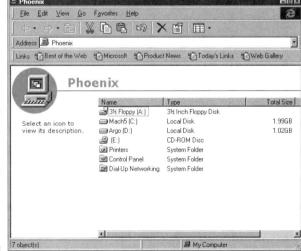

Figure 7-1:
HTML on
the top level
of your
Windows
desktop
menu. Oh
boy. . . .

A lot of people will avoid making the install, perhaps for that very reason. But, after giving it some thought, my take on what you're seeing is an interim upgrade to Windows 95. Windows 98 is coming in mid-1998, but Internet Explorer is really the first piece of software to be developed for that up-graded operating system. As a result, it looks like Microsoft bundled in the components that were necessary for Internet Explorer 4.0 — in effect giving people a sneak peek of things to come.

Remember, none of these features is accessible to channel builders who are using the Netscape Netcaster, because these Windows upgrades are not installed on their systems!

Lot's of things are different, both visually and programmatically, after you make the full switch with Internet Explorer. All in all, it's creepy — because you're not sure exactly how much has actually changed. Still, here are some of the highlights:

✔ **HTML is embedded in the Active Desktop layer.** Instead of just having a floating layer for windows objects (like icons and shortcuts) in front of the desktop background, there's now a layer that supports ActiveX controls and HTML. These layers, by the way, are behind the windows objects layers, so if you drag an icon over an HTML object on the desktop, the icon appears in front of the HTML.

✔ **The Explorer Tool Bar is built into all desktop windows.** It looks weird, there's no doubt about that. It works the same, kinda. Drop-down menus now exist for such things as Favorites (yes, from Internet Explorer 4.0), which can be accessed when Explorer isn't even open. In addition, the Explorer icon is now on every desktop window (this is the most annoying part, because I haven't found a way to turn it off yet). Click it, and — you guessed it — Explorer fires up to whatever your home page happens to be.

✔ **Some new features have been added to your Display Properties.** Microsoft really goes a bit overboard with these changes to the desk-top. You can choose to tone it down a bit by going to the Display Properties from within the Control Panel (shown in Figure 7-2), or by right-clicking the desktop. Here you can manage several pieces of the new desktop, including the Active Channel Bar, the Active Desktop, and the Active Screen Saver.

In the end, users really don't have much of a choice. They're going to get this upgrade eventually, assuming they all latch on to Windows 98, which they will because, well . . . is there really another choice? The big question, naturally, is what does all this have to with you? As you may have noticed, I threw in some new words, most notably *Active Desktop* and *Active Screen Saver.* I get into them in more detail in the section "I Like My Desktops Active," but they are key pieces to this new Microsoft architecture, and, here's the big payoff: They use CDF as their primary language interface!

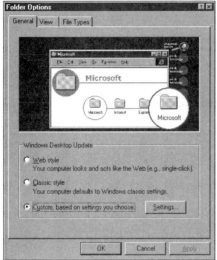

Figure 7-2:
You can
tone down
your Active
Desktop
settings
from
Display
Properties
in the
Control
Panel.

Roll out the barrels, and strike up the band! Microsoft has deemed us worthy of interfacing with Windows, via CDF! Even better, it's really pretty easy, and it uses a language that is not very different than HTML. Strange days, indeed.

Realistically, though, what do these new technologies offer you, the web-channel developer? The answer, I believe, boils down to *access*. I've watched a lot of people install Internet Explorer 4.0 during the course of writing this book, and over time, a number of them have begun to accept the new ways of viewing HTML-based content, whether it's from a web channel in a browser, or something going right to the desktop. Of course, let's not declare the browser obsolete just yet. Channel viewing isn't for everyone. But, for those who endeavor to try new things, the Active Desktop and Active Screen Saver will offer you a chance to gain greater access with the content you've already created.

I Like My Desktops Active

Figure 7-3 shows the Active Desktop in action. The best way I can think of to describe it is that it looks like background wallpaper that doesn't take up the entire screen and is always changing. It took me a while to get used to seeing it there, let alone looking at it for useful content. But, hey, that's progress, and who am I to stand in the way!

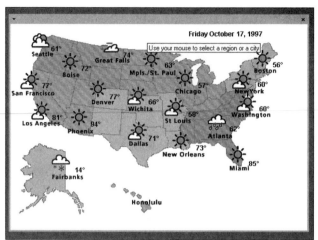

Figure 7-3:
Weather
updates on
my desktop.
Ya, but it
just looks
weird.

Why go to the Active Desktop?

Like web channels for Internet Explorer 4.0, the first thing you'll need to ask yourself when considering writing content for the Active Desktop is: "Why do I really want to get myself into this?" In all seriousness, though, it's a valid question, because there are some key differences between having a web channel and writing to the Active Desktop. The two biggest differences are:

- ✔ The Active Desktop is up and on all the time.

- ✔ The Active Desktop can be a full page — but is more likely a small box on the desktop. Most of your content needs to be set up to fit within smaller dimensions.

Let's face it. There's not a lot of room on the desktop for content, plus a lot is going on there already. The best way to think of the Active Desktop is as a summary of your channel content that links to your site on the Web when a user selects one of your summary headlines — which means that you'll be creating new content to support yet another component of web-channel broadcasting.

So, is going to the Active Desktop worth it? Some things to weigh in your decision:

- ✔ How many times a day do you update your content? If the answer is none, just move onto another format, because this one ain't for you.

- ✔ Do you have headlines or easily digestible content that people want sitting on their desktop all the time? Weather and sports scores are good examples of such things. Things like the Kelly blue book prices of used cars . . . probably not for you.

✔ Can you make your stuff small and light on the graphics? If so, get in there. If not, probably best to move on.

✔ Do you really want to set yourself up for calls from complaining customers when they think it's your Active Desktop item that keeps crashing their desktop. It happens. You're a likely target. Be ready.

Of course, it's not all bad. In fact, the Active Desktop can be quite good. If you meet the criteria, just think of the exposure you can have. You're always on! Whenever anyone drops out of an application to the desktop, there you are, with your message, and that of your advertisers (if you have them). Sure, there's a price, but the payoff could certainly be worth the additional work.

A brief primer on how the Active Desktop works

With the upgrade to Windows that comes with Internet Explorer 4.0, some modest (spelled Huge!) changes were made to the layers of the Windows desktop. The transparent icon layer, which houses all your shortcuts, was modified to accept HTML links, so that you could link to any web page from your desktop. No big deal there, because that feature was begun with Internet Explorer 3.0.

The second change was to add a second layer based on HTML. This layer is where the Active Desktop lives. All the files on the Active Desktop are controlled through a single file, Desktop.htm, which is controlled and edited by Internet Explorer 4.0. The file includes each of the tags for Active Desktop items, as well as an ActiveX control that handles the resizing of objects on the Active Desktop layer.

When you modify the Desktop Properties via the Control Panels in Display properties, you're also modifying the Desktop.htm file, just manually.

The Active Desktop can handle any number of web-friendly file formats through HTML, such as JavaScript, Java applets, graphics, or other ActiveX items that you may have in your site. The catch is simply this: Everything you create must be able to run when the user isn't connected to the Internet, as in Figure 7-4. The last thing you want to have running up there is a Java applet that starts barking at the user because the user can't find the Internet connection and therefore can't download content. Worse yet, many Java applets default to a gray screen when they can't find the data they need. Yikes, now a gray screen is going to look appealing!

Figure 7-4:
This ESPN
sports
ticker runs
without
needing
updates
from the
Internet.

One of the other interesting things about the Active Desktop is that it has no navigational component. In other words, no drop-down menus, no default buttons, no frames. Nada. To the developer, that simply means you won't be pushing any more than the one page you put on the desktop, and that pages itself shouldn't have any embedded navigation icons, except for hyperlinks that can send the user back to a web page.

Just one last thing. The Active Desktop layer uses the same 256 color palette as Windows. Thus, the graphics you use in an Active Desktop item also have to match that palette. If it doesn't, the graphics will most likely look bad, as if they had been painted with the wrong colors. Most graphics programs include the "System" palette as an option for taking higher resolution graphics and turning them into an 8-bit Windows friendly format.

Active Desktop and Active Channel CDFs: Are they different?

The steps to creating an Active Desktop item may look quite familiar, because they're nearly identical to those used to create a web channel in Internet Explorer 4.0 (see Chapter 5). Here are some basic differences, however:

- ✔ There's only one <ITEM> tag per CDF file, because there's only one page that goes to the desktop. You can have others, but they won't be shown in Internet Explorer 4.0.

- ✔ The <USAGE> function, called within the <CHANNEL> tag, needs to have "DesktopComponent" specified instead of an Active Channel. If you call other types, such as "Channel," in the CDF file, they'll be ignored.

- ✔ The desktop item needs a default size, and a specification as to whether or not a user can resize the window.

In creating your Active Desktop item, you need to consider some other items. First, only one <ITEM> tag is viewable to the user, no matter how many you have in the CDF file. Nevertheless, you can use other <ITEM> tags to specify other pages, even though information won't be viewable to the user. You would create more than one <ITEM> tag if you wanted to specify additional content that could be brought down to the user's PC. This content could be thrown into a cache, to be used when the Active Desktop is offline, meaning not connected to the Internet. A cache is simply a segment of disk space where data is held temporarily to be used for a specific application, in this case the Active Desktop.

Just your typical Active Desktop CDF

In Chapter 6, I show you what a typical CDF file looked like. Here it is again:

```
<?XML version="1.0"?>
<CHANNEL HREF="http://www.siteswank.com/channels/ie/
home.htm" BASE="http://www.siteswank.com/channels/ie/
cdf/ " >
<ABSTRACT> The web channel for Swingers, Hipsters and other
Loungy types. Leave your coat at the door, grab yourself a
Bombay Tonic, slip into your chaise lounge, and set your
attitude to cool.</ABSTRACT> <SCHEDULE>
<INTERVALTIME DAY="1" />
<EARLIESTTIME HOUR="7" />
<LATESTTIME HOUR="17" />
</SCHEDULE>
<LOGO HREF="http://www.sitewank.com/channels/ie/graphics/
icon.gif" STYLE="icon" />
<LOGO HREF="http://www.siteswank/com/channels/ie/graphics/
channel_menu.gif STYLE="image"/>
<ITEM HREF="http://www.siteswank.com/channels/ie/news.htm"
LASTMOD="1997-12-0100:00">
<TITLE> Swingin' News </TITLE>
<ABSTRACT> All the news that's fit to print </ABSTRACT>
</ITEM>
<ITEM HREF="o|tp://www.siteswank.com/channels/ie/
cocktails.htm" LASTMOD="1997-12-0100:00">
<TITLE> Smooth Cocktails </TITLE>
<ABSTRACT> Cocktail recipes for the ultra hip </ABSTRACT>
</ITEM>
<ITEM HREF="http://www.siteswank.com/channels/ie/music.htm"
LASTMOD="1997-12-0100:00">
<TITLE> Sound of Swank </TITLE>
<ABSTRACT> The classic toe tapping and finger snappin'
sounds </ABSTRACT>
</ITEM>
</CHANNEL>
```

If you've already created a CDF file for your Active Channel, getting the file to work for you as an Active Desktop CDF is a snap. If you haven't yet created a CDF file, refer back to Chapter 5 for a walk-through on creating your first CDF file. Just follow the steps I've outlined here and you'll be ready to fly.

1. **Delete the bottom two** `<ITEM>` **tags, as well as the two LOGO items.**

   Because you won't be needing more than one `<ITEM>` tag, you can get rid of the others. As for the logos, you don't need any for Explorer or the subscription process, so those lines can go as well. Everything else, in one form or another, you need.

2. **Delete the HREF and BASE functions in the** `<CHANNEL>` **tag.**

   You won't need these functions anymore. When building an Active Desktop item, the only thing Internet Explorer 4.0 cares about is the `<ITEM>` embedded within the `<CHANNEL>` tag, and it uses that `<ITEM>` as the place to look for content updates.

3. **Modify the** `<ITEM>` **tag to include desktop window parameters.**

   To create a desktop element, you need the following code snippet. I've used Channel Swank as an example (and my comments are in bold). Check out Chapter 5 for an introduction to Channel Swank and how it fits into CDF files if you haven't seen or heard of that name yet in the book. In addition I've modified the `<ITEM>` tag to represent an Active Desktop page, rather than the News item it was previously.

```
<ITEM HREF="http://www.siteswank.com/channels/ie
Active_Desktop/ticker.html" LASTMOD="1997-12-0100:00">
<TITLE> The Swank Ticker </TITLE>
<USAGE VALUE="DesktopComponent"> //This sets it up as
desktop item
<OPENAS VALUE="HTML" /> //You can also use an image here
<WIDTH VALUE="150" />
<HEIGHT VALUE="200" /> //Both of these values define
your screen real estate
<CANRESIZE VALUE="YES" />  //You can chose "No" as well.
that will lock the screen size
</USAGE>
</ITEM>
```

4. **Modify your schedule times for the Active Desktop.**

   I threw this step in as a reminder. If you're posting any less than a couple times a day, you should question whether this is the right thing to do.

That's it! Like I said, pretty much cake. When you're done, your modified CDF file should look a little something like this, and your Active Desktop items should look a little something like Figure 7-5:

Figure 7-5:
Channel
Swank . . .
really on
the desktop.

```
<?XML version="1.0"?>
<CHANNEL>
<SCHEDULE>
<INTERVALTIME HOUR="6" />
<EARLIESTTIME HOUR="1" />
<LATESTTIME HOUR="5" />
</SCHEDULE>
<ITEM HREF="http://www.siteswank.com/channels/ie/
Active_Desktop/ticker.html" LASTMOD="1997-12-0100:00">
<TITLE> The Swank Ticker </TITLE>
<USAGE VALUE="DesktopComponent"> //This sets it up as desk-
top item
<OPENAS VALUE="HTML" /> //You can also use an image here
<WIDTH VALUE="150" />
<HEIGHT VALUE="200" /> //Both of these values define your
screen real estate
<CANRESIZE VALUE="YES" />   //You can chose "No" as well.
that will lock the screen size
</USAGE>
</ITEM>
<CHANNEL>
```

Build, then post, but remember the catches

The posting and subscribing process for an Active Desktop item are exactly the same as for an Active Channel. Again, though, to do it right, you're looking at jumping on the Microsoft band wagon and registering as a member of their SiteBuilder network. The only difference between the two processes, really, is that you have a different icon, and users can modify their channels manually from the Display Properties area of the Control Panels.

Does HTML Make a Wonderful Screen Saver?

Active Screen Savers are reminiscent of the PointCast Smart Screens outlined in Chapter 6. With Internet Explorer 4.0, you have the ability, within your CDF file, to designate a web page as a screen saver page. That page is combined with similar pages to create a scrolling slide show of pages that pop up when the computer is idle. Figure 7-6 shows what this stuff looks like.

Active Screen Savers are a lot easier to develop than Active Desktop items. Like Channels and Desktop items, you can use all sorts of web content, including Java, JavaScript, and ActiveX components. But, unlike Active Desktop, you won't need to have a separate CDF file. You can simply add the Active Screen Saver item to the CDF file that you're currently using as an additional <ITEM>. Explorer does the rest.

One of the more unique things about the Active Screen Saver, besides the fact that it uses HTML, is that you don't disable it simply by moving your mouse. When you move the mouse, a menu and button appear at the top of the screen, even though the page is still being shown. What this action allows you to do is select a link from the HTML page that's being shown. When you select a link, a new web browser page is spawned, which then breaks the screen saver.

Getting your channel to support a screen saver is about as easy as it gets. Your best bet, and the one thing that will cause you absolutely no grief, is to take your top level channel page and declare *that* your screen saver page. To enable a screen saver page in your CDF file, you need the following code:

```
<ITEM HREF="http://www.siteswank.com/channels/ie/news.htm"
LASTMOD="1997-12-0100:00">
<TITLE> Swingin' Screen Saver</TITLE>
<USAGE VALUE="ScreenSaver"> </USAGE>
</ITEM>
```

Duplicating an <ITEM> tag and changing the USAGE VALUE from Channel to Screensaver will take my news page and show it both an item in the channel, as well as part of the rotating screen saver. When users subscribe to the channel, they get a special dialogue box asking whether they also want to subscribe to the Active Screen Saver, if that channel has an Active Screen Saver included with it. You can modify your screen saver properties from the Display Control Panel, shown in Figure 7-7. After that, the Active Screen Saver acts just like any other item in the CDF file, getting pushed when something on that page is new.

As with most things in Explorer, there is a catch. As of now, you can have only one item designated as a screen saver in each CDF file.

Figure 7-6:
You can call
an Active
Screen
Saver from
within your
existing
CDF file.

Figure 7-7:
Here you
can choose
which
pages to
include in
the Active
Screen
Saver.

Your Channel Update Is in Your Inbox

Both Microsoft and Netscape are selling their e-mail clients in their new web-channel environments. Netscape mail has been able to handle HTML for a while now, but only recently has Microsoft come to the e-mail playing field. With the latest version of Outlook Express, which comes with Internet Explorer 4.0, Microsoft is now offering integrated HTML support for e-mail.

The big payoff for developers here is that you can now send your channel updates via e-mail. If you've read Chapter 5, you may have noticed that one of the options on the subscription dialogue box was for the user to be notified by e-mail when changes to the channel were made. That was simply for notification. To actually send the update with the notification e-mail requires a small addition to your CDF file. Nonetheless, it's easy, and it provides a great way for channel viewers to get their content through a familiar interface.

Again, this is a pretty simple and straight forward addition to the CDF file. You should keep some things in mind, though. First, not everyone will have a compatible viewer, so the audience may be limited in that regard. In addition, no one wants e-mail that takes half an hour to download, so the operative words here are "teensy weensy footprint."

Those warnings aside, you can specify an item to be e-mailed to a user by adding the following code to your CDF file. You'll find that it looks pretty well identical to the code for a Screen Saver. Really, all you are doing is switching a variable — and Explorer does the rest, including asking for the e-mail address to send the update to. One last note: Like the Screen Saver, you can have only one of these items per CDF, so choose wisely!

The code to make it happen is right here:

```
<ITEM HREF="http://www.siteswank.com/channels/ie/news.htm"
LASTMOD="1997-12-0100:00">
<TITLE> Swingin' Screen Saver</TITLE>
<USAGE VALUE="EMail"> </USAGE>
</ITEM>
```

Part III
Webcasting the Netscape Way

The 5th Wave   By Rich Tennant

In this part . . .

*E*veryone knows that Netscape has an advantage, one called 60 percent of the market. You can't deny the simple math of the situation, and I keep coming back to that fact in this section. Like the reality or not, Netscape owns the browser market for now, and it's not planning on going down without a fight.

For that reason, you're wise to find out as much as you can about Netcaster and its kid sister from Marimba, the Castanet Tuner. By the end of this part, you no doubt are going to come to the same conclusion that I have about building my first Netcaster channel: Man, it's hard! You have a lot of little nuances and a lot of big chunks of JavaScript. Is Netscape's entry in the webcasting sweepstakes better than Microsoft's? You be the judge. Is a Netcaster channel harder to develop than a Microsoft channel. Oh yeah, you betcha! So roll up your sleeves, because the web-channel weather's gettin' a bit rough outside!

Chapter 8

Getting Acquainted with the Netcaster

*A*lthough you may think that referring to Netscape as a behemoth sounds a bit odd, that's exactly what the company's become. Netscape owns, at least for now, the lion's share of the Internet browsing world, much to Microsoft's dismay. In the past few years, Netscape Navigator has become one of the most recognizable symbols around the world. It is the mainstay of web browsing, having beaten out the likes of NCSA Mosaic and the Netcom NetCruiser. America Online and CompuServe have tried to bring the browser to their services, with modest but limited success. Try as they may, one by one, the competitors to Navigator have faded away, leaving Netscape the clear owner of marketshare and mind share.

And then you have Microsoft. If I'm Jim Clarke (the CEO of Netscape), and I see the big Internet Explorer animated world spinning in my rearview mirror, first I'm going to get nervous and then I'm going to feel as though I can never stop trying to one-up the competition with my product. By the way, is it a coincidence that Internet Explorer 4.0 uses the globe as its icon, or is Microsoft sending a subtle message to us all? As long as its tailing me, I'm going to feel that I can't screw up even once, because if I do, Microsoft is going to blow right on by. Welcome to the world of Netscape; please fasten your seatbelt.

You don't need to be a rocket scientist (though it certainly couldn't hurt) to figure out that Netscape releases software early and often in an effort to keep users feeling feature-rich and content with their Netscape software. That's the only way that Netscape can win the browser war and, by the by, make money.

All this buildup, then, leads us to Netscape Communicator 4.0. Now perhaps you've been wondering where Netscape Communicator 1.0 through 3.9 have been. Seems that they were always there, unbeknownst to all of us. They just happened to be called Navigator. In the past, Netscape has developed and released its browsers as "one-offs," meaning that the browser has stood by itself. With Version 4.0, however, Netscape decided to integrate several other of its products with the browser, including Collabra (the news reader), Messenger, and Netcaster (the webcasting tool).

Netscape Communicator has not exactly met with critical success thus far. Communicator continues to be buggy and has been beset with security problems. In addition to labeling Communicator a clone of Explorer, MIS and web types have griped continually about not being able to get Navigator separately from the rest of the package. Bowing to community pressure, Netscape agreed to separate all the other pieces of Communicator and ship Netscape Navigator 4.0 as a stand-alone product, as they did before.

Right off the top, that decision makes webcasting a somewhat dubious proposition for Netscape simply because you can get Navigator or Communicator without necessarily getting Netcaster. To get Netcaster, you must seriously want it, and by virtue of that, you must question just how committed Netscape is to their Webtop channel environment. I'm not saying, by the way, that Netcaster isn't a good product. It is. But, as is true of all things in the Internet world, you need to keep an eye on the situation before you jump right into webcasting using Communicator. The last thing that you want is for the company that you've invested your resources in to change strategy at the last minute.

Grabbing a Copy of Netcaster

You have two basic options for getting yourself a copy of Netcaster. You can download it either as a part of Netscape Communicator 4.0 or as a stand-alone component of Navigator 4.0. Stand-alone components don't automatically come with Navigator, so you will need to specify that you want Netcaster included. Nothing like making it plain and simple! Either way, you're probably going to end up at the Netscape site, as shown in Figure 8-1. Here, you can select your operating system, your download size based on the features you want (as for Microsoft Explorer, the download sizes are just plain huge — usually more than 10MB), as well as the language of the browser.

Unlike Microsoft, which insists that you download from a third party that maintains its servers, Netscape enables you to download from one of its 20 or so FTP sites. A number of mirror sites also carry the software. Your best bet for speed in downloading Communicator or Navigator is to forget the current version of your browser and use an FTP program, such as WS_FTP32 for Windows 95 or Fetch for the Macintosh.

Figure 8-1:
I'm sure
that you've
seen this
before: the
Netscape
download
page.

As with Explorer, you have a variety of installation options, all of which I outline in Table 8-1. The only real question, however, is whether you want a really big download or a monstrous download. With the really big download, you just get Navigator. From there, increasingly large installs include different permutations of Netscape Communicator. Among your options: Netcaster (webcasting), Messenger (e-mail), Collabra (news reader), Page Composer (HTML editor), and Conference (a real-time conferencing tool). You be the judge. From my perspective, if you're going to do the downloading, you may as well get them all.

Table 8-1	Variations on a Theme: The Many Ways of Downloading Netscape Navigator 4.0	
Official Title	*Products Included*	*Approximate Size*
Navigator 4.0 stand-alone	Navigator, Netcaster	6MB
Communicator Standard	Navigator, Collabra, Messenger, Page Composer	8MB
Communicator Professional	Navigator, Netcaster, Messenger, Page Composer, Calendar, and IBM Host On-Demand	15MB

One last thing! Netscape tries and tries to get you to use the Smart Update feature to download their software — but avoid it like the plague if you can. It's still buggy, particularly if you have a previously installed version and you're writing over it. Lots of key information is left in your Windows Registry, which can pose problems in downloading anything that checks the version of Netscape you're running.

So Just What Is Netcaster?

Netcaster is a web-channel viewer. By itself, that sounds simple enough. If only that were all, however, I'd be done with this section, popping champagne bottles, and your channel would be up on the Internet. End of story . . . or not. Netcaster, as things turn out, is a fairly complicated little piece of equipment, and although it may look like the Active Channel viewer in Explorer, the two are eons apart in terms of their technology and implementation.

Netcaster is basically made up of three parts: the *Webtop,* the *Drawer,* and the *Channel Finder.* Together, they create an environment that enables you to get content pushed to your desktop in the background while you're working on other applications. Each of the three parts works as a mini-application that controls a specific area of Netcaster. I provide more information on these areas in the following sections.

Netcaster is both separate from and equal to Navigator and Communicator. Netcaster is built on JavaScript and is designed to use basic HTML as the content that it pushes to the user. In that sense, Netcaster is a lot like Navigator. Netcaster, however, also makes use a wide array of application-specific JavaScript that you can't use with any other browser. And, although you launch Netcaster from within Navigator as a series of new windows that simply take over the desktop, the interface is such that it looks as though you've spawned a new program. The result, at least from the user's perspective, is that Netcaster is a completely new application. Figure 8-2 provides the highlights.

The Netcaster Webtop is your stage

Microsoft Explorer has the Active Desktop, which enables its web channels to interface directly with the Windows 95 desktop. (After Microsoft finishes with Internet Explorer 4.0 for the Macintosh, you can rest assured that it's going to have the same kind of effect on the Mac OS.) Netcaster attempts to do the same thing, without the direct integration of Windows 95 or the Mac OS desktop. The Netcaster version is called the *Webtop.*

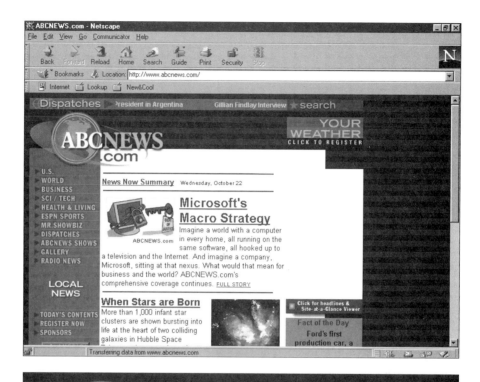

Figure 8-2:
Netcaster
(bottom)
and
Navigator
(top) are, in
fact, the
same
application,
although
they don't
really look
that way,
as this
comparison
indicates.

The Webtop basically sits on top of your desktop but behind all the other active applications, as shown in Figure 8-3. The idea, *à la* PointCast, is to have an active window that's always present, where information can be pushed from Netcaster to the user. The Webtop is also cross-platform, just like a web browser is, so it works with Navigator versions on Windows 95, Windows NT, the Mac OS, and UNIX.

Both JavaScript and HTML power the Webtop. HTML provides the content architecture, and the JavaScript handles the Webtop interface as well as all the animation and layering that's commonplace with webcasting. The JavaScript you hand to Netcaster as you're building the channel manages the Webtop interface — meaning everything from the size of the window to its position on the desktop.

Although this setup gives the developer a tremendous amount of flexibility, it's a significant departure from the Explorer 4.0 method. In Explorer, interfacing with the desktop is mostly a function of enabling a few key calls. Netcaster is quite different. Just to give you a taste of what I'm talking about here, check out Figure 8-4. The source file in the figure is the top page of the Netscape Channel on Netcaster. More than 300 lines of script is there just to handle that one front page. Just what's in all that script? Oh, nothing much; just the parameters for the entire Webtop, along with all the styles, the cascading layers, and all the channel properties! But don't panic. I go in-depth on how to make all this stuff easy in Chapter 9.

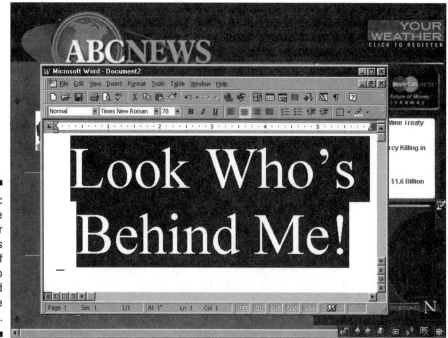

Figure 8-3:
The Netcaster Webtop sits on top of the desktop but behind active applications.

```
Source of: http://netcaster.netscape.com/channel/index.html - Netscape
// CONTSTANTS
ARTICLE_BUTTON_WIDTH = ARTICLE_BUTTON_HEIGHT = 13;
ARTICLE_HOME_X = CROSSHAIRS_X + ARTICLE_BUTTON_WIDTH + 5;
ARTICLE_HOME_Y = CROSSHAIRS_Y + ARTICLE_BUTTON_HEIGHT + 5;
ARTICLE_CONTROLS_X_OFFSET = ARTICLE_BUTTON_WIDTH + 5;
ARTICLE_CONTROLS_Y_OFFSET = ARTICLE_BUTTON_HEIGHT + 5;
ARTICLE_INC_OFFSET_Y = 25;
ARTICLE_INC_Y = HEIGHT - (CROSSHAIRS_Y + ARTICLE_INC_OFFSET_Y);
ARTICLE_INC_X = 10;

function article_scrollDown (){
        var articleToSlide = "article" + activeArticle;
        if (HEIGHT <
                document.layers[articleToSlide].clip.height +
                document.layers[articleToSlide].clip.top +
                document.layers[articleToSlide].top) {
                document.layers[articleToSlide].top -= ARTICLE_INC_Y;
                document.layers[articleToSlide].clip.top += ARTICLE_INC_Y;
        }
}

function article_scrollUp ()
{
        var articleToSlide = "article" + activeArticle;
        if (document.layers[articleToSlide].clip.top > ARTICLE_INC_Y) {
                document.layers[articleToSlide].top += ARTICLE_INC_Y;
                document.layers[articleToSlide].clip.top -= ARTICLE_INC_Y;
        } else {
                document.layers[articleToSlide].top = ARTICLE_HOME_Y;
                document.layers[articleToSlide].clip.top = 0;
        }
}

function article_scrollRight ()
{
```

Figure 8-4:
Yikes! Look at all that script — and just for one page!

Why so much script for a simple web channel? Unlike Explorer, which does most of the handling of windows and the desktop for you, Netcaster leaves all these nasty features for you to handle. The primary reason is that Netscape purposefully avoided getting directly into the Windows 95 or Mac operating systems. Although this hands-off approach ensures that the product is truly cross-platform, it also ensures that you're responsible for handling the interface commands by using JavaScript.

The good news is that the Webtop works pretty much like a web page. HTML provides the primary interface for designing channel content, so using existing material from a site to your channel is pretty straight forward, except for the interface design.

One of the most common mistakes that I've seen with Netcaster web channels is that developers decide to spawn new windows within their web channels, instead of maintaining the fiction of the web channel that takes over all of your desktop. This usually manifests itself when links that were originally designed to spawn a new window in the web browser end up in the web-channel viewer. You click the link, and then bang!, a new Navigator window instead of the Webtop.

Keep track of channels while dropping your Drawer(s)

The Webtop is your Netcaster stage. Its *Drawer* is more your on-screen, programmable-VCR kind of feature. The only major difference is that setting your web channels by using the Drawer is a heck of a lot easier than setting the clock on the VCR. Briefly, the following list tells you what features reside on the Drawer or that you activate from the Drawer:

- ✔ Channel status indicator
- ✔ Channel Finder bar
- ✔ Add Channel menu
- ✔ Options menu
- ✔ The Help menu
- ✔ The navigation bar

Figure 8-5 shows the Drawer as the user first sees it. As with the Active Channel display in Explorer, you can place the Drawer in Netcaster on either side of the screen and can minimize it to show just a small tab. The major difference is that the Drawer contains all the options that the users ever need. With Explorer, most of the Channel options that are located in a variety of places throughout the browser. In this regard, Netcaster is much more efficient. After you launch Netcaster, none of the Navigator menus bars remains on-screen. This change gives the users the perception that they launched an entirely new application.

Buttons and features fill the Drawer, but the most basic information that it delivers can be, well, confusing. You can find all your channel information in the My Channels area of the Drawer, but don't be surprised if you can't immediately tell that just by looking at the screen. I certainly couldn't!

More often than not, if you're looking at the Drawer, what you really want to know is the status of an active channel. Has it updated since you last checked? If so, when? If not, when can you expect it to do so? Call it poor design or the limitations of JavaScript, but this feature is the worst-designed aspect of Netcaster. Finding out key pieces of information, like whether or not a channel is being updated, requires a deciphering tool. Well, I just happen to have one, and it's in Table 8-2.

Figure 8-5:
The
Netcaster
Drawer, as
it first
appears to
users.

Table 8-2	Deciphering Netcaster Channel Status
What You See	*What It Really Means*
A little green animated line underneath the name of a channel	The channel is in the process of updating, and is viewable.
A little red animated line underneath the name of a channel	The channel is being updated but can't be viewed at the moment.
A little green dot next to the channel on the left	Your channel has been updated.
A little red dot next to the channel on the left	Your channel hasn't been updated.
A box to the right of a channel (and it's blue on the inside)	The channel is running in Webtop mode.
A box to the right of a channel (and it's green on the inside)	The channel is running in Webtop mode and is the currently selected channel.

At the bottom of the Drawer are the options for Netcaster as well as the menu bars. Although the buttons all have separate functions, choosing the Options button spawns a rather non-descript window that combines all of the options located at the bottom of the Drawer. From the Options menu, you can perform the following tasks:

✓ **Modify the properties of a channel.** Properties include the majority of the options including how the channel looks on-screen, how often the channel gets pushed, and how many pages deep Netcaster should go in order to bring back the content that you want.

✓ **Add or delete channels.** If you add a channel, you get to set the properties for the channel as well.

✓ **Manually update channels.** If you can't wait to get the latest update, you can push manually from this Options menu.

✓ **Modify the layout of the Drawer and set the default channel.** The default channel is the channel that is loaded whenever Netcaster is started up. When you first install the program, that channel is the Netscape channel.

✓ **Modify the security options for Netcaster.** Here you can specify how Netcaster interacts with Castanet, because Castanet support is built into Netcaster.

From the My Channels area of the Drawer, you can access a number of the features in the preceding list by right-clicking the channel (or Ctrl+clicking for the Mac fans out there). You'll get the same Options menu that I just described. You can start an update, modify the channel properties, and delete the channel.

The very bottom of the Drawer includes a button bar that gives you limited access to Navigator. Here, you can perform a number of the tasks that take Netscape Navigator nearly the entire screen to do. From this button bar, you can minimize or maximize the Webtop, navigate forward or backward through Netcaster pages, and spawn a new Navigator window. Figure 8-6 is a blowup of the menu bar.

Figure 8-6:
A blowup
of the
menu bar
at the
bottom
of the
Netcaster
Drawer.

Honey, where's my Channel Finder?

Perhaps the most significant part of Netcaster is not actually the Webtop or the Drawer but the *Channel Finder* — mainly because, well, you have no easy way to add channels to Netcaster. In fact, I'm probably being a bit on the gracious side, because I happen to like Netscape. The reality of subscribing to channels in Netcaster is that it's a royal pain the first time that you do it, so much so that it could possibly turn off a number of potential subscribers.

The Channel Finder: What is it?

The Channel Finder exists in two places, both of which are driven from the Netcaster Drawer. As shown in Figure 8-7, the Channel Finder in the Drawer is split into two tabbed sections, In General and Business Focus. You can toggle back and forth between these two sections by clicking either of the tabs. Like the Active Channel Bar in Explorer, this space is generally reserved for companies that have strategic relationships with Netscape. As such, you can expect to find companies like Disney and ABC News on the Drawer's Channel Finder.

Figure 8-7:
The Channel Finder is located primarily in the Netcaster Drawer

After you select a channel from the Channel Finder area of the Drawer, an icon appears, as shown in Figure 8-8. As is true of the Active Channel in Explorer 4.0, the icon is merely a graphical representation of the channel, mostly for show. At the bottom of the icon are two buttons: Add Channel and Preview Channel. If you choose Preview Channel, a new window generates and a promo page appears showing the channel's contents. If you choose Add Channel, the subscription process begins (as I describe in the following section).

If you take a quick glance back at Figure 8-7, you see that a button labeled More Channels appears at the bottom of the Channel Finder. If you choose that button, another new page appears that includes a number of other new channels, along with their corresponding preview pages. This page, too, is the Channel Viewer, although it's a completely new window that is not physically attached to the Drawer. This part of the Channel Viewer is shown in Figure 8-9. I know it sounds a bit weird, but the way in which Netcaster works is that they revolve companies from the larger Channel Finder window onto the more exclusive Channel Finder on the Drawer. It's called marketing!

A graphical representation of the channel you select.

Figure 8-8:
Selecting a channel from the Drawer Channel Finder reveals an icon and two buttons.

Figure 8-9:
Channel
Finder II:
the sequel.
You access
this page by
choosing
the More
Channels
button.

If there were a shortcut around all the revealing layers and new windows spawned by the second in the Channel Finder, I'd offer it up to you, but honestly, it doesn't exist. This setup isn't so bad if you know what's going on, but all these features are new, so you're going to need some time to get comfortable with them. The best advice that I can give is to have a little patience, and if you get frustrated, go grab some coffee, take a walk, and come back later!

The kind of subscribing that only a doctor should do

Before you can even start subscribing to channels, you must jump through several hoops. (By the way, I'm walking you through this process for two reasons: one, to identify how bad an idea this setup was on Netscape's part, and two, to highlight and underscore the fact that every user of Netcaster must go through this process as well before any user can subscribe to the first channel.) In the short term, anyway, you may want to think about putting the following "steps to subscribing" on your web site just to help users out:

1. **From the Channel Finder (in either location) click the Add a Channel button.**

   This action begins the process. After you perform this step, a new window is generated and you can see a preview of the channel.

2. Choose the Continue button.

An alert similar to the one shown in Figure 8-10 appears, asking whether you're a part of Netscape's Member Services. At this point, you're not, so choose the Sign me Up option and then choose Continue again, and head to Netscape Member Services.

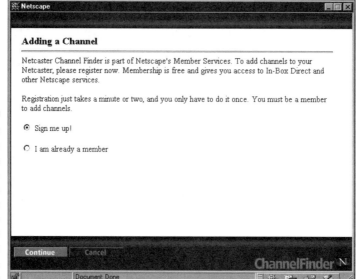

Figure 8-10:
Expect to see this alert the first time you try to subscribe to a channel.

3. Fill out the information requested on the Member Services form that appears and then choose Continue again after you finish.

All this information is necessary to create a *Verisign certificate* for you. This certificate eventually authenticates who you are for secure online transactions and the like. Thankfully, you need to go through this step only once. After you finish the form, choose Continue to begin to process your certificate. From there, a new window appears on-screen.

4. If you want, fill out the membership survey and then choose Continue again.

This survey is optional. To skip it, just choose Continue.

5. Select submit from the next window, and get the certificate sent to you.

After you're done with this string of windows that make up the registration process, you're asked to provide a personal password; then, within a few minutes, Verisign sends an authentication e-mail back to you, as shown in Figure 8-11. Here's the last tricky part. The e-mail includes some information about you and then enables Verisign to embed the certificate within Navigator so that you don't need to see it again. However, this service can only be performed if you're using Netscape Messenger mail. If you're using something else, such as cc:Mail or Eudora, you must actually visit the Verisign web site and follow their instructions to finish off the process.

The Verisign web site is located at www.verisign.com

After you go through this process, you're pretty much in the clear. You get asked if you want to send the certificate, to which you say Yes. Here's one of those things, though, that they never tell you about in the manual. For this system to work right, you need to shut down Netcaster (and, preferably, your computer), and reboot before the certificate will work properly. If you don't, you may find yourself going though Steps 1 and 2 again. After you reboot Netcaster, though, the certificate should automatically be recognized and transferred when you subscribe to a channel, without you having to do any work!

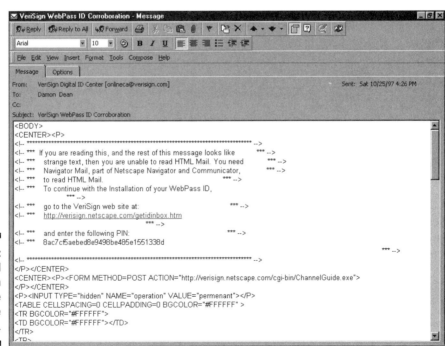

Figure 8-11:
This e-mail is a sign that you're in the home stretch.

How Does Castanet Fit into Netcaster?

The *Castanet Tuner* is essentially a bolted-on component to Netcaster. Castanet Channels are more often than not Java applets. Built into Netcaster is support for Java applets. As a result, you can subscribe to any Castanet Channel through the Channel Finder interface. Figure 8-12 shows the Marimba Castanet Channel Guide.

The real question is whether subscribing to Castanet channels provides any real added value to Netcaster, and the answer thus far has been "No." Because Castanet Channels have yet to catch on as a strong web-channel format, the benefit to having them accessible through Netcaster is minimal at best. In the future, this situation may, of course, change. Castanet has been getting more popular, and as developers begin to understand its tools a bit better, more popular web channels may begin to surface. If this event does happen, the chances are good that support for these channels in Netcaster is going to prove a benefit to users and developers alike.

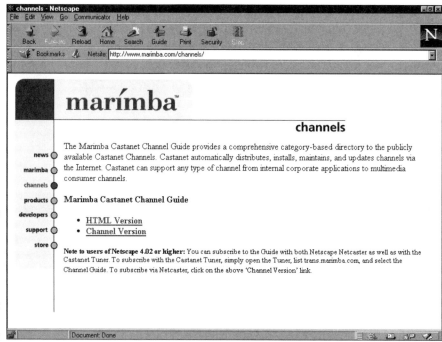

Figure 8-12:
By using
Netcaster,
you can
subscribe
to Castanet
Channels.

Is it Worth Developing Channels for Netcaster?

Netcaster has some very basic problems, including those in the following list:

✔ It's SLOW, even on machines connected to the Internet via a T-1line (a super faster Internet connection) or higher.

✔ It's not included in every version of Communicator 4.0.

✔ It's cumbersome to install and get running.

✔ Subscribing to channels is a hassle.

✔ The controls are confusing and counter-intuitive.

✔ The basic product documentation for users and developer stinks.

How slow is slow? Netcaster is based on Java and JavaScript, both of which are slow in their own right. Every successive version Java and JavaScript gets faster, but because they are cross-platform, and because they have some odd conventions that programmers and developers aren't necessarily used to considering when they write code, a lot of applications built in this language tend to be RAM hogs. Many seemingly simple Java applications, like those sports tickers you see a lot of, can fill up the RAM buffer on PCs and Macs if left running for long periods of time, and bring the entire system to a near crawl. The best solution. Reboot.

All those things said, one simple fact is very hard to ignore, and that's the installed base figure for Netscape users. Like the situation or not, this company owns the majority of the Internet browser market. That market dominance doesn't mean that every version of its product is a winner, however, and as everyone has seen at one time or another, Microsoft isn't about to let Netscape just take the market for itself.

Ultimately, the decision is yours. Some people go with Netscape because it's not Microsoft. As you can see in Chapter 9, getting a Netcaster channel up and running isn't that difficult, but the process can be tedious. As a starting point, Explorer is a whole lot easier to use — something to keep in the back of your mind as you weigh the decision of choosing a platform to start with.

Chapter 9

Netcaster Journalism

· ·

In This Chapter

▶ How much of that Explorer channel will be useful in Netcaster

▶ Just enough JavaScipt to get your channel up and going

▶ Using the unsupported but nonetheless efficient Netcaster Channel Wizard

▶ More Wizards, this time with Webtops

▶ Promoting your channel after it's complete

· ·

*I*t kinda stinks to be number one. Everyone's always after your number one slot, and no matter how hard you try, good (or even great) is never good enough. Just ask Netscape. In building Netcaster, they pushed JavaScript to its limits and basically created a new application within their current web browser.

All that work, and what did they get in return? Industry types and pundits complained that Netcaster was confusing and too hard. They were right, by the way. Long story short, over the past couple of months, Netscape has feverishly been adding new "How to" documentation to their DevEdge Online center, in an attempt to show developers just how easy it is to create a Netcaster channel.

And you know what? Netscape got it right, because now it is easier to create a Netcaster channel. Granted, more "Wizards" are now on the Netscape site than at the Excalibur in Las Vegas, but at least the Netscape ones don't cast spells that make you lose twenty hands straight at the blackjack table! Arguably, with the latest Wizard additions to the Netscape site, making a Netcaster channel may be nearly as easy as making a Microsoft channel.

Ah, I can hear you all muttering "Prove it, smart guy." All right then, I will!

About All That Content I Already Have

Assume for just a second that you built a web channel for Microsoft Explorer 4.0 (see Chapters 4 and 5). You built the CDF file, subscribed to the Microsoft SiteBuilder Network, and added a few fancy Dynamic HTML add-ons to create kicking web channel. You did it, because, well, it was pretty easy and you didn't have to change much of your content.

But you also know that, right now, Microsoft doesn't own the marketshare that Netscape does. You've got this web channel, and you're beginning to wonder (a) how hard would making a Netcaster channel really be and (b) how much of my current web site can be used in a Netcaster channel. Good news! The answer to (a) is that it's not that hard (which I know I keep repeating), and (b) is that quite a bit of your current web site content can be reused for a Netcaster channel.

The basic difference between the Microsoft and Netcaster channels lies in the front end, meaning the area where you do the subscribing and setting up of the channel. Microsoft relies on CDF and some very specific HTML operations to do all the work. Netcaster relies on some Netcaser specific JavaScript and some very specific HTML to do exactly the same functions. Beyond the CDF file and your channel front page, a Microsoft channel can basically be an existing web site. Beyond the JavaScript and the Webtop (your channel front page), a Netcaster channel can basically be an existing web site.

Figure 9-1 illustrates this concept. The channel on the top is the CNET channel on Explorer 4.0. The channel on the bottom is the CNET channel on Netcaster. Though the channels are different at the subscription page and top level, below they are the same!

Rapunzel, Lay Down Your Hierarchy!

Netcaster and Explorer share a very similar subscription structure, even though their elements are different. Explorer controls the spawning of a channel by using the CDF file. The Netcaster equivalent is a subscription page. Figure 9-2 shows how Netcaster uses this subscription page to set up the channel. This page includes all the relevant information about the channel, including:

- ✔ Webtop (channel) location
- ✔ The channel description
- ✔ The channel size
- ✔ The channel delivery schedule

In turn, the subscription page controls the spawning of the initial Webtop and loading of the channel from the server to the user's desktop. By the way, the subscription file is just a regular HTML document like any other on your web site, though it contains Netcaster-specific JavaScript that handles both the process of subscribing, as well as the spawning of the first page in the channel.

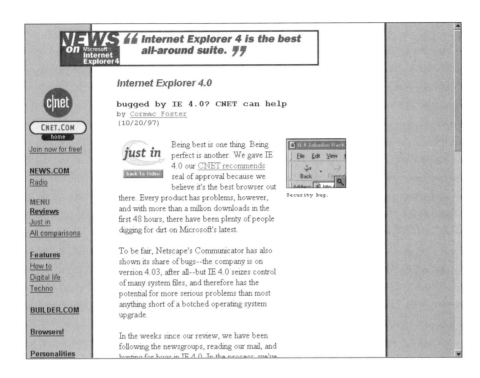

Figure 9-1: The CNET channel on Explorer (top) and on Netcaster (bottom).

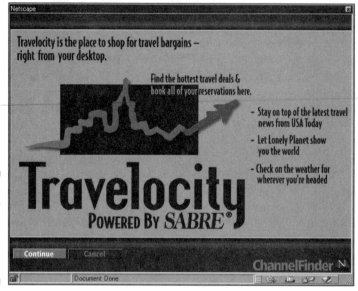

Figure 9-2:
A Netcaster subscription page in the Channel Finder.

The Netcaster subscription page, like the Explorer CDF file, can be started just by referencing it in a link from any web site. Although the Netscape Channel Finder is by far the best way to promote your channel, all you really need is the link and a copy of the Netcaster logo (which can be found at developer.netscape.com/one/netcaster/index.html).

Just Enough JavaScript to Subscribe

Take a gander at Figure 9-3. It shows the subscription page for Channel Swank. This page, like every other Netcaster subscription page out there, attempts to accomplish three very important tasks. They're so important, in fact, the I've listed them right here:

✔ Selling your channel

✔ Setting the channel properties

✔ Calling Netcaster to set the channel up

If you're just looking for the JavaScript by itself, without all the dramatic prose and walk-through, you can skip to the "I got it! Now what?" section, later in this chapter.

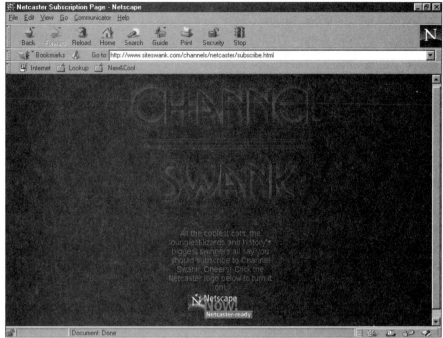

Figure 9-3:
The
Channel
Swank
subscription
page.

Without the subscription page, there is no Netcaster channel, which makes it a pretty important piece of the overall webcasting puzzle. Kinda like math, though. You never wanted to do it, but you needed math to get into a good school, so you did it, begrudgingly. The subscription page is by no means the sexiest of pages (or is it?), but it is perhaps one of the most important.

If you've got it, flaunt it!

I bet you didn't know it, but your subscription page has two personalities. The left brain side of your Netcaster subscription page is concerned only about JavaScript and subscribing to channels. Boring, but functional stuff, really. Don't worry, though, there will be plenty of time for that.

The right side, however, is more of a rebel. It just wants to party, stay out late, and talk about itself to anyone who'll listen. Which is the more important side of your subscription page? Functionally, the left side is more important, but JavaScript doesn't sell nearly as well as, well . . . uh . . . you know what sells. I don't have to tell you that. Nevertheless, for your Netcaster channel to be a success, the right side of your Netcaster subscription page needs to put in a little overtime and start selling.

The Hecklers Online subscription page shown in Figure 9-4 illustrates my point. Underneath the content is all the JavaScipt necessary for creating the Hecklers Online channel. To the untrained eye (spelled "user"), it looks like a promotional page, and it is! Of course, you don't have to do a promotional page. You could just put up the JavaScript with a link. Sort of a Beatles white album kind of thing. That could be cool, but not if everyone does it!

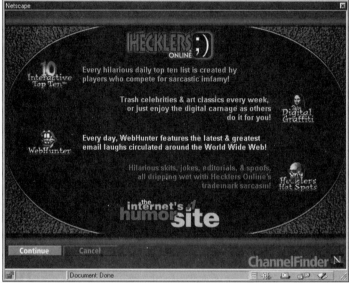

Figure 9-4:
Promote your channel, and I promise I won't tell anyone about all the JavaScript under there!

Property values are going up . . . or was that under?

Behind all the flash that is your subscription page lies the key to human understanding — or at the very least your channel properties. The properties you set here give Netcaster all the information it needs to set up and configure your web channel. All the channel property information is contained in some JavaScript that runs when the page is created.

After all the JavaScript is in place, you may think that the whole subscription process would just run itself. It doesn't. What happens if someone doesn't want your channel? Auto loading the channel would certainly be more efficient, but users may not appreciate it much. So, instead, all the information is kept there until the user calls Netcaster, usually by selecting a link. More on that in a few paragraphs!

You have two basic ways to do the subscription page. The cleaner way, at least insofar as your HTML looks nicer, is to reference the JavaScript in a separate file and simply read it when the page loads. If you do it this way, you can include all the channel property values in a hidden form that automatically gets posted to the Channel Properties window when the user selects the subscribe link.

Alternatively, you could simply embed all the JavaScript in your subscription page. That's the way I've done it here, to illustrate the process more clearly. However, either way is equally acceptable.

I've noticed that channels in the Netscape Channel Finder all seem to use the external .js file and then the hidden form. If you plan to promote your channel through that venue, you may want to consider using that method.

Calling all Netcasters! Calling all Netcasters!

The way Netcaster is built, you first have to call it and tell it that you and your channel are waiting to get it. It's kinda particular that way. The way to get Netcaster's attention is to enable two functions that allow you to both create a channel and then add that channel. Specifically, these functions are called getChannelObject and addChannel.

You can call getChannelObject and addChannel in a number of ways. Whichever way you chose to do it, however, the basic syntax has to do the following:

- ✔ Initialize the subscription/adding a channel function
- ✔ Retrieve all the components that Netcaster needs to create a channel
- ✔ Figure out whether or not the browser supports Netcaster
- ✔ Import the getChannelObject and addChannel features

To meet all the preceding requirements, Netscape recommends using the following script. (My comments are in bold.)

```
<SCRIPT LANGUAGE="Javascript1.2">
function addMyChannel(name,url) {
    var nc = components["netcaster"]; //calls the
    Netcaster components to be used in creating the channel
    nc.activate();  //activates those components
    if(nc.active == true) { //checks to see if the
    browser supports Netcaster
        import nc.getChannelObject; //gets the Channel
        creation object
        import nc.addChannel; //gets the object that allows
        you to add a channel
```

A channel by any other name . . . isn't a channel

Every channel needs a name. That shouldn't be a big deal since you've probably already got one in mind. But you need to let Netcaster know what it's going to be called — if for no other reason than Netcaster has to know what to put in the MyChannel area of the Channel Drawer. In addition, though, you need to let Netcaster know where the Webtop page is located as well as provide a brief description of the channel itself. This description is seen when people move the mouse over your channel in the Channel Finder.

For the purposes of a demo, I've used Channel Swank, the Netcaster version, in the locations where having a real name or URL is appropriate. I hope you don't mind! Here's the script:

```
channel = getChannelObject(); //the properties you define
after this line will be fed to getChannelObject
        channel.url = "http://www.siteswank.com/channels/
            netcaster/index.html"
        channel.name = "Channel Swank"
        channel.desc = "The web channel for Swingers,
            Hipsters and other Loungy types."
```

Telling AbsoluteTime and IntervalTime

Here's yet another way in which both Netcaster and Explorer are alike. In the CDF file for Explorer, you usually provide a default (or preferred) set of channel update times for the user. In Netcaster, you do the same thing. Of course, the numbering is totally different, but in a strange way, it's a bit easier to understand.

The two basic time parameters are AbsoluteTime and IntervalTime. Absolute time is the exact time in which a channel should be updated, such as Monday morning at 7:00. Interval time is a range time in which the channel should be updated, such as every 30 minutes. AbsoluteTime works in minutes, starting with Sunday at midnight. Interval time works with kooky integers that have no other useful connection, except that they're negative and in a row.

For AbsoluteTime, here are some handy conversions for you:

- One day: 1440
- Wednesday midnight: 4320
- Friday at 7:45 p.m.: (7200 + 1140 + 45) = 8685

For IntervalTime, here are the conversions for their negative integer scale (and no, neither –1 or 0 have any meaning).

- ✔ 15 minutes: -2
- ✔ 30 minutes: -3
- ✔ 1 hour: -4
- ✔ Daily: -5
- ✔ Weekly: -6

To set `IntervalTime` and `AbsoluteTime` in your subscription, you can use the following script:

```
channel.intervalTime = -5; //daily
channel.absoluteTime = 8685; //Friday at 7:45 pm
```

Hey man, how much cache you got on ya?

This is one of those functions that I'm glad Netcaster asks if the developer wants to set, but frankly, it doesn't seem to matter much, because Netcaster is such a memory hog to begin with. Who cares what the cache is? The entire system memory cache bursts at the seams faster than Homer Simpson's pants. Come on! On the plus side, the function is optional and not needed to set up your channel.

There are two cache parameters that you can specify for your channel: `estCacheSize` (estimated) and `maxCacheSize` (maximum). Both are measured in bytes, which means big numbers for everyone! For `estCacheSize`, you can also set the value at –1, which means you're not sure of the cache requirements. If you're so inclined, you can drop the following script in your subscription page for cache parameters:

```
channel.estCacheSize = -1; //I'm not sure!
channel.maxCacheSize = 1024000; //about 1MB
```

Just how low can you go?

One of the more interesting parameters you can set in Netcaster is the crawl depth. *Crawl depth* is simply the number of layers deep you'd like Netcaster to go when updating the channel. As a rule of thumb (whose rule or thumb, I have no idea), you probably should try to keep this number lower than, say, three levels. The reason is simple: download size. The deeper the crawl, the longer the download will take. The crawl depth is represented by an positive integer in the following script:

```
channel.depth = 3; // three layers deep
```

Note: Netscape uses their own site-crawling tool that goes to the top level of the channel and then follows the links downward according to the number you specify in the script.

No, over to the left a little

To specify your channel front page, you have five parameters to consider. The first, and most important, is the *mode setting,* which specifies whether you think your channel should default to a Navigator window or to a full-screen Webtop. While the decision is up to you (as are they all, actually), let me suggest using Webtop. It looks much, much cooler, and it promotes the TV style prevalent in web channels.

The other parameters all have to do with your channel front page in Window mode, which is the non-Webtop mode. Called *Hints* (I really wish I knew why they're called Hints, but I don't know), these commands allow you to set the horizontal and vertical offsets of the web channel front page, as well as the size of said front page. The horizontal and vertical offsets are all taken from the top-left corner of the screen, and all measurements are in pixels.

If you decide to use the Webtop mode, be sure not to use the Window parameters!

For the Webtop mode, all you'll need is the following addition to your script:

```
channel.mode = "webtop"
```

For the Windows mode, you'll modify the mode setting and add the other parameters, as follows:

```
channel.mode = "window"
channel.topHint = 0;     // no offset
      channel.leftHint = 0; // no offset that way either
      channel.widthHint =  600; //window width
      channel.heightHint = 391; //window height
```

Beam me up, Server

You know I couldn't get through a technology book without a *Star Trek* reference. It was just a question of when! The last bit of the subscription script requires that you set addChannel so that, when the channel is added, all this great information gets put into the right place.

I've thrown in the last little bits that finish off the script as well, but to set addChannel and specify all your channel parameters, it looks like this:

```
addChannel(channel); //this takes all your paramters and
sets them in the addChannel function
    }
  }
}
</SCRIPT>
```

I got it! Now what?

Congratulations, with that, you've got all the JavaScript you need to get a channel up and running. The completed script should look a lot like the script that's right here (if it doesn't, oops!):

```
<SCRIPT LANGUAGE="Javascript1.2">
function addMyChannel(name,url) {
var nc = components["netcaster"];
nc.activate();    //activates those components
    if(nc.active == true) {
        import nc.getChannelObject;
        import nc.addChannel;
            channel = getChannelObject();
        channel.url = "http://www.siteswank.com/channels/
            netcaster/index.html"
        channel.name = "Channel Swank"
        channel.desc = "The web channel for Swingers,
            Hipsters and other Loungy types."
            channel.intervalTime = -5;
        channel.absoluteTime = 8685;
            channel.estCacheSize = -1;
            channel.maxCacheSize = 1024000;
            channel.depth = 3;
            channel.mode = "webtop"
            addChannel(channel);
    }
}
</SCRIPT>
```

Just a friendly reminder. The script should be wholly contained in the `<HEAD>` tag of your subscription page.

After you've got the JavaScript in your subscription page, you'll still need a way to run it. There are any number of ways to do this, but the easiest way is to simply have a link that calls the subscription function. The most effective way is to get a copy of the animated Netcaster logo (you can get it at `developer.netscape.com/one/dynhtml/images/ncnow.gif`) and use that as your active link.

To add this function, just add the following HTML in the `<BODY>` of your subscription page:

```
<A HREF="" onCLick="addMyChannel(); return false;">
<IMG SRC="http://developer.netscape.com/one/dynhtml/images
ncnow.gif" WIDTH=117
    HEIGHT=55 BORDER=0></A>
```

After you select the Netcaster Now! image, the subscription function is called, and a dialogue box like the one in Figure 9-5 appears. It includes all your default channel properties in their proper slots. Hopefully, users will select OK, and you're channel will be ready to roll!

Figure 9-5:
The
Channel
properties
box, filled
with the
subscription
page
defaults.

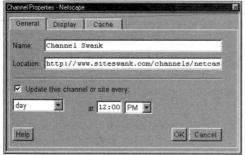

Can a Wave of the Wand Eliminate All This Work?

Now that Netcaster version 1.0 has been released, Netscape is supremely interested in getting as many people as possible to use it. Using it means having a large number of channels. To have a large number of channels means making channels to be pretty straight forward. Hmm . . . sounds like a great place for a Microsoft-like *coup de software.*

Netcsape's answer, shown in Figure 9-6, is the Add Channel Wizard. Officially, the Add Channel Wizard is not supported by Netscape. However, it's on their web site, and they're promoting the heck out of it. If only I had that kind of non-support! By the way, you can find the Add Channel Wizard at `developer.netscape.com/one/netcaster/index.html`.

The Add Channel Wizard does pretty much what I just finished telling you all about, so you may well ask if it does anything that makes it worth looking into. The Add Channel Wizard does two additional tasks that I didn't cover here. First, it writes the subscription page JavaScript so that it detects whether or not you're running on a Netcaster supported browser — something that I omitted. This is a nice feature, but the script is kind of ugly because it's long and has a whole bunch of conditions to it. It would be a far more important feature if Netcaster crashed or something when you tried running it with Internet Explorer 4.0, but it doesn't, so I'm not convinced you need to have that in your subscription script.

Figure 9-6:
The Add
Channel
Wizard
builds a
Netcaster
subscription
file for you.

The second (and more important, I think) thing that the Wizard does is submit your channel for consideration to be put in the Netcaster Channel Finder. This doesn't seem like such a huge benefit, I know, but if you've tried to find the Channel Finder submission area on the Netscape site lately, you'll soon find out why this is a pretty big deal. The Channel Finder submission area is not there!

So you be the judge. Go for the upside and get some extra script you don't really need. Or go for the simpler script and try to find the Channel Finder submission area. I went for the latter — I'm still looking.

Instant Webtops: Just Add Water

Now that you've got the subscription page set, it's time to turn your attention to your Netcaster channel itself. First, though, the truth. The truth is that you don't need to do anything else. If you simply reference your existing home page in your subscription file, you're basically done. Like Internet Explorer 4.0, you can simply take an existing web site and make it a channel.

Now, the question is, could you live with yourself if that's all you did? I know, it would take some time, but you'd probably find a way to get over it. On the flip side, though, if you take a look at the other available Netcaster channels, you'll notice that very few of them are just web sites in disguise.

Or are they? In fact, most Explorer and Netcaster web channels are web sites in disguise, but they're able to get away with it because they're using Dynamic HTML to make their introductory front pages look, well, sexy. All of that talk back at the beginning of the book about looking and feeling like TV is true — up to a point. That point, if I'm not mistaken, appears to be about two clicks deep into the average web channel.

Netcaster, like Explorer, offers support for Dynamic HTML. Dynamic HTML is being heralded (everything about the Internet is heralded, in case you were curious) as the next wave of content development. Dynamic HTML allows you to do some very clever things, including:

✔ Layering of text and graphics

✔ Hiding and showing of text and graphics

✔ Setting a wide variety of font types and characteristics

✔ Animating

While this all sounds nice, you may be wondering why I'm bringing it up now. After all, I could just stop the chapter right here and move onto Marimba! You've already got everything you need to make a channel — except a little sizzle. Remember, the point of this nifty webcasting thing is to create a more TV-like experience for users, and for you to get the most out of the effort you put into creating content.

Of course, you can't forget about ease of use. This stuff should be easy, as well as compelling. Enter the Netscape Webtop Wizard (shown in Figure 9-7), a Java applet that does your Dynamic HTML work for you and creates a quasi-custom Webtop for your Netcaster channel. The Webtop Wizard is literally right next to the Add Channel Wizard, located conveniently at a Netscape Developer site near you (`developer.netscape.com/one/netcaster/index.html`).

Figure 9-7:
The Webtop
Wizard,
at your
service.

The Webtop Wizard can help add appeal to your Netcaster channel. It works by using a standard set of Webtop templates and then creates buttons with on and off states, as well as tab menus that hide and show depending on whether you've selected them or not. If you already have a good handle on

Dynamic HTML, the Webtop Wizard probably won't tell you anything you don't already know. However, if you're looking to add a little life to your channel Webtop but don't want to bone up on Dynamic HTML, the following sections may just be what you've been waiting for!

Wizard hard drive trickery

There are just a couple of things that you should know going in. One, the Webtop Wizard uses a tab format, so all the information for you channel is contained on one form that eventually generates your channel Webtop. Second, the Wizard is going to want to access your hard drive to create a couple of folders. Now, I don't know about you, but I'm always a nervous wreck when that Java Security window like the one in Figure 9-8 starts popping up. In this case, though, you need to do what I did, which was to just take a deep breath and let the Wizard do its magic.

Figure 9-8:
The Wizard needs to access your hard drive to create some folders. Don't be alarmed!

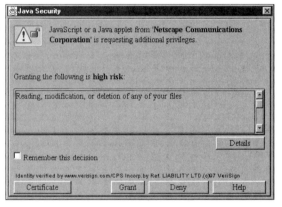

We're off to see the Wizard

The Title section is the first part of the Wizard. Not surprisingly, this is where you put the title of your channel. In the final Webtop, it turns out to be 72-point type, so chose your words, uh, sparingly.

The Styles section, shown in Figure 9-9, lets you chose from three basic types of Channels. Actually, the biggest distinction is in color, though there are some functional differences. However, these types all have a similar approach, in that they all split the Webtop into two areas, a content area and a navigation area.

Figure 9-9:
Do you like khaki, or pinstripes?

Reveal to me your sections, my dear

The content area is represented by the Sections tab, as shown in Figure 9-10. In this area, you specify any number of pages on your web site. Each gets a name and corresponding URL. The Wizard then creates a button for each section that is shown on the Webtop. When the user selects one of the buttons, the content from the page that you specified is revealed. Select another button and that layer is revealed, while the previous one disappears.

Figure 9-10:
In the Sections tab, you specify the web pages you want shown on demand at the Webtop.

Hide your drawers

Every Webtop needs to have some sort of navigation bar. In the Wizard, you create this navigation bar from the Drawers tab (see Figure 9-11) — not to be confused with the Drawer described earlier in this chapter and in Chapter 8. They must have had naming burnout at Netscape that day. How else could you end up with two totally different items with the same name?

Figure 9-11:
Different
drawer,
same basic
concept.
Here's
where you
build it.

Anyway, this Drawer does work similarly to the one built into Netcaster. First, you define the name for a tab, which is always on the Webtop. When the user selects the tab, the Drawer opens up to reveal a series of icons. These icons are links to different parts of the channel, where users get sent if they click the icon.

Poof! There's your channel

One last thing before you press that Generate Webtop button. You can also specify a ticker for the bottom of your channel. Personally, I think adding another string of text running across the bottom of your channel is both busy and makes your channel look like CNBC in the morning, and who wants that, really? It's up to you, but I recommend avoiding this part of the Wizard.

After you filled in all the loose ends, all you really need to do is press the button, and the Wizard does the rest. The finished product may look a little something like the graphic in Figure 9-12. It isn't the sexiest Webtop around, but it's functional, and — better yet — you can hack it and make a better one if you like!

Promoting Your Netcaster Channel

Like Internet Explorer 4.0, you won't need anything fancy to get your channel set up. You don't need to be part of the Netcaster Channel Finder (shown in Figure 9-13), though, like the Active Channel Guide, it's pretty much the only gig in town at this point for Netcaster channels. Finding an application for the Channel Finder on the Netscape site appears to take an act of congress, so your best bet is to use the Add Channel Wizard to get your channel considered for inclusion. If, however, you are accepted, be prepared to change some of the content on your subscription page, in order to meet their requirements for fitting within the Channel Finder.

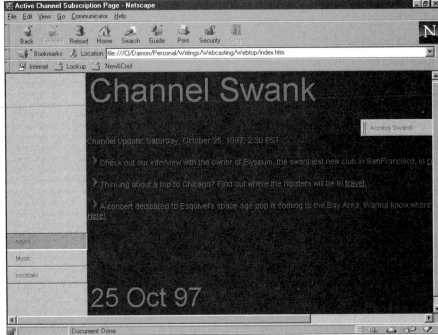

Figure 9-12:
The
Channel
Swank
Insta-
Webtop

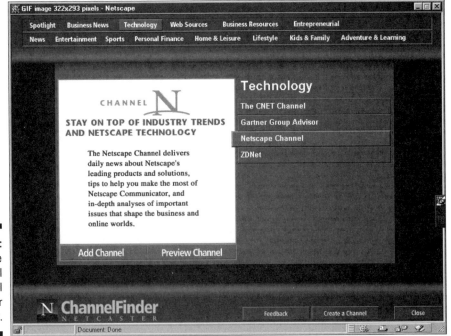

Figure 9-13:
The prime
promotional
real
estate for
Netcaster.

One of the best things you can do to get your channel noticed is to join the Netscape DevEdge online program. There's no fee for a basic membership, and you gain access to a number of newsgroups and newsletters. By participating and collecting these items, you keep in touch with what's going on with Netcaster, and, in addition, begin to get contact within the developer community. This contact should increase the overall exposure of your business, as well as your Netcaster channel.

Chapter 10

Using Castanet to Push Your Message

• •

• •

Castanet is the most powerful technology available for creating channels. You can call on all the capabilities of the Java programming language in creating Castanet channels; plus, using the Castanet Transmitter, you can send the user regular updates to the channel's code and data.

But all this power comes at a price. Unlike most other channels, which feed information from Web pages to users, creating a Castanet channel usually requires programming. You can learn the Bongo user interface scripting language, or the Java programming language, or both, but in any case it's no walk in the park to create a Castanet channel.

In addition to the price of doing real programming, there's the price of . . . well, price. To support a Castanet channel you need to run a piece of software called a Castanet Transmitter. There's a trial version for free, but for any real channel you'll need at least one copy of Castanet Transmitter, which costs at least $995.

Marimba, the developer of Castanet, has not done as good a job as PointCast, Microsoft, or Netscape in getting the word out to developers on how to create Castanet channels. Because of this lack of publicity and because Castanet is different from other web-channel technologies, developers have been slow to adopt it. There are many fewer Castanet channels in existence than there are PointCast or Netcaster channels. (You can view Castanet channels in Netcaster, but Castanet channels are different from Netcaster-specific channels.)

Because you can do almost anything with Castanet, and "almost anything" is too much to cover in a single chapter, I've created a simple path through the maze of possibilities that will show you how capable Castanet is without requiring you to do Bongo scripting or Castanet programming. I start by taking a look at the Castanet Tuner and some existing Castanet channels.

Getting Castanet Tuner and More

Getting Castanet Tuner is easy: It's on the CD, along with Bongo and a sample version of Castanet Transmitter. You can also download this stuff from the Marimba Web site. Just go to www.marimba.com and follow the instructions. I know you've done this kind of thing before, so I'll just point out a couple of things.

First is that you have to register before you get the software; the registration page is shown in Figure 10-1. It only takes a minute or so to fill out. At the bottom of the registration page you choose the products that you want and the operating system you use.

Figure 10-1:
Registering
to get the
Tuner
download
software.

Netscape

Download Marimba Software

news
marimba
channels
products
developers
support
store

You can download evaluation versions of our software by filling out the form below.

If you would like more information about our products, take one of our self-guided tours.

Name:
Email:
Phone:
Title:
Company:
Address:
City: State:
Zip: Country:
(OPTIONAL: ☐ Download via HTTP protocol)

Software Products:
☐ Castanet Tuner   ☐ Castanet Transmitter
☐ Castanet Proxy   ☐ Bongo

Operating System:
Select Your Operating System ▼   Download

Document Done

Now here's the trick: You can save yourself time and trouble by downloading all the pieces you need at once. Here's how to decide what to download:

✔ If you just want to look at some Castanet channels you can do so using either Netscape Netcaster or Castanet Tuner. But Castanet Tuner is smaller, faster, and easier to use. So I suggest that you download Castanet Tuner even if you already have Netcaster.

✔ To create an interface for a Castanet channel, download Bongo.

✔ To test your Castanet channel, download the sample version of Castanet Transmitter.

You can download as many or as few pieces of software as you want on each visit to the download page.

You can download all the Marimba software you want simultaneously. Choose all the products that you want on the registration page. This will bring up a page with links to all the products, as shown in Figure 10-2. Then click each product's link in order. All the products download simultaneously. Do this just before going to lunch, or going home for the evening, and all the products will be downloaded when you come back to your computer.

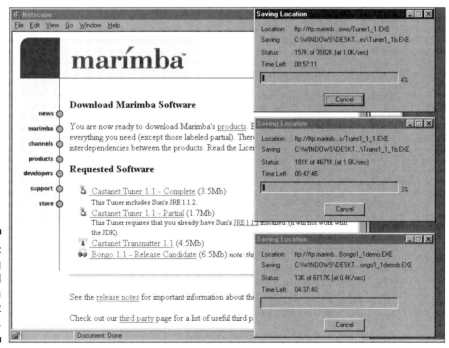

Figure 10-2:
Downloading several Marimba products at once.

My experience is that my computer is more likely to crash when I'm downloading several files at once. To avoid having problems, try to not do anything else with your computer until the downloads are complete. (Downloading the Tuner, Bongo, and the Transmitter sample version took me less than an hour with an ordinary 28.8 Kbps modem.)

What is Castanet, Anyway?

Castanet is what a fisherman does, right? Sorry! Actually, Castanet is a technology for using the Internet to keep computer applications updated with the latest code and data. Marimba, as the Castanet developer, is trying to make Castanet the industry standard for application development and delivery.

As a result, learning more about Castanet, even developing a sample channel with it, may be worthwhile to you even if you don't end up doing larger projects with the technology later.

Attributes of Castanet

Castanet channels are *client-server applications*. Even if you're familiar with the term, it might be worth refreshing your memory: Castanet channels are computer programs (applications) that depend on regular interaction between many user machines (clients) and a computer that provides a service to the user machines (server). The architecture of a Castanet application is shown in Figure 10-3.

The Castanet architecture is nothing if not diverse. It's also quite flexible, in that it gives developers the luxury of building a wide variety of applications, through the Bongo development tool. Here I've listed some of the distinguishing characteristics of the Castanet architecture:

- **Java emphasis:** Marimba was launched as the first Java software company, and in the beginning Castanet only worked with Java, not with more widely-used languages such as C and C++. For additional money, you can now include non-Java language support in your channel.

- **Cross-platform:** Both Java and Castanet are intended to be cross-platform technologies that work equally well on all versions of Windows, Macintosh, and many different flavors of UNIX.

- **Push model:** Like most technologies that are described as part of the movement toward push, Castanet uses a timer on the user's computer to periodically request updates from a server, which then downloads updated files in a single Internet connection to the user's computer.

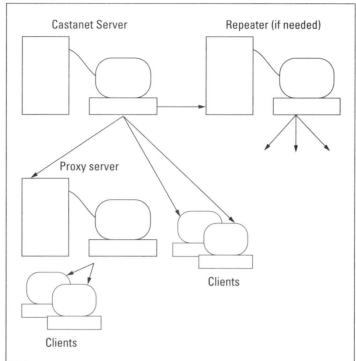

Figure 10-3:
The
architecture
of a
Castanet
application.

✔ **Differential updating:** To reduce connect time and bandwidth usage, Castanet implements differential updating, in which only files that are new or changed since the last update are transmitted.

✔ **Partnership with Netscape:** Marimba has partnered with Netscape to support Castanet channels in the new Netscape Netcaster push client and to resell Castanet server software. This partnership with Netscape greatly increases Marimba's ability to reach out to large numbers of end-users and to reach deep into large corporations.

✔ **Security emphasis:** Upcoming versions of Castanet will offer greatly improved security features. Castanet seems to be listening to customers who value security features over other possible improvements like support for other languages than Java or greater ease of development.

Castanet can support HTML-based channels as well as Java-based channels, but it's simpler and cheaper to deliver HTML-based channels using the CDF format supported by PointCast, Microsoft, and others. Only use Castanet for more robust channels that need the power of a programming language like Java.

When to use Castanet

So given the specifics of how Castanet works, and the fact that its lack of popularity makes using it risky, what kinds of applications is it still suitable for? Here are a few characteristics of projects that may be suitable for implementation in Castanet:

✔ **Intranet-based:** For World Wide Web applications, you can't be sure that users have a client that can use Castanet channels — Internet Explorer users can't — or that users are willing and able to connect to the Internet often enough to allow the channel to update itself. On an intranet, users can more easily be provided with Netscape Netcaster or Castanet Tuner to receive the channel.

✔ **New:** Castanet channels must be created using Bongo scripting and/or Java, both of which are new, so it's logical to reserve Castanet channels for new development. A good compromise here is to use the Castanet channel to create a new interface to existing information, such as information stored in corporate databases.

✔ **Small:** It's generally dumb to use new technology for big projects until you have experience with it, and Castanet, which is new in and of itself and is based on the still-new Java language, is no exception to this rule. (Corel's failed attempt to deliver a complete office applications suite in Java is just one of the dead bodies you'll have to step over in doing Java development.) Pick a small project with a well-defined purpose and a high chance of success.

✔ **Fun:** You usually have a lot more latitude in choosing and defining small projects as opposed to large ones. Part of the reason that push technology has become so popular is that there is a strong element of fun to using and developing it. You'll enjoy life more, and also be more likely to get the best work from all involved, if you pick something that sounds like fun.

Trying Castanet

Before you create a Castanet channel, you should try using some of the existing ones. Using existing Castanet channels will familiarize you with the technology and with the options that your users have when they use Castanet channels you create. Follow these steps to try Castanet channels:

1. **Download the Castanet Tuner (as described at the beginning of this chapter).**

2. **Install and configure the Castanet Tuner.**

3. **Subscribe to Castanet channels.**

4. **Manage Castanet channels.**

Install and configure the Castanet Tuner

To install the Castanet Tuner, close all open applications. Find the Tuner installer, which was called Tuner1_1 when I downloaded it, and double-click it. Follow the instructions that appear onscreen to proceed with the installation. One choice you will be given is a Typical installation, which uses default directory names, or a Custom installation. Choose Typical so that you can be sure that utilities like uninstall programs can find all the parts of the Tuner.

At the end of the installation process, a dialog box called the Installation Complete dialog box appears, as shown in Figure 10-4. I recommend that you check yes to the first option and but not to the second:

- ✔ **Launch the Castanet Tuner now to configure it.** Clicking yes on this option means that Castanet Tuner will be automatically launched when you close this dialog box so that you can configure the Tuner.

- ✔ **Launch automatically when the system boots.** I have to admit, I'm biased against applications automatically starting up when I turn on my PC. Clicking yes on this option causes an alias to be added to the Windows StartUp folder which will cause Castanet Tuner to be automatically launched each time you start your computer system. This wouldn't be so bad, except that Tuner, like most Java applications, is a memory hog. Once it starts up, about ten minutes later, you'll be asking yourself "Gosh, why is my system running so slow?" It's the Tuner. Better to launch it only when you want it.

Figure 10-4:
Make the
right
Castanet
installation
choices.

When you complete the installation process, Castanet Tuner will launch immediately if you clicked the checkbox telling it to do so. If not, start Castanet Tuner now to begin configuration.

To configure Castanet Tuner, specify the kind of modem connection you want to use, as shown in Figure 10-5. If you use a modem connection, choose one of the existing dialup connections on your system from the scrolling list that appears. Change the Idle Timeout value; the default value, 1 minute, is too short. I recommend 3 minutes as a good starting point. Then enter your user name and password for the connection.

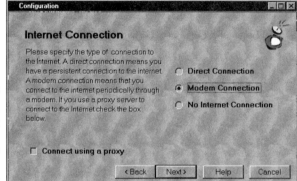

Figure 10-5: Set the right connection method for Castanet.

If you are using a proxy server, enter the proxy server host name and port number as well as your user name and password, if needed.

When you've entered all the information needed, the Castanet Tuner connects to update itself to the latest version. When it's done, click Finish to complete the configuration process. The tuner then launches itself.

Subscribe to Castanet channels

Castnet Tuner is shown in Figure 10-6. It's an unusual application in that it doesn't use a full-size Windows window. The Tuner also doesn't support typical Windows Alt-key menu shortcuts such as Alt+F+S to save a file; you need to memorize the Ctrl-key shortcuts listed on the menus instead. Think of the Tuner as a kind of remote control keypad for finding and managing Castanet channels and you won't be far off.

To begin the process of subscribing to Castanet channels, click the Marimba Channels button from the Marimba tab of the Tuner. The Tuner connects to the main Marimba transmitter, trans.marimba.com and switches to the Listings tab to show the channels available. Figure 10-7 shows the Listing tab and the channels.

Figure 10-6:
Castanet
and catch
the Tuner.

You can view Castanet transmitters as Web pages. Just enter the transmitter's URL, such as `trans.marimba.com`, in your Web browser.

To get a brief description of the contents of a channel, click the + symbol next to the channel name. The + symbol will change to a –, and the channel's description will appear. To hide the description again, click the –, which will change back to a +.

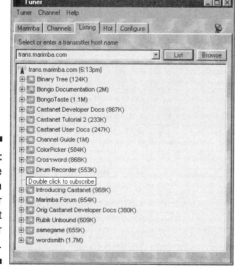

Figure 10-7:
Make the
Marimba
transmitter
your first
stop for
channels.

To subscribe to your first channel, double-click the icon Channel Guide. The Channel Guide is a list of Castanet channels. When you double-click the Channel Guide icon, Castanet Tuner connects to the Internet and downloads the channel. While doing so, it switches to the Channels tab and displays the progress of the download, as shown in Figure 10-8. The progress bar next to the channel displays its download progress; at the bottom of the Tuner window, the download's progress is shown in more detail.

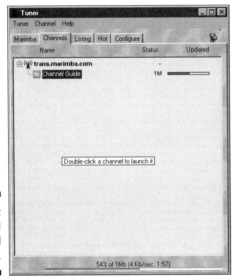

Figure 10-8:
Download the Channel Guide first.

The Marimba transmitter is a great resource for Castanet development. Subscribe to all the relevant channels such as Bongo Documentation, BongoTaste, Castanet Developer Docs, Castanet Tutorial 2, and Introducing Castanet to get a jump-start on developing Castanet channels.

You can download several channels at once. While the Channel Guide channel is downloading, click the Hot tab. You'll see a list of featured channels, as shown in Figure 10-9. The Spotlight Channel appears at the top with a description. Below that are Featured Channels and Transmitters. Move the mouse cursor over the icon for one of these channels to see a description for it appear.

Last and least are the Other Transmitters and Channels in the pull-down list at the bottom of the window. Pull down the list to see a list of transmitters and channels; to find out more about one of these transmitters and channels, choose it from the list. You won't immediately start downloading anything; instead, the list will retract with the transmitter or channel select, and its icon and description will appear. You can then click the icon to access the transmitter or channel.

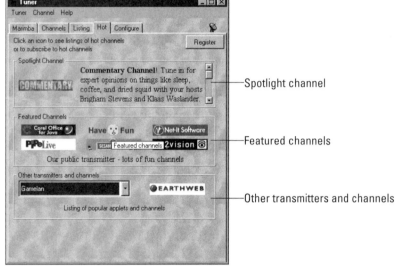

Figure 10-9:
The Tuner
gives
you Hot
channels to
choose
from.

Choose a couple of channels and download them. (This would be a good time to get the developer-related channels I described earlier in this section.) That way, you'll have a few channels to practice managing.

When a channel finishes downloading, it launches. See the next section for information on what to do with channels once you have them.

Managing channels

The Marimba Castanet Channel Guide, shown in Figure 10-10, gives you an organized guide to many of the existing Castanet channels. (Try the TV Guide channel, it's localized to your Zip code and customizable as well.) You can use it to subscribe to as many Castanet channels as you want.

Castanet channels each have their own built-in update schedule. This works fine if you have a persistent Internet connection, such as a network-based connection; the updates happen invisibly to you. However, if you have a dial-up modem connection, scheduled updates don't happen until you connect. Then all previously scheduled updates occur.

To manage channels, use the Channels tab in the Castanet Tuner. The Channels tab lists all the channels that you've downloaded and not yet removed. To start a channel, double-click it. To perform any other management functions, click a channel to select it, then click the Channel menu to display options. Figure 10-11 shows the Channel menu options that are available with a channel selected. Options include:

- **Channel Description (Ctrl+D)** and **Channel Properties (Ctrl+P):** Brief information about the channel's update status, size, and type.

- **Start (Ctrl+X), Stop, Create Shortcut:** You can start a channel running if it's not already; stop it once it's been started; or create a shortcut to the channel.

- **Subscribe (Ctrl+S), Unsubscribe:** You can unsubscribe from a channel, which leaves it on your hard disk and in the available list of channels, but stops it from being updated when Castanet Tuner updates the channels you have subscriptions to.

- **Update (Ctrl+U), Download Remainder (Ctrl+F):** You can begin an immediate update of a channel, or complete a previously interrupted update.

- **Remove (Ctrl+R):** You can remove a channel, which deletes it from the channel list and from your hard disk.

Because the Castanet Tuner is designed to work the same on all platforms, it doesn't support right-clicking a channel to access properties and options. (Macintosh users typically have a one-button mouse and so aren't able to right-click, so for consistency Castanet doesn't support this capability for Windows, either.)

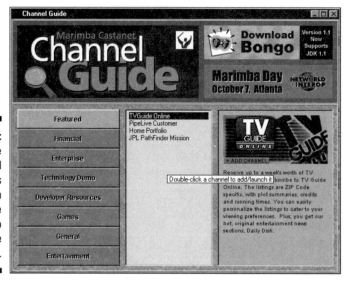

Figure 10-10: The Channel Guide gives you even more channels to choose from.

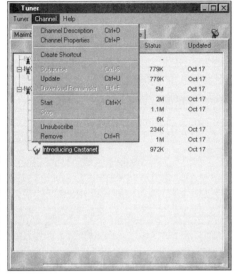

Installing the Transmitter

The Castanet Transmitter is the server application that hosts Castanet channels. When any Castanet channel gets updated, it connects to a Castanet Transmitter. The Castanet Transmitter can run on any computer that can run Castanet Tuner and that is connected to the Internet. (Unless you're using the Castanet Transmitter only for testing purposes, you'll want to run Castanet Transmitter on a machine that's connected to the Internet full time.)

In order to test your Castanet channel you'll need a copy of the Castanet Transmtter. The Castanet Transmitter costs money; though it gives away much of its software for free, Marimba makes money by selling the Transmitter. However, there's a special development version that's free. The development version of the Castanet Transmitter supports up to five tuner connections per hour. (An entire channel update usually occurs in a single connection, so five tuner connections is more than you might think.) On the Web, by contrast, which requires a separate connection for each HTML file, each graphic, each sound file, and so on, five connections might not be enough to download a single Web page.

If you want a version of Castanet Transmitter that supports more than five connections per hour, you'll have to pay up. Table 10-1 shows the current pricing structure for the different licenses available for the Castanet Transmitter.

Table 10-1 Castanet Transmitter and Bongo Licenses Cost Money		
Software	*Number of connections per hour*	*Price*
Bongo	N/A	$495
Castanet Transmitter	5 connections per hour (trial version)	Free
Castanet Transmitter	Unlimited connections, Java-only	$995
Castanet Transmitter	Add plug-ins, non-Java support	More

To install the transmitter, close all open applications. Double-click the installer icon; the version I downloaded was called Trans1_1_1. Follow the instructions that appear onscreen to complete the installation.

After you've installed the transmitter, you then have to set options for it to use. Launch the Castanet Transmitter. The Castanet Transmitter Administration screen appears.

Enter a directory for your channel's files. (I used c:\marimba\test for my test channel.) Then enter the tranmsitter host name and port number. For a test channel, enter the name localhost, as shown in Figure 10-12. For a real channel, enter a host name and a port number. The host name must include your domain name. You can prepend your domain name with trans in order to form the host name, such as trans.mydomain.com. The port number should be 80, unless the transmitter will be running on the same machine as a Web server. If the Castanet Transmitter and a Web server will be running on the same machine, set the Transmitter port number to any number that's easy for you to remember and that's greater than 1024.

Figure 10-12: Set up the Transmitter hostname and port.

For your next step, enter a password to protect transmitter access. Also enter a list of hosts that can publish to the channel. (Don't leave the list of hosts blank unless you want any host to have access.) Then enter the e-mail address to which the Transmitter will send notifications when a channel is published. The default value is a Marimba address; for publicly accessible channels only, Marimba would like to know about new channels so as to help publicize them. To notify yourself, put in your own e-mail address; for no notification, leave the e-mail address blank.

When you complete these steps, you'll come to the end of the transmitter setup process, as shown in Figure 10-13. If you wish, you can set advanced options before leaving setup. You should leave these values alone while creating and testing your channel, and then experiment with them when your channel goes into active use in order to provide the best server performance you can to your users.

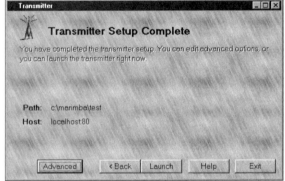

Figure 10-13:
Finish the
Transmitter
setup
process.

When you've set all the options you want to, click Launch to start the Transmitter, or Exit to complete the setup process without launching the Transmitter.

Publishing a Channel

Before you create a channel, you should publish a channel. Why? Because publishing a channel is something you'll be doing a lot in Castanet channel development, and because publishing a channel first takes more unknowns out of the overall Castanet channel-development process. After you know how to publish, subscribe to, and view Castanet channels, as described in this section and previous sections of this chapter, you can then concentrate on the problem of creating them.

The Castanet Transmitter comes with several sample channels, shown in Table 10-2. I'll show you how to publish the SameGame channel, because I'll be using that for my Bongo example later.

Table 10-2   Demo Channels That Come with Castanet Transmitter

Channel	Purpose
Crossword	Daily crossword
GraphLayout	A version of a Java sample program
Headlines	Current news
HTML Sample	A sample HTML-only channel
PluginDebugger	A channel for testing and debugging plugins
SameGame	A game

The process of publishing is rather simple. You specify various options for your channel using Castanet Publisher. Castanet Publisher then copies the channel files to the transmitter and publishes the files using the options you specified. Then you have a channel!

Castanet Publisher allows you to publish directly from the subdirectory in which you do channel development into the transmitter directory. Castanet Publisher even allows you to exclude certain files from being copied; you can name specific files and kinds of files to exclude, such as files ending in .bak (backup files) or .java (Java source code files). But even with these exclusions, it's easy to copy files you don't want to the transmitter, or conversely to accidentally exclude files you need. (If you exclude .txt files, for instance, you'll exclude the properties.txt and parameters.txt files that help define your channel.) Consider creating a directory in which to store your publishable files only, then publish from that directory instead of your development directory.

Start the Castanet Channel Publisher by choosing Start➪Programs➪ Castanet Transmitter➪Castanet Publisher from the Windows desktop. The Castanet Channel Publisher appears.

Click the Channels button, and then click Add. The Add/Create a Channel panel will appear. Enter the pathname of the channel you want to publish. The pathname for SameGame is C:\Program Files\Marimba\Castanet Publisher\developers\channels. (I know, I know, Marimba should provide a Browse button so you can find the file on your hard disk and don't have to type all this!) Double-check the pathname, and then click Add.

Now you'll see the main dialog box for Castanet Publisher, as shown in Figure 10-14. Following are some highlights from among the many options available for the different tabs:

- ✔ **Transmitter:** Specify transmitter and channel options, including passwords. The Ignore field allows you to specify files not to be copied to the transmitter.

- ✔ **General:** Enter the name of the channel and its type: Application, Java Applet, Bongo Presentation, or HTML channel. SameGame is an application.

- ✔ **Update:** Change the Update Frequency for both inactive (not running) and active (running) channels from never to weekly, or to even more frequent updates.

- ✔ **Description:** Click the Hide checkbox until you're ready to have the channel listed in a publicly accessible list of Castanet channels.

Though there are many other features available in Castanet Publisher, these are the only ones you'll need to set for testing a channel locally. When you've set these fields appropriately, click the Publish button. The channel will be published to the host.

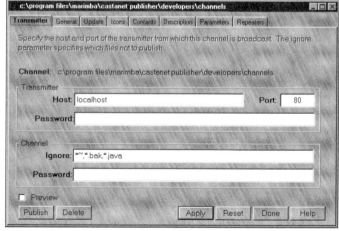

Figure 10-14: The Castanet channel publisher puts out the word for you.

Planning Your Channel

To have a successful experience developing your first Castanet channel, it's important that you plan the channel first. That means you should figure out the purpose of your channel, how frequently it needs to be updated, and more. A good way to get a bead on your Castanet channel plans is to use existing Castanet channels as models.

As you use Castanet channels, you'll see that they are all over the map. (The MapQuest Channel is shown in Figure 10-15, ha-ha.) Castanet channels range from simple, use-once presentations like Introducing Castanet to standalone applications like the Sesame Street channel to update-driven applications like the TV Guide channel.

As you consider your own plans for a channel, consider the breadth and scope of the work you want to do, and consider carefully each of the items discussed in Chapter 3. Then find several existing channels that are similar to yours. Figure out what the purpose of each channel is — and if you can't figure out the purpose, that's a good sign of problems in the channel's design and implementation right there. Then evaluate how successful the channel is in fulfilling its purpose. What did the channel's developers do right? What could they have done better?

Then, plan your own channel. Decide on a simple application that you can develop easily — a one-person job first, followed by a larger pilot project later. Sketch out the user interface, and figure out how often you want the channel to be updated. Look first at the needed data update frequency, and then at the needed code update frequency. If you're not sure, plan to update your channel once a week, which is how often the Castanet Tuner application is updated.

Figure 10-15:
The MapQuest channel is an ambitious Castanet channel.

Using Bongo to Modify a Castanet Channel

The easier way to try creating, publishing, and using your own Castanet channel is to create the channel with Bongo. (I didn't say the easiest way because Bongo, though easier than Java, still requires scripting. Scripting is a form of programming, and programming isn't easy for most of us.) You can download a free version of Bongo from the Web, as described at the beginning of this chapter. When you create an application with the free version, it puts a message across the user interface screen saying so. For a version, with no built-in message, you pay $495.

Bongo is a tool that makes it easy to create user interfaces for Java applications — the windows, menus, buttons, and other visual elements that the user sees and interacts with. You then use Bongo scripting and/or Java to add functionality, to make the menu elements and buttons actually do something.

The first step in using Bongo is to install it. Close all open applications, and then find and double-click the Bongo installer. (The installer I downloaded was called Bongo1_1demo.) Follow the instructions onscreen to install Bongo.

Follow these steps to modify the SameGame Castanet channel.

1. **Start Bongo by choosing Start➪Bongo➪Bongo from the Windows desktop.**

2. **Choose File➪Open Presentation (Ctrl+O).**

   Figure 10-16 shows Bongo with the File menu open. The Windows Open dialog box appears.

3. **Open the SameGame about box presentation file using the path C:\Program Files\Marimba\Castanet Publisher\developers\ channels\samegame\about**

   A warning appears stating that changing the file will make it unplayable on older 1.0 and 1.1 beta versions of Castanet Tuner. Click OK to acknowledge the warning. Then a window containing the About box for SameGame appears, as shown in Figure 10-17.

4. **To add your name to the About box, choose New➪Text➪StaticText.**

   A text box with the words StaticText in it appears.

5. **Drag the new text box to the center of the empty area below the word "Marimba."**

Figure 10-16:
Getting
started with
a Bongo
presentation.

Figure 10-17:
Get ready to
change the
About
box for
SameGame.

6. **Click on the Bongo window to bring it to the forefront.**

   The Bongo window appears.

7. **Next to the word "text" in the Property column, change the Value to "plus my changes."**

8. **Next to the word "align" in the Property column, use the pull-down menu to change the Value to "center."**

9. **Next to the word "style" in the Property column, use the pull-down menu to change the Value to "boxed."**

10. **Click the Apply button.**

11. **Click the about* window to bring it back to the front.**

    The about* window comes back to the forefront with the changes shown, as shown in Figure 10-18.

12. **Click the Bongo window to bring it back to the front, then choose File⇨Quit (Ctrl+Q).**

    A window appears asking if you want to save the changes to the about box.

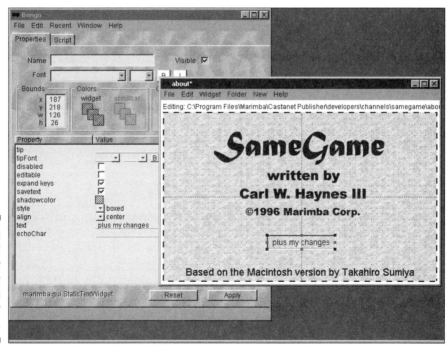

Figure 10-18:
The about*
window
now
reflects
your
changes.

13. Click Yes.

14. Use the steps described earlier in this chapter to publish the changed channel to your local transmitter.

15. Use the steps described earlier in this chapter to subscribe to the changed channel on your local machine.

Congratulations! You've taken the first steps toward creating your own Castanet channels.

Going Further

Going further with Castanet requires quite a bit of learning. Many books and training classes exist for Java and, to a lesser extent, for Castanet. I suggest you build up your Java skills first — they'll be useful no matter what — then work on learning more about Castanet.

Marimba also has several resources available. You can take training classes at Marimba itself, and Marimba provides several useful example applications with Castanet, such as Bongo Taste. Include training time and a learning curve in deciding whether developing Castanet channels is worthwhile.

Part IV

Maintaining and Upgrading Your Channel

In this part . . .

1 can hear the comments from the crowd:

"Whew! I'm glad that's all over with. Can we go home now?"

Sorry. There's just another little something I have to cover.

"Oh, no — not another technology."

No — no more technology. Just maintaining and upgrading your web already.

"Already? But I just built it!"

Well, yeah, sure, but you're probably going to have to do it sometime, don't you think?

"Well, probably, but do we have to cover it now?"

If not now, when? If not by me, who?

"Okay, Churchill, get off the soapbox and get to it."

I thought you'd never ask.

Chapter 11

They Came. Now Make Sure They Come Back.

• •

In This Chapter

▶ Using teams of writers to generate compelling and diverse content

▶ The jam session and what it gives you

▶ Seven ways to keep your subscribers interested in your channel

▶ What do you really need to know about your audience?

• •

*W*hat makes a web site thrive on the Internet? What makes NBC better than CBS or ABC? The proverbial bottom line in programming of any kind is *content*. No shocker there. *ER, Seinfeld,* and *20/20* are successful for a reason: The shows' writers know their audience and they hit the mark almost every time. Nevertheless, TV history is also full of TV shows that hit the mark the first time, only to fade into oblivion just as quickly. Some recent examples include *Max Headroom* and, more recently, *Grace Under Fire.* What those shows failed to do was to reinvent themselves constantly and provide fresh perspectives on their basic recurring themes.

Let me put it a different way: How many times have you heard George Castanza tell Jerry that he can't get a date? A ton. How many patients have they saved on *ER*? A couple million. How many times have you seen the exploding car or the crash test dummies slamming into walls on *20/20*? Two or three times a year. Successful programming is really two things: One, content. Two, reinventing content in new ways. Chapter 3 is about the former. This chapter dares to take on the more formidable task of the latter.

Assembling Your Team of Channel Experts

Most movies and TV shows are the idea of one person. Most movies and TV shows are not, however, written by one writer. Movie scripts can go through rewrite upon rewrite to get just the right sense of tension or the perfect balance of action. Some writers know dialogue. Others know how to brilliantly set up a scene in 25 words or less. TV shows — comedies in particular — are nearly all made up of writing teams for the same reasons that companies have team meetings and brainstorming sessions: The more people who are involved, the more ideas that they generate.

One of the basic rules of channel design is to create persistent content, which is to say continual content. Imagine trying to come up with a new content every day of the week for a channel based on, say, network routers, or acoustic guitars. No matter how good you are at your field, at some point, you're probably going to run out of ideas or get burnt out along the way. In the end, you sacrifice the channel — and you don't want to do that! You worked too hard to get it running in the first place!

The best way to avoid burnout is to treat your channel as if it were a TV series and get a team of people together to help you out. Clearly, if you're a magazine channel, such as the Forbes channel shown in Figure 11-1, you've got a built-in editorial team who can help establish content for the channel. But what if you're not a magazine or a media company at all? Here are some things to consider in searching for the right mix of people to create a content team:

- ✔ **Take volunteers first.** Cajoling people who don't want to be there into helping you is totally pointless. Enthusiasm is the key to success, so send out those e-mails asking for volunteers. If you think people aren't going to want to help, just take a look at an example such as The Mining Company (at www.theminingcompany.com), which is driven completely by volunteers!

- ✔ **Don't take people from your own backyard.** If you're in a small company and in, say, the marketing department, and you're trying to create a channel to promote your products, go outside marketing for help. Your best insights often come from people who don't think about channel development the same way that you do.

- ✔ **Don't re-create yourself.** The corollary to going outside your department is not to look for people who are just like you. Your best resources are those people who complement you, not mimic you.

- ✔ **Keep the group small.** Ever tried negotiating with nine people on where to go for dinner? Exactly. So what makes you think that would be a good number of people to create a web channel? Have no more than five on a team, although you may want to set up a way to get insights from others outside the group.

Figure 11-1:
Media
companies
have built-
in teams of
people who
can direct
content.

I'm thinkin' that a good number of you may just want to know how to make a channel for yourself and don't necessarily have a staff to turn to for content help. Don't forget your friends and family. I see no reason that your wife, husband, kids, or even grandparents can't help you. Everyone has ideas. Whether those ideas are any good, well, that's a different story.

Jam Session: Nerf Weapons Needed

We used to sit around our offices and try to come up with cool game ideas. We had about five or six people on the production team, and we'd spend hours arguing about what were good game ideas. After about an hour, we started bringing out the Nerf firepower. Nerf guns, Nerf sticks, Nerf anything — just as long as it could be thrown. The more we threw, the more interesting our ideas became. But even as dumb as some of them were, we always designated one person to write everything down, because we knew that somewhere in there was our next game.

Of course, that company went out of business, but that's not the point! The point is that brainstorming, in whatever form it takes, provides you with a list of things that you can do with your channel. From that list of ideas, of which perhaps 20 percent are useful, you can develop your content strategy. For each of the main sections of your channel, you should be prepared to design a rollout plan for content that's at least six to eight weeks ahead of today, if not longer. If you think that's too long, just remember that magazines project their issues at least six months ahead, and usually it's more like 10 or 12 months.

I know that sounds like a long time, but what's the risk to your channel if you don't do it? Even the news shows such as *20/20* plan out their entire season (sometimes two if they do those undercover expose-type stories) and then leave themselves the flexibility to adapt if some huge story pops up.

If you've ever lived in Los Angeles, you've probably had someone approach you and ask whether you want to see a test-screening of a new TV show or a movie. If you haven't lived in LA, let me assure you that it gets annoying after a while. Networks and studios love to try out their shows on audiences before they go on the air. That way, they get a better idea of how the show may fare. Your brainstorming sessions will no doubt lead to an editorial calendar for your channel. You have no reason not to put that calendar on the channel for people to preview.

Previewing your programming has a huge upside and some downside. The upside is as follows:

- ✔ Previewing can get people excited about what's coming to the channel.
- ✔ Previewing enables you to solicit feedback on the content and perhaps make some changes.
- ✔ If the preview peaks interest, it can solicit a return visit to the channel.
- ✔ If you've got channel advertisers, you can use the channel feedback to induce more excitement about the schedule.

On the downside, putting out your programming schedule does leave you exposed, which is why a number of media companies avoid it. If I have a magazine, and you have another magazine on a similar topic, finding out exactly what I'm covering is in your interest. That way, you can scoop me and get your story out quicker. This point is a good one and quite relevant to anyone who owns a business and wants to make a channel. The question you need to ask is whether the promotional value outweighs any potential risk to the business or risk of losing the channel's audience.

Seven Ways to Bring 'Em Back

All righty then! You've got the channel and got your design working something fierce. You've people coming into the channel and subscribing. You're the service that people turn to if they're looking for whatever you're providing. To borrow a couple of cliché sports phrases, you're in the Zone and blowin' up.

Now what?

Can you just keep doing what you do and expect to keep everyone coming in? For a while, this approach may work. After a while, however, the news, the features, and the columns begin to seem the same. That's to be expected. So then what happens? Your channel's gonna need a pick-me-up, so the following sections provide a list of seven things that you can do to jump start that channel that's reached the flat-line.

Seven really good tips follow this one, but to be honest, the most important thing that you can do to make sure that people come back to your channel is to have a sense of personality that makes the channel seem more real to people. Of course, you want to be professional, but as with web sites, some of the best web channels are the ones with the right personal touch and attitude. In this regard, web channels and web sites are no different.

Give away the good stuff

No doubt about this one. Contests are king, particularly if the payoff is good. Check out almost any channel, and you find that something is always being given away. If you've got a restaurant channel, give away a dinner. Toss in some CDs for the music channel. For Channel Swank, the draw is the free martini glasses, as shown in Figure 11-2.

A word of caution about promotions, however: Don't give away the ranch the first time you have a promotion. Otherwise, what's the incentive for the user to come back the next time you have one? Start small and then build up over time. Try to have promotions at least once a month if possible. Additionally, try to get other people to pay for them. Look for sponsors wherever possible, unless, of course, you're giving away your own products.

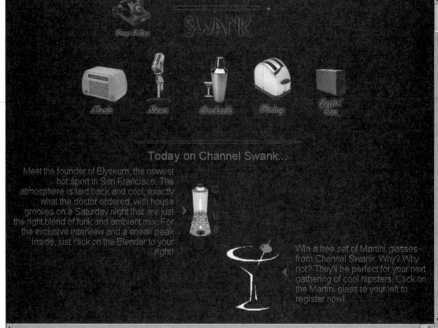

Figure 11-2:
Martini
glasses?
How much
more
lounge
could
you be?

"Please take a moment to tell us about you." Promotions are the best time for getting some demographic information on your audience, including such characteristics as age, sex, time online, and other channels to which they subscribe. Experts tell you that, if you collect information this way, the information's likely to skew your view of your audience, because you were giving something away. I say, "Bollix!" I've done research both ways and the skewing was so minimal that I kicked myself for not doing more when I had the chance.

The daily X

Perhaps the best example of this approach is the Top Ten List on the David Letterman show. I can't tell you the number of times I've hit the Letterman show at 11:18 (in Northern California), just in time to catch the Top Ten List. People are ritualistic to the point of obsession where the Top Ten List is concerned. They go to bed right after it, but not a moment before.

Many web channels employ a similar tactic in that they try to find that one thing that brings people back day after day. Some of the more common approaches include the following daily tidbits:

✔ Quotes (as shown in Figure 11-3)

✔ Recipes

✔ Songs

✔ Sound and video clips

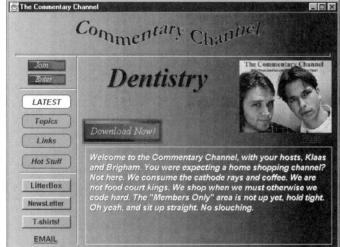

Figure 11-3: Random quotes. You see these everywhere, including here, on the Commentary Channel.

Yeah, it sounds corny. I can't lie to you on that one. But some people eat this stuff up, and using these things is an easy way to make sure that your channel always has something new. Nonetheless, I'd recommend trying to keep your daily offering in the same vein as that of the channel. Bass-o-the-Day may not play so well on the Duck Calling Channel.

Testing the pulse of your audience

Americans love to toss out their opinions. I'm an American, so I can say that! If anything, our political process embraces the poll, and the media . . . well, don't get me started about *their* polls. But have you checked out ESPN on the Internet lately? It's doing polls, as shown in Figure 11-4. And, my oh my, it's getting the kind of voter turnout that most municipalities would kill for — and *that* could help out voter turnout, too, come to think of it.

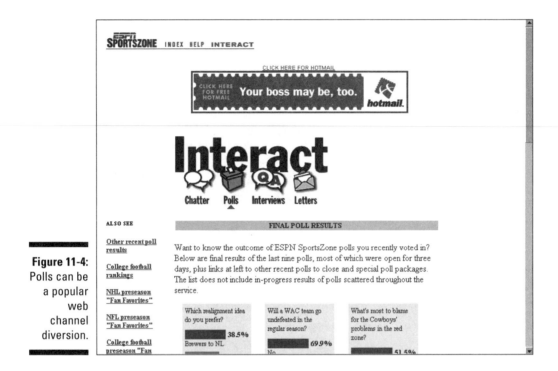

Figure 11-4:
Polls can be a popular web channel diversion.

Polls have two very good payoffs for anyone willing to make the investment in time and resources: One, they increase the interactivity of the site, and two, they almost always ensure return visits, assuming, of course, that the polls are any good. The downside, as you may have figured, is that polls can require a lot more work to build and then tabulate than, say, a random quote. That said, polls can be a very good way to get people involved in the channel and then to see for themselves the other kinds of people who are also subscribing. Instantaneous feedback . . . one of the advantages that the Internet offers over movies and TV.

You can download Java applications that enable you to create graphs automatically from user inputs. Point your browser to www.inserthere.com to download one.

Have some company

Nothing's quite like a little high-priced talent to bring people back to your web channel. Oh, what's that? Tight budget? Oh, no budget. Well, so much for the George Bush comeback spot on that restaurant channel you were planning on starting. Truth is, you don't need big names to bring people back to your channel. What you may want, however, is an expert — someone who knows the field that your channel serves.

The best way to get enthusiasts — and face it, most of your web channel subscribers fall into that category — is to give them some sort of an expert. Channel guests add credibility, as well as some interactivity, to your channel. Now, I know you're probably wondering about how to get someone to be a guest and to set them up to chat live with your audience.

First up, getting the guest. I'm just guessing, but I think that you already have a pretty good idea who you want to be a guest for your channel. For me, with the Lounge Channel, clearly Wayne Newton would be somewhere near the top of the list. He fits all the basic criteria for a good guest. He's hip; he knows the topic; and he's got a good sense of humor. How do I bag him? I sell him on my audience (hence the need for demographic information), his ability to sell his stuff to that audience, and the PR value in it for him. Does it work? Maybe not, but that's basically what you're selling to any guest of a web channel. Something's got to be in it for the guest, even if it's just being seen by an audience that wouldn't usually see that person.

After you bag the guest, setting up the chat part is easy. Your best bet for a fast implementation is to use a form-based chat client that enables people to post questions to the channel and then have the responses follow the questions on the same page, as shown in Figure 11-5. For more information, as well as freeware chat client software, I'd suggest the following web sites:

- ✔ www.developer.com
- ✔ www.internet.com
- ✔ www.cio.com/resources/
- ✔ www.stars.com

Logistically, you need to keep a couple points in mind in thinking about using a message-board style chat client to support a guest appearance. First, remember that you're a channel, and you need to continually push the page on which the guest chat is taking place. That means either updating the CDF header in Explorer or adding a dynamic page update to Navigator. In addition, you probably want to suggest to your audience that, before the guest chat takes place, they may want to increase the frequency of their channel updates to a rate that's more manageable, such as between one and five minutes.

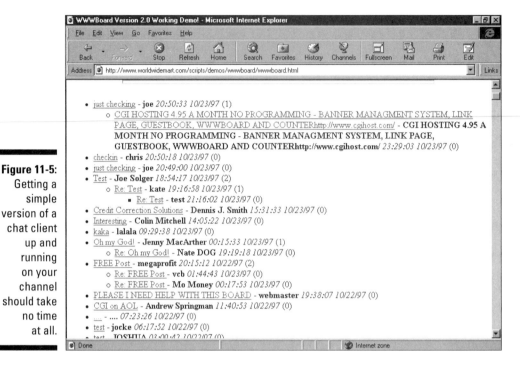

Figure 11-5:
Getting a
simple
version of a
chat client
up and
running
on your
channel
should take
no time
at all.

Oh yeah, one last thing. Don't forget to promote the heck out of your guest appearances! You can post your guest schedule through most of the channel-events pages maintained by Microsoft, PointCast, Netscape and Marimba. In addition, however, you may want to point your browser to one of the more general web events sites such as the one at `www.webevents.com`.

Whet their appetite by using a tag

This one is perhaps one of the oldest tricks in the books, but it works, so why not use it? In the preceding section, I mention that you should promote guests through services and on your channel. Well, don't stop with just the guests! The best way for you to peak interest in your channel is to preview the coming content and throw a "Coming On <insert date here>" tag somewhere in the channel. Such a tag constantly reminds people that, on the date in question, they need to keep an eye on your channel. If you're really trying to get people's attention, try counting down the days until you reveal the content, as shown in Figure 11-6.

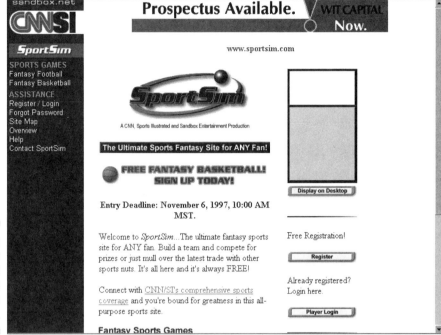

Figure 11-6:
A good trick
is to count
down the
days until a
big event.

Never underestimate the integrated application

Just recently, I was looking for property in the city of San Francisco, a task I'd never wish upon anyone. I was checking out the hundred or so web sites that are out there for Bay Area property. (*Memo to readers:* Someone please start a real estate channel in the Bay Area!) On a few of them, I came across a simple application that enabled you to input the amount of your loan, and it would give you back how much your monthly payment would be, based on the loan amount. I bookmarked the site that had this feature so that I could always refer back to it if I found something I liked.

The point here is that you can add value to your site by having an ancillary application that isn't necessarily directly related to your content. In Figure 11-7, for example, you see the Quicken channel on Internet Explorer. Intuit is a financial software manufacturer, but it has a tool that enables subscribers to track their own stocks on the channel. It's not the world's most perfect fit, but it works well, and it provides a good reason for me to keep the site as an active part of my channel viewing.

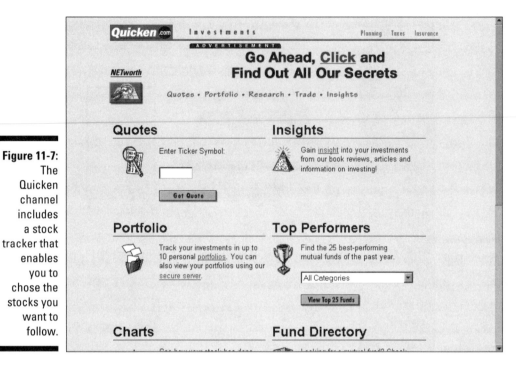

Add a feature

No, you can't just add a new feature every day, but you'll find over time that you are going to want to introduce some new features on your channel. When the channel needs a new area to meet the growing needs of your audience base, however, you want to make sure that you promote that new feature. Many magazines simply introduce a new section or a redesign in the issue in which it appears without much of any warning. The bottom line is that's usually not a good idea.

I've never understood that way of thinking, however, and I worked in the industry! If you're going to spend the time investing in a new feature on your channel, you should promote it to your audience in advance of its arrival. Of what promotional use is a redesign if it just shows up one day? People are most likely to just say, "Huh?," and move on. If, however, you peak their interest beforehand, they're going to be looking for it, just as with the date trick. Users no doubt want to give the new feature a test drive and provide some feedback. Your job is to provide them with enough information to ensure that they understand what you're delivering and then to provide a way for them to spout off about it after it's on the channel.

You Push Your Survey In; You Push Your Survey Out

Surveys are good and bad. (The survey in Figure 11-8 is a pretty good one.) They have the potential to tell you a great many things about your subscribers. For magazines, newspapers, and even network executives, subscriber surveys can determine what gets saved, what gets cut, and what gets a chance to make good in the big leagues. Nevertheless, surveys usually have horrifically low response rates because, well, most people don't like to fill out forms unless someone forces them to do so.

Earlier, I mentioned that you may want to try to slip some demographic surveying into your promotions. Doing so is certainly a good idea, but sometimes you simply want to know more about your audience, promotion or not. Who wants to know this stuff, anyway? Several people, including the following:

- **Prospective advertisers:** This group is the obvious one. Advertisers want to know that they're getting their money's worth. Part of that equation is knowing that their marketing is hitting the right target audience. Surveys are the usual method for determining this kind of information.

- **Your audience:** Strangely enough, I've noticed that people like to know with whom they're consorting. My take is that such information gives people a sense of place and an idea of how the community looks and feels.

- **Yourself (and your new team of writers):** Information, even if you have too much of it already, is your friend where surveys are concerned. The more that you know about your audience, the easier you can tailor your content to their needs and the more likely they are to come back.

What do you really want to know today?

You have only the following three reasons to conduct a survey at all:

- To get to know more about your audience.
- To find out what your subscribers like.
- To find out what your subscribers don't like.

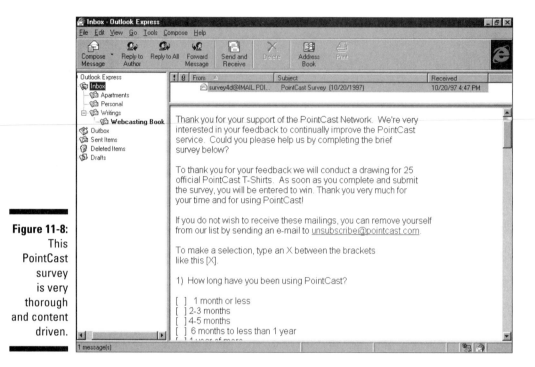

Figure 11-8:
This
PointCast
survey
is very
thorough
and content
driven.

After that, pretty much everything else is gravy. A host of other questions, however, follow these "simple" goals: How much information is too much? What are the right questions to ask your audience? How much time can you actually expect a subscriber to spend on a survey, if at all? Ugh, the whole thing just gets uglier and uglier the deeper you go. That's why I've constructed the following list of areas that I hope gets you headed in the right direction:

✔ Get the basics first: age, sex, geographic location.

✔ Find out what your subscribers like about the channel content.

✔ Ask about the design and the user interface. Do they work? Are they too complicated or deep?

✔ Ask whether the channel has enough content.

✔ Find out whether you're updating the channel too often or not often enough.

✔ Ask about the things the channel needs work on and what new things would make the channel better.

✔ Find out what other resources your audience uses to get the same information that your channel provides.

✔ Find out your audiences' opinion on issues relevant to the fields that the channel serves.

✔ Finally, try to cull some information about how much money your respondents make, what their interests are, and what kinds of products they intend to buy in the next 6 to 12 months.

You need to be exceptionally careful with polling your audience. The web community tends to be very interested in maintaining its privacy. As a result, surveys may to some appear invasive. On the other hand, they are subscribers and are interested in what you're providing. The best solution is to give users the option to simply ignore the survey — and, above all else, be polite!

With some questions from each of the preceding areas, you can establish the profile of your user, plus what works on the channel as well as the parts that need work. In short, you get a picture of where your channel stands in relationship to others out there and a tool for adapting your channel over time to keep the audience happy.

To keep yourself honest and to get a good-sized sample, you should try to get at least 5 percent of your subscriber base to respond to the survey. If you have a smaller subscriber base, I'd set 50 as the absolute lower limit of the number of surveys you need to paint an accurate picture of your subscribers.

It's all in the delivery

Okay, so you're ready to rumble. You've got the survey all planned out, and you're ready to find out everything you ever wanted to know about your subscribers, except one thing — how they get the survey.

In this area, you have basically two options: e-mail and posting. If you already track your subscribers, you should have their e-mail addresses. If so, you may want to consider simply sending the survey to them. Given concerns about invasion of privacy and the general animosity of web users toward "junk e-mail," posting may be the better way to go.

Either method, however, has a catch. If you use e-mail, you're more than likely going to need to send out a large number of e-mails, and you should expect a response of between 1 and 5 percent. Ouch! I know that hurts, but it's true: That's the average response rate. You could throw in a promotional angle, but even those kind of surveys don't usually get much more than a 5-percent rate of response.

If you decide to post your survey, you have just the same problem, with an additional twist. Usually, posting a survey to the channel gets a much lower number of responses, because people must want to fill it out, and the number of people who want to do so is much lower than those who return a survey sent by e-mail.

In addition, however, posted surveys tend to be self-selecting, which simply means that they're usually biased in favor of the group doing the survey. The people who go looking for a survey are usually either really happy or awfully disappointed with the site, and if they're really disappointed, they probably aren't subscribers any more. Regardless, you're always going to be better off doing your surveys through e-mail and leaving the channel area "content pure."

Chapter 12

When It's Time for a Face-Lift

*C*hange can begin with a series of e-mails from subscribers. Sometimes you may simply realize that you're suddenly trying to push too many pages. Perhaps, just perhaps, the Retro-'70s look starts to fade, replaced by the — uh, boy — Euro-'80s look, and your channel is just that quickly out of style. How your channel gets dated happens really doesn't matter — just that it does. You wake up one morning, and bang! Reality hits you: Your channel needs a once over.

If you've worked with web sites, you've come to know the feeling. Just as you start to think that you have the old image map problem solved, animated buttons become the rage. Just as soon as HTML gets pretty cozy, here come cascading style sheets. I, for one, am waiting for the solid strip down the left side of the web page to go out of style.

As the old cliché goes, the only constant about the Internet is that it's always changing. Web channels are no different. So you wake and decide that the time has come for something new — or worse, your boss wakes up and decides for you to make something new. What then? How can you make the transition painless? What if you need to change channel development environments? And, oh yeah, one last question: Do you really even need to change anything?

You Have Change . . . and Then You Have CHANGE

Somewhere along the line in this book, you made a decision. The question was "For whom do you want to develop your channel today?" As I see things, you had one of the following four options:

- ✔ Design your channel for Microsoft's format (the easy but not too snazzy way).

- ✔ Design your channel for Netscape's format (the not too taxing and kinda snazzy way).

- ✔ Design your channel for some other technology (the hard way with no installed base).

- ✔ A combination of the first three options (the *really* hard way that took you an extra month to get right).

If you're just starting out, you probably chose the first option. If you really disdain Microsoft, you probably chose the second option. If you have a deal with one of the other web channel companies out there, you probably chose the third option. And if you're just a glutton for punishment, you chose the last option.

Changing your channel can manifest itself in one of two ways, one of which requires changing your answer to the preceding question. You can change within the context of the technology you're currently using, and then you can move up the old web-channel food chain, in which you must . . . gulp . . . reassess all your content and figure how to build your channel all over again.

The former is palatable. The latter . . . well, I get to that in a moment. Web-site re-designs happen all the time. People know that re-designs are inevitable and accept them. A web-channel re-design can work exactly the same way. In the worst case, a subscriber wakes up one morning and needs half an hour to download the channel because you remade the entire interface. Your subscribers may grumble at first, but after they see that you have a whole bunch of new graphics and perhaps even a new architecture, they're likely to adapt to the change and hope that you don't redo it again tomorrow.

Changing platforms, however, has more ominous overtones. Here's what you need to consider in such a change:

✔ **Platform:** If you change platforms, you have no guarantee that your current subscribers have the software necessary for your new platform. And adding platforms means needing to support more than one channel, so you're very likely to end up doing a lot of the same work twice.

✔ **Time:** Internet Explorer is far and away the easiest web-channel development environment. Just create your CDF file and you're ready. As you move into more complex systems, the process gets more time consuming. In the end, that increased complexity may translate to fewer updates.

✔ **New Tools:** Explorer and Netcaster use pretty much the same tools you've always used for channel development. For Castanet, BackWeb, and, to a lesser degree, PointCast, you use new tools. Again, the change translates to time, as you need to learn a new set up software tools.

In the end, changing the web-channel development environment you're currently using in favor of another may not be worth the effort. If the goal is to add to the number of people who can see your channel, adding platforms is fine, as long as you're prepared to add resources to maintain them all. Otherwise, I'd pass and look at ways to improve the channel you have, which is exactly what the following section is about! (Who knew?)

Remaking Your Channel

You can do lots of little things to reinvigorate your channel that don't suck up a lot of bandwidth. You can also do some things that totally harpoon your bandwidth. In the best of all possible worlds, you begin with the former and then end with the latter, since adding bandwidth and making your channel slower is the least desirable course of action. I know things don't always work that way, but I'm an idealist, so for now, I'm going to assume that they do.

Touching everything but the kitchen sink

First up, the little things. Check out Figure 12-1, which shows the opening page of the sample Channel Swank on Internet Explorer. This page is pretty well off-limits, because anytime that I change it, I'm going to need to push a lot of graphics to the user all over again. I don't want to do that just to add, say, a new feature section. Remember that changing even just one graphic may mean pushing the entire front page or Webtop all over again.

Here's another factor to consider. Suppose you just want to change the

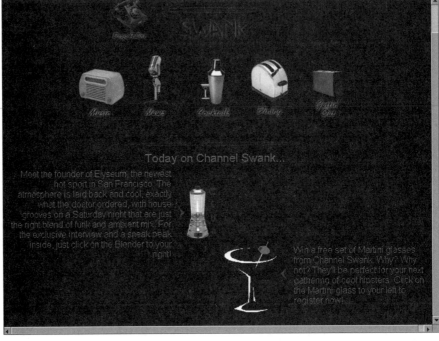

Figure 12-1:
You don't
want to
touch the
top page
of your
channel
unless
you're
going to do
a major
overhaul.

JavaScript on the front page of your channel. This may be more dangerous than you may initially think. The more JavaScript you have on a web page, the slower that page runs. Both Explorer and Netcaster do a relatively poor job of caching memory to handle large amounts of JavaScript. As a result, adding JavaScript may be as detrimental as adding more graphics to your web channel front page!

At this point, you may be asking, "Sure, but how is changing the front page any different from changing the other pages?" Presumably, the front page of the channel is the user's biggest download, because it's the most graphically intensive part of the channel. The only reason to avoid touching the channel's front page is to save users a big download. By the way, if your channel's front page has a really small footprint, you may not even need to worry about this problem. The point is that you really shouldn't touch the graphics architecture of the channel unless it's absolutely necessary.

Touching everything and the kitchen sink

Okay, so not touching the Webtop or the front page is a nice idea, but what if I'm just plain sick of the channel. I'm tired of the way it looks; the navigation isn't working for me; and the content's all bad. At that point, you're best off just sandblasting the old channel and starting over again.

The important point to remember is that this decision isn't the kind that you make in a vacuum. You have subscribers, and they have a right to know if the bandwidth is going to hit the fan, so to speak. In the case of Explorer and Netcaster, you also have the dilemma of not being able to really test your channels until you put them up. Re-designing a channel can get a bit messy, so I offer the following list of steps to walk you through the process to minimize the pain. Each of the following points applies equally to channels created in Explorer, Netcaster, and PointCast:

1. **Do the redesign on paper first.**

   Make sure that you know exactly what you're going to change, because the worst thing that you could possibly do would be to change the entire architecture and then realize that you forgot something.

2. **Warn your viewers.**

   I'd pull a small countdown routine or at least take a very emphatic shot across their bow on two occasions. That way, people know that the redesign is coming and can skip the channel that day.

3. **Bring up the new channel hidden.**

   As with a web site, you need to test the channel to make sure that it works. You need a server to do so, and although using an HTTP utility may seem like a good way to fake your computer into thinking that it's both a server and client, your best bet is to simply post your new channel material to your ISP and keep the links hidden so that you can test it.

4. **Bring down the old channel; Put up a placeholder.**

   You need to take everything off of the old channel and then get the correct links for the new channel before you can put it up on the server. In the interim, you want to throw up a temporary holding page, similar to the one shown in Figure 12-2. This page is simple to post, and if someone hits the channel while you're finalizing your remake, they don't get caught in the middle.

5. **Fire up the new channel.**

   After you have everything ready and the links set, take down the placeholder and swap out the new front page.

Changing the Marimba's big diapers

The process for changing a more advanced channels — for example, a Castanet channel — is a little bit different, but the basics remain the same. You're still going to tell your users that the channel is coming down soon and that you're making changes. You also still need to test the revisions before putting them up and then swap out the channels.

Figure 12-2:
When your
channel
goes down,
let your
subscribers
know.

Castanet, however, enables you to test channels locally a lot easier than do Netcaster and Explorer, so the switching out of the old channel and putting up a placeholder isn't really necessary. What you need to be more careful with, however, is the actual front page itself. Castanet relies heavily on a large singular download at the beginning of the channel, in many cases one more than 1MB in size. This situation means that, every time you want to make a major facelift, your users are looking at a serious download, as shown in Figure 12-3.

The lion's share of the size in Marimba channels generate from Java, the scripts, and the graphics. And, unlike with the Explorer and Netcaster channels, you don't have the luxury of pushing just the areas of the channel that are down below the front page. That's why you're best off leaving these kind of the channels alone. After you create a Castanet channel, try to keep it as clean as possible and avoid large updates.

Note: People wonder why Castanet channels aren't updated as often as some of the types of channels. This lack of updates is really because of a size problem. Castanet uses so much Java, which is slow and can be large in size, that pushing just the new content is nearly impossible without resending the front page of the channel. The end result is that people have gotten frustrated with Marimba and don't give their channels the kind of attention that users deserve.

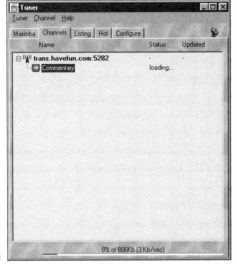

Figure 12-3:
Castanet
Channels
are
notorious
for their
large
downloads
for a simple
update, as
in this case.

Is Movin' on Up (Or Down) Worth The Work?

Deciding whether or not it's worth adding channel types is perhaps the hardest and most frustrating part about webcasting. You have no real way of knowing who's going to come out on top of the whole webcasting war. Right now, you have two safe bets: Microsoft and Netscape are in this game for the long haul, and you can expect them to continue to throw resources at their implementations until the other side blinks.

As a developer, the first question that you need to ask yourself is which company you think has the best approach to webcasting, regardless of the environment on which you developed your first channel. My take is simply that Netscape has better technology than Microsoft but that Microsoft is more accessible. By going with Microsoft, almost anyone can make a channel. Using Netscape requires more work, but in the end, the channel that you create feels different than a web site — unlike the case with Explorer. Everyone else, including PointCast, Marimba, and BackWeb, is sure to find a bandwagon and jump on. At the moment, Explorer has the stronger position, even though Netscape has the installed base advantage.

Following are five quick questions to ask yourself before you even think about changing from one channel platform to another:

- ✔ How many subscribers do I currently have? Is that amount enough for the goals I've set for the channel?

- ✔ Does changing platforms get me more subscribers while keeping those I already have?

- ✔ Do I want to learn new development tools?

- ✔ Do I want to build two versions of my channel?

- ✔ Does changing platforms make me more competitive or give me an advantage?

These five questions should give you the answer right away — and only you can be sure of the right direction for your channel, after all. Something else to consider, however, is the path of least resistance. My experience with channels thus far has been that people like them but that they don't want to work at getting them. Channels are being treated just as is TV, which to me is classic! This situation is exactly what you'd expect and makes the case for an advanced channel from Castanet not nearly as compelling as one of the more mainstream web channels.

Web sites thrive because they're a least common denominator of the Internet, much as e-mail is. Web channels, if they're to be successful, must abide by those same rules.

When moving down is moving up

Many people love Java and like to tinker with it. This tendency extends to web channels. Something that's typical in the world of Castanet are Java applets passing as channels. People who enjoy writing Java applets have found a way to distribute them by using Castanet, under the guise of calling these applets a channel. Not only is this practice misleading to users, but it hurts other developers who are using technologies like Java and JavaScript for what it was designed for — namely, building web channels!

This situation would seem to indicate a couple things. First, lots of people don't know how to use the tools, and second, many people don't have a lot of respect for the development environment. In a way, that leaves those who originally develop channels for the Castanet environment out on a limb of sorts, hoping that the technology, and by association their channels, catch on with web users.

The first option is to hope that someone views your channel (no doubt one of the good ones if you've read Chapter 10) through Netcaster. To be rather blunt, that's not a good way for someone to view a Castanet channel. Castanet channels look way out of place — not to mention ugly — against the Netcaster environment. The second, and better option, is to simply develop a new channel for either Netcaster or Explorer.

In general, if you create a channel for one of the higher end environments, you should seriously consider moving down. Your audience increases. Your design and graphics options increase. You get more feedback and more support from the Internet community at large. I have no doubt that the number of useless channels isn't going to decrease. But you're also going to be surrounded by a stronger number of higher quality channels, which gives you a larger base of channels from which to draw tips and tricks.

What's best for the business

Until this point in the chapter, I could have been talking about both business and personal channels. Briefly, however, I want to just touch on some of the other issues that could affect a business decision to move to a new channel environment, because the factors are slightly different.

If you have a small business, exposure is your best friend. That, by itself, almost precludes using anything but Netcaster or Explorer. If you start with one of these channel types, stick with it, and just redesign your channel whenever necessary. If you want to maximize your exposure, you may want to consider using the other web-channel format (the one you're not using, whether Explorer or Netcaster) as well. Some things to consider, if you're thinking along this line, follow:

- ✔ You can use similar looks and similar content across the two different channel formats.
- ✔ You're maintaining two different channels.
- ✔ One channel can be a part-time affair. Two channels, however similar, most likely cannot, given the increase in traffic and feedback.

So what if you've got a larger business, one in the thousands of people and millions of dollars category? The key word of the day there is *intranet,* and web channels are often espoused as a great way to keep the work force informed with up-to-the-minute information, whether on site at the company, or connected from a remote location.

At that level, a web channel using Explorer or Netcaster may or may not be the right answer for your situation. Many companies already have internal intranets built by using Netscape or Explorer. If such intranets already exist, the only thing that you really need is to upgrade everyone to the latest version of Communicator or Explorer and you're one good webmaster away from having an intranet channel for the company.

If your goal is scalability, flexibility, and tools designed to enable the salesforce to access lots of data while on the road, the traditional browser turned web channel may not be the best route. In that case, upgrading to a product such as BackWeb makes sense. With the BackWeb acquisition of Lanacom, the company now supports a wider array of corporate solutions for webcasting. And although many would argue that you're better off going with a larger and more cumbersome system such as Lotus Notes, BackWeb is both more affordable and more targeted, making it a realistic corporate alternative to enterprise communication.

Part V
The Part of Tens

The 5th Wave   By Rich Tennant

"QUICK KIDS! YOUR MOTHER'S EMBEDDING JAVA APPLETS IN HTML."

In this part . . .

Movies have the Oscars. TV has the Emmys. ...For Dummies books have The Part of Tens. Here's my chance to show you the best web channels, give you the biggest pitfalls to avoid in making your own channel, and even recommend the best JavaScript to use in bringing your channel alive. You can even find some JavaScript and Dynamic HTML resources in this part as well as a ten-step process to a Dynamic HTML page.

So grab some popcorn, curl up on the couch next to the fire, and without any further comment, "The envelope please. . . ."

Chapter 13

Ten Web Channels That You Need to See

. . . .

In This Chapter

▶ Ten web channels, some good and some that may annoy you a bit

. . . .

*P*erhaps the best thing about the Internet is that it's a community where you learn by doing. Part of that process of learning is looking at the organizations that spend a lot of money investing in new technologies such as webcasting. These companies make mistakes just as everyone else does, but they have the resources to work through their mistakes quickly and efficiently. On the other side, that capability means that their end products — the channels that you and I see — are also cleaner, more sophisticated, and easier to use.

This chapter focuses squarely on those companies and highlights their web channels. Certainly, a number of well-designed and compelling personal web channels are available out there for your perusal. For a company looking to create its first web channel, however, a better course, I think, is to take a look at the big kids on the web channel block and see what they're doing. Many of the bigger companies are setting de facto standards for the look and feel of web channels across all the major platforms.

The Mining Company

I begin with the Mining Company not because it provides the best sites with the most sophisticated interfaces. Quite the contrary, actually: The Mining Company's many sites are often pretty much plain vanilla as far as design aesthetic goes. The Mining Company is, however, most definitely prolific. The company offers web channels on just about everything from chemistry to Harleys to social policy. To give you an idea of just how widespread these channels are, I've listed some of the more interesting in Table 13-1.

Table 13-1	An Absolutely Random Sampling of The Mining Company's Mountains of Web Channels
Category	*Web Channel*
Sports	snowboarding.miningco.com
Entertainment	nonfiction.miningco.com
Science	physics.miningco.com
Travel and Leisure	camping.miningco.com
Politics	uspolitics.miningco.com
College	campuslife.miningco.com
Cultures	religion.miningco.com

Purely for the sheer magnitude of content that the Mining Company guides push on a daily basis (on more than 450 channels), this company is one that you want to look at very closely. Its interfaces are generally simple, and although the company offers a plethora of diverse channels, its design remains fairly consistent. The result is a sense of familiarity in every Mining Company channel, which automatically reinforces the idea in the user's mind that each Mining Company channel is going to meet certain standards.

Want to get your Dummies content pushed to you from The Mining Company on a daily basis? That's right, IDG Books has a Dummies channel on the Mining Company, the *Dummies Daily*. To subscribe, just jump over to nonfiction.miningco.com.

By using the Microsoft CDF format, the company's also been able to implement its channels on both Internet Explorer and PointCast Connections, as shown in Figure 13-1. This flexibility gives the company the capability to reach an exceptionally broad audience and do the work only once. In addition, the company's been clever with the way in which it pushes content. Every channel that I looked at was pushing no more than five pages, while everything else still sat on the Web site. Push the important stuff and leave the rest up to the user — an efficient philosophy.

Figure 13-1:
The Mining
Company
dominates
all web
channels on
the Internet.

ABCNews.com

I know I've used ABC News as an example quite frequently in this book, but really, the recognition is well deserved. In fact, ABC News is probably the best-designed and -implemented web channel out there among the major news companies. ABC has made a big commitment to using the Netscape Netcaster, which, in all honesty, I think is more a function of the Microsoft and NBC partnership than anything else. (Check the Netscape home page if you don't believe me on that one.)

What the Netscape and ABC partnership provides you with is a look at what the technology can do (see Figure 13-2). You can figure that, if Netscape and ABC are in cahoots, the web channel that ABC makes is probably going to use every last piece of the Netscape technology that it can shove in. And, in fact, that's what the channel feels like. The interface design is slick, and the channel contains more JavaScript than you can shake a stick at.

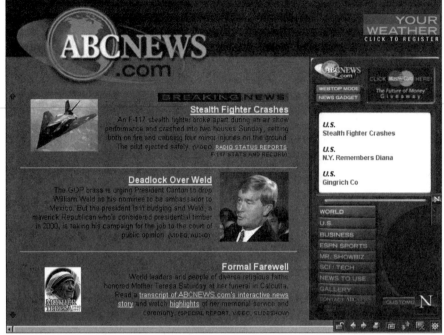

Figure 13-2:
The ABC
News
channel is
the luxury
sports
sedan of
Netcaster
channels.

The end result is a great channel — one that far and away outshines all the others currently available through Netcaster. Clearly, ABC set out to beat MSNBC and, more specifically, the NBC channel available on Internet Explorer. Whether it actually beats the competition is a moot point, just as long as you and I can learn how to make better channels from it!

MSNBC

Now, after everything I just said, why cover yet another media company? If ABC is the best media company using the Netcaster web channel viewer, MSNBC wins hands down for Internet Explorer. And it should win for Explorer. You can't get much closer than Microsoft and NBC have gotten, and these close ties show in their web-channel design (see Figure13-3).

By using layered graphics, interactive hierarchical menus, and a design that's both simple and complete, MSNBC provides every possible feature you could want in a great channel. If this channel has a knock, it's that it tries to do too much at the top level. The menu bars obscure the other content, and trying to follow them is a bit clumsy, but those are really trivial complaints. On the whole, the channel is very solid, and you should definitely check it out just to see how well the company's integrated all the components into a very compact space.

Figure 13-3:
A lot of
information's
packed into
a very small
space on
MSNBC,
but it works
quite well.

The Media Channels

Oh, so you've never heard of the media channels! That's okay, because I made the name up. On the Internet you find a series of web sites that all basically look the same. The content, in some cases, may be radically different, but the overall look and feel are nearly identical. Several of these sites have become web channels in Internet Explorer. Although adding a web channel is an easy addition for these companies to make, in particular because they have such large web-development teams, their cookie cutter approach tends to blur the line between what is a channel and what's a web site.

I find channels such as these a bit annoying, although the content is usually very good and the design works. No doubt, that's why so many companies have adopted the format (see Figure 13-4). Table 13-2 gives you an idea of what I'm talking about. It includes, a brief list of some of the players on the media channel list:

Table 13-2	Media Channels
Web Channel	**URL**
ESPN SportsZone	www.espn.com
CNET	www.cnet.com
CMPNet	www.cmpnet.com
ZDNet	www.zd.com
CNN	www.cnn.com

What all these channels have in common is the amount of information they're managing and the frequency with which they present it. All the channels in Table 13-2 are news companies, and they've designed their channels to provide a lot of information quickly and easily. Where I think they suffer, against channels such as NBC and ABC, is in their graphic design and overall visual appeal, something to consider very carefully in planning your first channel.

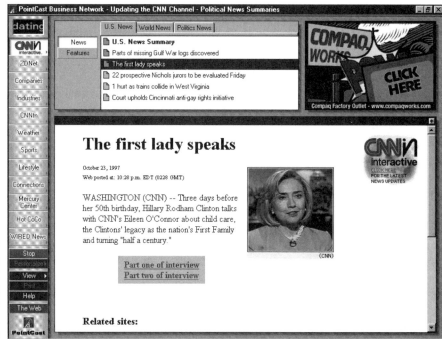

Figure 13-4: The CNN page on the PointCast network.

Developer.com

A lot of Web sites dedicate their content to teaching people about the Internet. Not many channels take a similar course. Nevertheless, the Developer.com web channel on Internet Explorer is both a competently designed channel and a useful resource for any developer looking to get the latest information on the Internet.

Developer.com provides a good combination of news and access to applications. As a developer of channels specifically, and of web content more generally, you're not always looking just for news. The addition of a featured resources list provides a good balance of usable software and digestible industry news. That's what sets apart the Developer.com channel from its everyday web site. To make the information more compact and useful, the company's eliminated some of the layers between you and the actual downloads.

If this site has a downside, it's that I haven't seen the frontpage change yet (see Figure 13-5). Although I've grown used to bypassing it, if the user doesn't need the page, why have it there in the first place? Other than that complaint, however, the site is handy, useful, and a good model for the beginning web channel developer.

Figure 13-5:
For Internet-related news and cool software for creating great channels and great web sites, Developer.com is a great choice.

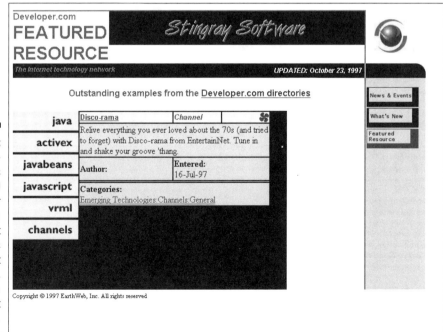

The Wall Street Journal

The Wall Street Journal holds a unique place in the American psyche, I think. Viewed as a sophisticated tool for the Wall Street businessman, *The Journal* strives to provide the kind of key information that enables those in the business world to make good decisions. Essentially, that's what its web presence is also trying to do.

The Journal's two web channels, one for Explorer and the other for Netcaster, aren't going to win any style competitions (see Figure 13-6). They tend to be very straightforward, somewhat dry, and fairly text heavy. Under normal circumstances, that would probably be the kiss of death for a web channel.

This style is exactly what *The Journal* readers usually see in *The Journal* itself, however, and, in large part, is what they expect, which highlights a key component to any good web channel design: understanding your audience. The folks who developed the channel's design understand that their audience isn't interested in a flashy channel with lots of graphics and sounds. Instead, they're interested in persistent and solid business information, delivered right to the desktop. Yes, it looks a little dull, but, man, does it work. (You can find *The Journal*'s channels at `www.wsj.com`.)

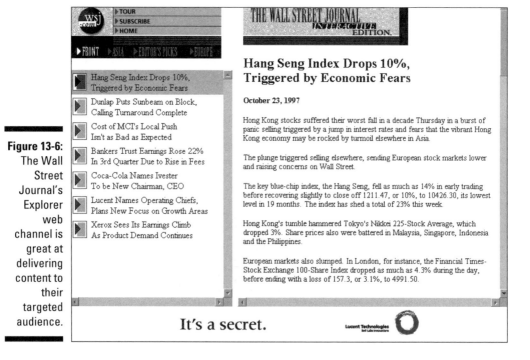

Figure 13-6: The Wall Street Journal's Explorer web channel is great at delivering content to their targeted audience.

The New York Times

The New York Times stands out among the nation's newspapers in as far as its developed a very well-designed and thorough web channel on the Internet. Although several newspapers have developed web sites, only *The New York Times* and a handful of other papers have gone the extra mile to develop web channels to push content to users. You can find *The New York Times* channel at `www.nytimes.com`, through Internet Explorer.

What sets *The New York Times* apart from its competitors is its design and functionality. *The New York Times* web channel uses a mock front page as its motif, as shown in Figure 13-7. Headlines and wire reports are constantly updated, so the user can quickly and easily scan headlines or access the entire site simply by selecting a story or a section.

Figure 13-7: The mock newspaper front-page design works to help set *The New York Times* web channel apart.

If you chose to visit the site, you're asked to fill out a subscriber form, but you need to do so only once. What makes *The New York Times* web channel more compelling than, say, that of CNN, is that its developers actually designed the site for the web-channel medium. From purely a content perspective, the company doesn't add any more than that you can find on a lot of other news sites. What appears on the channel, however, is presented in such a way as to be appealing to both *The New York Times'* subscriber base and those people who appreciate a well-designed web channel. That's what makes this channel worth checking out!

If you're more interested in local Bay Area news, the *San Jose Mercury* News Channel on PointCast is an equally good choice. Displaying a more regional flavor, the *Merc* has become one of the most admired papers on the West Coast. You can check out its channel at `www.sjmercury.com`.

The MapQuest Channel

The MapQuest channel is the only channel I've included from the Marimba Castanet family of channels. In large part, this lack of coverage is because of the lack of mainstream channels available for Castanet. Many of the Castanet channels are, in fact, Java applications that don't do much more than one or two things, such as play the radio over the Internet or provide a Java-based chat client.

Nevertheless, the MapQuest channel, as shown in Figure 13-8, is pretty darn handy, which is why it ended up in this chapter. From this channel, you can get directions to thousands of locations across the country. After you choose a location, you can find out what points of interest are available within that area, based on category. You can also set your own markers for locations on a map and then retrieve the maps at a later date.

I know that MapQuest stretches the definition of the word channel, because it's more interactive than most channels. I decided to grant a little leniency here, however, given the lack of good Castanet channels and the overall usefulness of this one. You can find the MapQuest channel at `trans .mapquest.com`. Download the client and give it a try the next time you need to go someplace. I think you're going to like it!

Figure 13-8:
The
MapQuest
channel
helps you
figure out
where
you're
going.

The Frommer's Guide

Travel channels are an interesting breed. Most of them that I've found tend to focus too heavily on the airline prices and fail to give enough space to new travel destinations and advice on planning an entire vacation experience. That's why I was so pleased to see that Arthur Frommer, the man whose books I've come to depend on when traveling abroad, had built a web channel.

As shown in Figure 13-9, the Frommer's Guide channel includes travel tips, an ongoing series on vacations destinations, plus a host of airline and hotel deals based on location and time of travel. For the intrepid traveler, the Frommer's Guide also provides unique local insights for several locations around the world. The bottom line is that this channel is a lot like the books — but delivered to you on a daily basis.

The Frommer channel falls into the category of a small to midsized channel, which makes it a novelty on this list. It's also strictly a PointCast channel, which is also a bit unusual. That limitation doesn't, however, diminish the fact that this channel is a solid one and is a good reference point for any small company looking to build its first channel. You can subscribe to the Frommer's Guide through the PointCast Network.

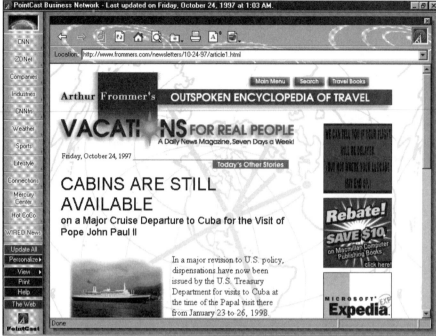

Figure 13-9:
Arthur
Frommer's
web
channel
provides
lots of
travel tips
and great
deals for
even the
beginning
traveler.

Wired

I must admit, I'm not that much of a fan of the latest Wired channels, which are available through Internet Explorer and Netcaster. Even for me, they're too loud, hard to follow, and generally not that interesting. All that said, you need to put that kind of thinking aside for a moment, because these are good channels to get to know.

What Wired lacks in design aesthetic, its makes up for in technology prowess. Wired is committed to using all the new technologies available to maintain its audience's perception of it as the hip leader of the digital revolution, as shown in Figure 13-10. What this commitment means to you is that you can see a number of web-channel viewers like Netcaster and Explorer pushed to their natural, if somewhat illogical, limits.

THE WORLD IS
ACCELERATING.
LiveWired delivers the
future
in 20 seconds:

Figure 13-10:
Wow, loud
channel
ahead.

Check out the channel variations, which you can subscribe to through Hot Wired at www.hotwired.com. In particular, make sure that you notice the differences between the Explorer and Netcaster versions of each channel. Although they offer roughly the same content, their implementation is different, which provides a unique opportunity to compare and contrast the two browser channel viewers.

Other Channels to See

You can find a ton of other web channels out there (seriously — I've weighed them), and each one can probably teach you something a little different. My recommendation is to start with the channels that I describe in this chapter and then keep going until you find a channel that fits into the paradigm of the kind of channel that you want to build.

Ultimately, the biggest thing to look for is the content. If you find a channel that delivers content in a way that fits your needs, that's the channel design you should go with. Just make sure that you remember the list I've given you here, because you can find a lot of good and some bad in these examples. Your channel can be substantially better if you learn the lessons of these companies before diving into your own very first channel.

Chapter 14

Nearly Ten Simple JavaScript Tricks That Make Your Channel Great

. . . .

In This Chapter

▶ Pull-down menus that jump

▶ Changing the status bar text

▶ The automatic redirect

▶ Animated buttons

▶ The interactive billboard

▶ Animations in Navigator

▶ Automated New!

▶ Remote Controller

. . . .

*H*ave I got a chapter for you! And luckily for both of us, it just happens to be this one. I can tell that you've had enough of the easy stuff and now you're ready to jump-start the old channel with some hard-core JavaScript! Uh . . . was that a gulp I heard? Don't worry. How could you not trust a face such as mine . . . even if you can't see it! Within this chapter you find some of the more interesting JavaScript scripts that I guarantee can take your channel out of the ordinary and set it apart from other web channels on the Internet.

Some of these scripts are a breeze. Just drop in the script and go. Others may take some mulling over before you get that "Aha!" flash of insight that makes putting the script into the channel a snap. Now, before I get too far into this discussion, I'm going to make a suggestion: Don't try to use all these scripts in the same channel. Although that course may give you the most eye-catching collection of content on the face of the planet, it's also bound to cause you to make endless errors — and besides, it'd probably look *really bad*.

But enough about what you shouldn't do. You're ready for the fun part —
the kind of stuff that you get to put into your channel and then tell your
friends, "Yep, I did that. And for $70 an hour, I can do it for you, too." Oh,
wait. That's for the consultants. Sorry. 'Nuff said. Time to get it on.

Pull-Down Menus

No need to drown you on the first one. This little script can help you get
people to other areas of your channel after they see the content on the front
page. It's simple. It doesn't take up a lot space, and most important, it makes
you look pretty darn professional. And who doesn't love that?

The first thing you need to do is to create an array with your various
sections and the corresponding pages where someone can find them. An
array is simply a collection of items that you plan to do something with — in
this case, put into a menu. All this information needs to go within the
<HEAD> tags on the page where the pull-down menu appears. Just follow
these steps:

1. **Create the** <HEAD> **tag and set the function that controls all the
   variables in an array.**

   This script creates an array using the JavaScript function command.
   The function, in this case, is makeArray. An array, by the way, is just a
   collection of items, in this case, sections and URLs. The function
   creates an array that can handle a number of sections and their corresponding URLs. Both the sections and URLs are variables, which are
   defined in the next point.

   ```
   <HEAD>
   <SCRIPT LANGUAGE = "JavaScript">
   <!—
   function makeArray() {
   var args = makeArray.arguments;
       for (var i = 0; i < args.length; i++) {
       this[i] = args[i];
       }
   this.length = args.length;
   }
   ```

2. **Set two new variables, one for the names of the locations and a
   second that includes the URLs.**

   Now that you've defined an array, you can specify the items to go in the
   arrays. There are two sets here, sections and URLs. Sections includes
   each of the locations that you want users to jump to when they select

that item from the pull-down menu. The second variable, URL, includes the URLs for each item in the pull-down menu. To create the array, I'll use the JavaScript function, makeArray.

I've used Channel Swank as an example here. This drop-down menu would redirect users to the three most popular areas of the channel.

```
var sections = new makeArray("Select a Page",
                             " News",
                             " Cocktails",
                             " Music",
);


var url = new makeArray (
              "/news.html",
                 "/cocktails.html",
                 "/music.html",
);
```

3. Jump the user from the drop-down menu to their requested page.

To do this, you first need to create a piece of script that tells the browser to jump to the requested page. This can be done with the function command. Here, I've defined a function, goPage, that will look in a form. When the script is called, it looks in the form and finds the item that the user has selected. Then the script finds the corresponding URL and sends the user there. You can just cut and paste the following script, which, by the way, also includes the tag that ends the script and then closes the </HEAD>. That's done with the </SCRIPT> tag. The script for all of this is right here:

```
function goPage(form) {
i = form.menu.selectedIndex;
    if (i != 0) {
    window.location.href = url[i];
    }
}

//->
</SCRIPT>
</HEAD>
```

That takes care of the `<HEAD>` area. Now, in the `<BODY>` of the script, you must call all that information in the form of a pull-down menu. The following piece of script does that for you. Specifically, this is another piece of JavaScript that creates a form and then places each of the elements that you specified in the head into a drop-down menu. When an item is selected (noted by `onChange` in the script), the array is checked for a location and a URL. To see what this one looks like in action on the Channel Swank, check out Figure 14-1.

```
<SCRIPT LANGUAGE = "JavaScript">
<!-
document.write('<FORM><SELECT NAME = "menu" onChange =
"goPage(this.form)">');
    for (var i = 0; i < sections.length; i++) {
    document.write('<OPTION>' + sections [i]);
    }
document.write('</SELECT></FORM>');

//->
</SCRIPT>
```

Figure 14-1:
The Lounge
Channel's
pull-down
menu.
Voilà!

Status Bar Change

I kinda like looking at URLs on the status line at the bottom of a browser. Then again, I'm kind of a geek, too, so I like that kind of stuff. Your average, everyday, run-of-the-mill, ordinary web-channel user may not be so excited to see such things. So, to impress your new channel viewers with your brilliance, I respectfully submit a simple little script that enables you to change the markers in the status area to display whatever you want them to.

To begin, you need to place the following little script snippet within the `<HEAD>` tags on your channel page. All this script does is tell the browser that you want to take over the status bar, which is the bar in the bottom-left corner of your browser that usually shows the URL. This script tells the browser to let go of the status bar when the function `windowon` is called and then put the text in the parenthesis that follows the function into the status bar. The script also builds in a time delay of five seconds (represented in milliseconds, as if anyone keeps time that way!) before the text appears.

```
<HEAD>
<script language="JavaScript">
function windowon(txt){
            window.status = txt;
            setTimeout("windowoff()",5000);
            }
    function windowoff(){
            window.status="";
            }
</SCRIPT>
</HEAD>
```

That was pretty painless, wouldn't you say? Now, the hard part. You're going to hate me for this one. Ha! I'm joking! The following script is the easiest part of the book, scout's honor! Come to think of it, this one is so simple that I should have put it before the pull-down menus. Ah, well, too late. I'm going to set it up so that when the users put their mouse cursor over a link, the status bar text changes to what I want it to be. To do that, I'm going to use the HTML command `onMouseOver`. When the mouse rolls over a link, I call the `windowon` function and put the text I want in the parenthesis following `windowon`. For Channel Swank News page link, the HTML would look like this:

```
<A HREF="/news .html" onMouseOver = "windowon('The Channel
Swank News Page');return true">YOU CAN USE TEXT HERE</A>
```

Automatic Redirect

Hmm . . . now why would you ever want to redirect someone to another part of your channel. Practically speaking, you wouldn't. But people change URLs, people change ISPs, people change *(insert favorite abbreviation here)*, so this little script helps you out whenever that happens to you. And say that you're doing a special promotion on the channel and you absolutely want someone to see it right away. By using this little script, you can direct users to that place without any say on their part.

Yikes! Now *that's* power. You need to be very careful with this one. Most people don't like being taken places without their consent. It's sort of the American way — land of the free Internet travel, home of the brave browser user . . . that sort of thing. If you go pushing people around the channel every day to try to pawn off your goods, people soon head for the hills. For, say, a guided tour of the channel, however, this script is the perfect tool!

All right, enough debating the moral implications of the script. Follow these steps:

1. **Set up the page to switch from one page to another by creating redirect and switch functions in the** $\langle$HEAD$\rangle$ **tag of your HTML document.**

   Here, you'll need to create two functions, one which tells the page that it's going to change (redirect), and another function that includes the location of the new page that will be loaded (switch). The redirect function also includes a variable, setTimeout, that is the time after which the page switches over to the new one.

   ```
   <HEAD>
    <SCRIPT LANGUAGE="JavaScript">
    function redirect () { setTimeout("switch()",10000); }
    function switch ()    { window.location.href = "/
          Wherever_you're_switching_them_to.html "; }
   </SCRIPT>
   </HEAD>
   ```

2. **To get the switch to occur automatically, you can call the function when the page is loaded.**

   Within HTML, there's a command called onLoad that lets you specify an action when the page is initially loaded. The onLoad command is nested in the $\langle$BODY$\rangle$ tag of your HTML document. Here, I'm using the onLoad command to call the redirect function that I specified within the $\langle$HEAD$\rangle$ tag.

   ```
   <BODY onLoad="redirect()">
   ```

Animated Image Menus

Until now, I've been dishing out the easy ones. Now, I'm dishing out the easy ones that look really cool, too. All that coolness and, man — you're the king of swank. The channel rats are gonna swing, while the other web-channel cats have no choice but to sit back and purr the blues, ya dig? You don't? Check out Figure 14-2, and let this channel be kickin'.

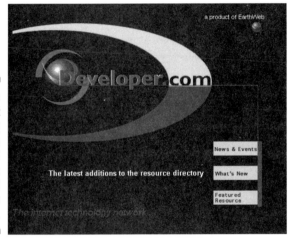

Figure 14-2:
Nothing but
nothing
brings the
channel
alive like an
animated
image
menu.

Swank is an animation state of mind, where the mouse and JavaScript act as one. After the mouse hits an image, the image changes to show that the mouse is over it. After the mouse leaves the image, it changes back to its original state. It's sweet. It's so sweet. Here's what you gotta do:

1. **Collect all the on and off states for your animation and place them within the** `<HEAD>` **of your HTML document.**

   You could do this script a couple of ways. You could create an array, which I talk about earlier in "Status Bar Change," or you can keep the items as a simple list. I've chosen that route, because I think it's easier to keep them working with your images this way. Although I'd usually recommend writing a function to check for the browser type and version first, my assumption is that you're creating this script for either Explorer 4.0 or Communicator 4.0, in which case checking isn't necessary. The following script defines each image's on and off state by assigning a name that the script looks for when you want the image to be switched on or off. As before, I use Channel Swank as an example. For each image, you need the following syntax:

```
<HEAD>
<Script Language="JavaScript">
    {
      newsOn= new Image();
      newsOn.src = "/newsOn.gif";
cocktailsOn = new Image();
      cocktailsOn.src = "/cocktailsOn.gif";
musicOn = new Image();
      musicOn.src = "/musicOn.gif";
```

(continued)

(continued)

```
newsOff= new Image();
        newsOff.src = "/newsOff.gif";
cocktailsOff = new Image();
        cocktailsOff.src = "/cocktailsOff.gif";
musicOff = new Image();
        musicOff.src = "/musicOff.gif";
}
```

For this script to work properly, you need to make sure that whatever you name your images for the on and off states, they include the extensions on and off with each image. The reason for this is that in the following function, those extensions will be looked for to control the on and off states of each image.

2. **Create a function that calls the source images after the roll-over occurs.**

Although you call the animation's start and stop later, you control the animating function here. To create the animation, your need to activate both the on and off states for each image and specify the circumstances under which the images will switch. Therefore, I've created two functions, activated and deactivate. Each function looks for a list of images with either the on or off extension at the end of the name which describes that image. Each of the functions also looks for the corresponding graphics file associated with the image. Here's the syntax:

```
function activated(imgName) {
    if (document.images)
    imgOn = eval(imgName + "on.src");
        document [imgName].src = imgOn;
        }
}

function deactivate(imgName) {
        if (document.images)
    imgOff = eval(imgName + "off.src");
        document [imgName].src = imgOff;
        }
}

</SCRIPT>
</HEAD>
```

3. **Use the** `onMouseOver` **command in HTML to call the on and off states for each image that you want to switch.**

   At this point, you're pretty much ready to roll. What's left is to call the on and off states from within your HTML document. To do that, I use `onMouseOver` and `onMouseOut`, two HTML commands. Because I'm creating a table of contents, I'll call them from the `<A HREF>..<A>` tag. When the mouse rolls over a link, in this case an image, I'll call the activate function. When the mouse leaves the area of the link, the `onMouseOut` calls the deactivate function. As a default image, I'm going to use the off states, so that it appears to be turning on when the mouse glides over the link. The syntax is right here:

   ```
   <A HREF = "news.html"
   onMouseover = "activated('news')"
   onMouseout = "deactivate(news)">
   <IMG NAME = "newsOff" SRC = "/newsOff.gif" ALT = "Chan-
         nel Swank News"></A>
   ```

4. **Repeat the preceding code snippet for each object that you include in the original list.**

Billboards

Now, the first question I'm sure you're asking here is "Why not just use an animation to create a billboard?" You could, but what if you wanted to send a user to a different area of the channel for each image on the billboard? Hmm . . . suddenly, the old GIF animation begins to look a little less useful. This script, on the other hand, enables you to scroll through a series of images and have each image represent a different link.

Here's what you need to do to make this script work:

1. **Within the** `<HEAD>` **tag, use the array function to make a list of the images that you want to be in your billboards.**

   For this part, I'm going to create an array called billboard. In addition, I'm creating another array, called `URL`. Like the array in "Status Bar Change," I'm going to use these two arrays to switch between billboard items, and then bounce the user to another URL when he selects one. As you may have noticed, this is a slightly different way of creating an array, but it's equally as effective! I've also created a variable, `boardNum`, and set it equal to zero. As you see in the next step, `BoardNum` is going to keep track of each of the images in the billboard array. The only catch here is that the images all must be the same size. If they're different sizes, they get out of proportion as they're loaded.

```
<Script Language="JavaScript">

var boardNum = 0;

    billboard = new Array;
    billboard[0] = new Image(144, 144);
    billboard[0].src = "/fancy_image.gif";
    billboard[1] = new Image(144, 144);
    billboard[1].src = "/second_fancy_image.gif";
    billboard[2] = new Image(144, 144);
    billboard[2].src = "/last_fancy_image.gif";


    url = new Array;
    url[0] = "/fancy_image.html";
    url[1] = "/second_fancy_image.html";
    url[2] = "/last_fancy_image.html";
```

2. **Set up the billboard's scrolling and interactivity by creating two functions in the** `<HEAD>` **(the tag which controls these elements).**

   I have two functions that I want to create. One is `showBoard`. It looks for each of the elements in my billboard array and cycles through them using the `boardNum` variable. This function also switches the billboards every five seconds using a `setTimeout` function. I also create a function called `boardLink`. This function controls the URL that is associated with a given billboard image. You end the script and the `<HEAD>` tag afterward. Here's the script

```
    function showBoard() {
    document.billboard.src = billboard[boardNum++].src;
 if (boardNum==3) boardNum=0;
setTimeout("showBoard()", 5000);
    }



    function boardLink() {
    window.location.href = url[boardNum];
    }

</SCRIPT>
</HEAD>
```

3. **Within the** ⟨BODY⟩ **tag, use the** onLoad **function shown here to call the** showBoard **function.**

```
<Body onLoad="showBoard()">
```

4. **Using an HREF command in a link, load the billboard and its associated links.**

This script also goes in the ⟨BODY⟩ tag. You treat the billboard the same way you would treat any other link on a web page. The only difference is that here, you've connected that link to a number of functions that you've described. In the HREF, you need to set an image, so you may as well set it to the first image in the array. You use the command javascript:boardlink() to reference the links that are specified in the boardLink function defined two steps ago. After you've got it down, it should look a little something like Figure 14-3.

```
<A HREF = "javascript:boardLink()"
    onMouseover = "window.status =
       url[boardNum];return true;"
    onMouseout = "window.status = '';return true;">
    <IMG BORDER = 0 HEIGHT = 144 WIDTH = 144 SRC = "/
       fancy_image.gif" NAME = "billboard"></A>
```

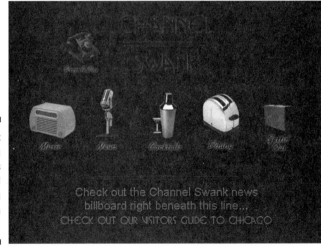

Figure 14-3:
By using this billboard script, you can flash messages!

Animation

Want to shock some people? Try animations. Nothing surprises people more than a good animation that requires no graphics, virtually no loading, and varying font sizes. Make no mistake, the coding necessary to pull off a fully loaded animation, with layers, flying objects, and dynamic links, is by no means trivial. This entire script animates the word *Falling* and makes it fall from the top to the bottom of browser window, as shown in Figure 14-4.

The script begins by defining your text properties by using *Cascading Style Sheets,* or *CSS.* Cascading Style Sheets are simply a new way of defining the attributes of HTML. They're supported by both Netscape and Microsoft and effectively eliminate the `<LAYER>` tag in Navigator 3.0. CSS include text point size, color, whether the object is visible, and where the text resides in relation to other text on the page. To begin with, take a look at the CSS for the text and the background. (For simplicity, I've labeled the style sheet `mystyle`.)

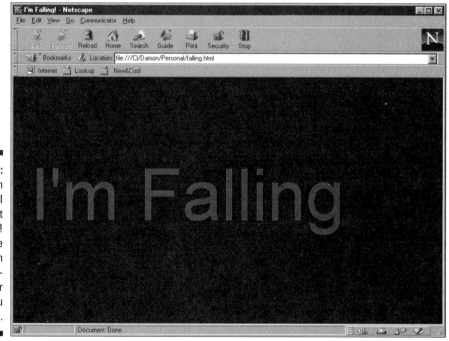

Figure 14-4:
Help! I'm falling and I can't get back up! Some animation in Communicator 4.0, if you please.

```
<HEAD>
<STYLE>
. mystyle{
font-family:      arial;
font-size:        128px;
color:            #006666;
position:         absolute;
top:              0px;
left:             30px;
visibility:       visible;
z-index:          1;
}

BODY {
background:       #000000;
}
</STYLE>
```

You can see from the script that the style sheet includes several parameters, some of which you don't use. I've also put the basic color for the background in the <HEAD> tag as well. From here, the next step is to add a function that animates the HTML. The animation function is set up to move the text from the top of the page to the bottom in 10-pixel increments per 75 milliseconds. The code for that is as follows:

```
<SCRIPT LANGUAGE = "JavaScript">

    function animate (from, to) {
            if (from < to) {
   falling.top = (from += 10);
                setTimeout('animate(' + from + ',' + to +
           ')', 75);
                }}

</SCRIPT>
</HEAD>
```

After you get this function in place, you're done with the <HEAD> tag and set to call the animation. From the <BODY> tag, you need a couple items to complete the animation. Just follow these steps:

1. **Decide what text you want to animate, and place it within a `<DIV>` tag.**

   Here, I use the words `I'm Falling` within a `<DIV>` tag. The `<DIV>` tag, by the way, is another way to represent text with Cascading Style Sheets. Eventually, I'm going to need to be able to reference this piece of text, so I can identify it by using the ID command. This text is labeled `fallnow`. I'm going to call this ID with JavaScript in the next step. In addition, I've applied the `mystyle` style sheet to the text. The script looks like this:

   ```
   <DIV ID = "fallnow" CLASS = " mystyle"> I'm Falling
         </DIV>
   ```

2. **Now, set up JavaScript to take the text and make it fall by creating a variable that enables the text to fall from the top of the screen to the bottom.**

   First, I need to define the variable `falling` that was set up in the animate function defined previously. In this case, I want it to look for the ID `fallnow` that I gave to the "I'm Falling" text. To accomplish this, I'll set the variable falling equal to `document.fallnow`.

   After I've done that, I need to specify the start and top locations for the text. Because "I'm Falling," I want the text to move from the top of the screen to the bottom. The top of the screen is a pixel location of 0. The bottom may vary, depending on the user's display settings, but about 350 should be sufficient. After you have this little bit of script in there, you're ready to fall:

   ```
   <SCRIPT LANGUAGE = "JavaScript">
       var falling =  document.fallnow
   animate (0, 350);
   </SCRIPT>
   ```

Automated New!

I really like this script, because it can make life easy on you. Say that you have some new content and you want to tell people that it's new. Before, you'd probably have thrown in one of the millions of "New" icons and then left the icon there until . . . well . . . uh . . . have you checked your channel lately?

Thankfully, this script can take care of that . . . with a hitch or two. The script essentially looks at today's date and compares it against the date set in the HTML. If the difference between the two dates is below a certain threshold, which you set, flagged items on the channel page have a "New" icon inserted next to them. If they aren't, the "New" icon goes away.

I'd like to thank Martin Webb for this script. I've seen several date and time scripts, most of which are forgettable. This script and his site, No Content, however, are both very clever and quite useful! The difficult part of the script is his. I just simplified it at the end to help fit it into a web channel. I'm giving him a shameless plug by showing his web site in Figure 14-5.

The first part of the script is a date interpreter. It takes Universal Coordinated Time (UTC), which is the total number of milliseconds elapsed since January 1, 1970 (why it uses this date, I have no idea), and translates that obscenely huge number into a more conventional-looking date. The code for this script follows.

Figure 14-5:
Martin Webb's No Content web site — a great place for JavaScript information.

```
<HEAD>
<SCRIPT LANGUAGE = 'JavaScript'>

 function check_if_new(then) {
     var today = new Date();
     var difference =
         Date.UTC(today.getYear(),today.getMonth(),today.getDate(),0,0,0)
         -
         Date.UTC(then.getYear(),then.getMonth(),then.getDate(),0,0,0);
```

Two other pretty important items follow the interpreter function. One is the variable (var days_difference) for the desired difference to check for between the current date and the date specified in the script. The second is what happens if the dates fall within the range set in the days_difference variable. Right now, it's set to find and place the GIF image I'm new. The code for this part of the script is as follows:

```
var days_difference = difference/1000/60/60/24;
     if (days_difference < 14)
         return '<IMG SRC=" New.gif">';
     else return '';
 }
```

Now, you can't have a date script without setting the date, unless of course you want to use another script, but I'm pretty sure that you don't even want me to go there. So you can use the following code to round out the <HEAD> tag:

```
date = new Date(year,month,date);
 document.write(check_if_new(date));
</SCRIPT>
</HEAD>
```

And now, the body! From here, you're on easy street. To run the script on a piece of text or a link, you need to carry out the following steps in the <BODY> of your script:

1. **Create an ID tag that appears in all links or text blocks that you want the script to check**.

   In the following code, I chose Check as the ID. This ID is needed for JavaScript to reference the text or link that needs to be checked to see if it's new.

   ```
   <A HREF= "\new.html" ID = "Check"> Am I new?</A>
   ```

2. Use JavaScript to create a simple script that looks for the specified ID and then runs the `check_if_new function.`

This script looks in the document for items with the `Check` ID and then applies the `check_if_new` function. If it does happen to be new, the `new.gif` image is put right next to the text or the link.

```
<Script = "JavaScript">
var check = document.check
check_if_new;
</SCRIPT>
```

Remote Controller

I saved this one for last because, well, it kind of goes against what I was saying earlier in the book about not falling into the habit of using too many web-site conventions to create web channels. Even though a number of web sites use the floating remote, however, I think that having it on your desktop could be a good way to provide a nice navigation tool for your channel viewers. And what's a web channel without a remote?

So, even though I'm feeling a little guilty about this one, here are the steps to create it (and, yes, it really *is* this easy):

1. Create the remote control by making a JavaScript function that spawns a new window.

How's that for oversimplification? The remote control is basically the spawning of a new window in your browser. When I do this, though, I can control the look and feel of that window. Thankfully, JavaScript has a command for creating new windows, so the script is pretty straight forward. Basically, I'm going to define the function `makeRemote`, and then set the remote parameters and then select an HTML page to go into the new window. The script goes within the `<HEAD>` tags, by the way.

```
<SCRIPT LANGUAGE = "JavaScript">

function makeRemote() {

remote =
        window.open("","remotewin","width=350,height=400");
remote.location.href = "My_Channel_Remote.html";

    if (remote.opener == null) remote.opener = window;
remote.opener.name = "opener";
}
</SCRIPT>
```

2. To run the script and launch the remote, call the script from within a link in the `<BODY>` **tag.**

The `javascript:makeremote` tells the browser to look for some JavaScript in the HTML file with the function `makeRemote`, and then run that script. Here's how your link should look:

```
<A HREF = "javascript:makeRemote()">Open Remote</A>
```

The best remotes that I've seen (and liked — which are about two) have combined the remote function and the animated-button function that I describe earlier in this chapter. Doing so makes the remote more dynamic and really makes it appear more professional. If you're going to build the remote, try adding the animation and see whether you like it!

Chapter 15

Ten Web Channel Boo-Boos
That Make Users Mad

. . . .

In This Chapter

▶ The mistakes, mishaps, and pitfalls of web-channel design

. . . .

My first web channel was a fiasco. Nothing worked the first time I tried it, and after I finally did get something up there that worked, I figured out that I'd forgotten a ton of stuff. It was a reasonably fun web channel (at least for me), and I got to put up all sorts of stuff that I thought was interesting. Every now and then, however, I'd get an e-mail from someone who'd subscribed to the channel and would comment about some small thing that, on reflection, I should have thought about as I first built the channel.

So, naturally, after I started researching other channels for this book, I looked for a lot of the same little things. Imagine my surprise to find that a large number of channels had made the same mistakes I did. If nothing else, it made me feel better. Nevertheless, the thought occurred to me that, in this mad rush to get content to the user, channel developers may be forgetting some of the little things that could make users happier about their web-casting experience. With that consideration in mind, I've compiled a list of the most common boo-boos that I've encountered in web channels and some solutions that may inspire users to thank you in the long run.

Remember the Date

This single item — the current date — is perhaps the most easily forgotten in all of webcasting, although it's something you really should never forget. Nevertheless, I've seen a number of channels without it, including my much-praised ABCNews.com, and few omissions are more annoying to the user than a missing date.

Here's why: Say that you fire up your channel viewer to take a look at some content. You know that you've set it to update every three hours. A day has passed since you look at the channel. If it displays no date, however, you have no idea whatsoever whether that channel's been updated since the last time you had it pushed to you.

Obviously, the easiest way to rectify the problem is to make yourself a note and remember to include the last date you updated the channel as part of your page. You can, however, use JavaScript to put the date on the page automatically so that, whenever a user gets the page, the date appears. The following code example gets the job done:

```
<SCRIPT LANGUAGE="Javascript">
<!-

// Array of day names
var dayNames = new Array("Sunday","Monday","Tuesday",
         "Wednesday","Thursday","Friday","Saturday");

// Array of month Names
var monthNames = new Array("January","February","March",
         "April","May","June","July","August","September","October",
         "November","December");

var now = new Date();
document.write(dayNames[now.getDay()] + ", " +
monthNames[now.getMonth()] + " " + now.getDate() + ", 19" +
now.getYear());

// ->
</SCRIPT>
```

Test Your Channel Before You Post

Testing your channel before you post it is another consideration that seems as though it should be a no-brainer, right? You'd think so, but . . . more than half the channels I subscribe to (and, by the way, that number is more than 50 now) currently either have scripting errors or crash bugs in them. Some of the crash bugs are in the channel viewers themselves, but in most cases, the cause is pilot error, as shown in Figure 15-1.

The sad truth is that, no matter how simple a channel is, it can always be broken. The reasons are nearly infinite. Some of the problems may be beyond your control. But if you keep the following simple, if somewhat long, suggestions (which I stole from my own software Q&A guidelines) in mind before you set up any content to push, you should be all set.

Figure 15-1:
JavaScript
errors
are not
uncommon
sights
in web
channels.
Make sure
that you
test before
you post!

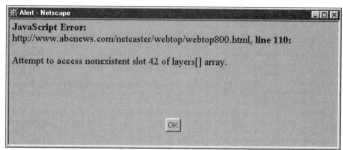

- Test all the new and old elements of your content on your machine first. Usually, testing can be simplified to pressing all the links and engaging all your JavaScript to make sure you don't get any syntax or link errors.

- If you're setting up a multiple-viewer web channel (such as for Explorer and PointCast), make sure that you check all the viewers to make sure that the channel is working on all of them before you post.

- If you have other machines, either at work or perhaps at a friend's home, that you can also test your channel on, you should do it there first. Testing on a different machine is always a good second phase test of your content for accuracy and mistakes.

- Post your content to an area on your web server that users can access from either your current channel or web site. That way, you can test it live from the Internet before turning it on for others to see!

- Again, grab those neighbors. Have them go to your secret area on your web server and try getting the content pushed to them. It's another way to check to see if the channel is working on a non-production machine.

I know these guidelines sound like a lot of steps to take, but in the end, this procedure offers the best way for you to ensure that what you push to other people is free of errors.

Check Your Spelling

I know, I know — now I'm sounding like your sixth-grade teacher here, but you'd be surprised how many web sites and web channels have typos in them. I'm just going to keep this one short and sweet, however. I could show a screen shot, but that would be embarrassing — mostly for me, because it would be my channel!

Push in Parallel

I've seen this one a lot at the various news web channels. A lot of times, channels have headlines within the page, as well as a scrolling banner somewhere on the channel displaying the same basic information. I'm convinced that you don't need both, but — hey, what do I know?

Anyway, I've seen this sort of thing occur a number of times, where one of the two examples gets updated before the other. (And by *before,* I'm talking hours and days, not minutes.) I've recreated this phenomenon with the Channel Swank Lounge Channel, as shown in Figure 15-2, to give you an idea of what it looks like. Besides looking pretty unprofessional, this discrepancy creates confusion among your customers, because a viewer can't be sure whether the channel is working correctly.

The best solution to this mess is to just change both headlines at the same time. Although that fix may seem simple, it can prove a more arduous task than you'd think, depending on the complexity of the channel's front page. You may end up needing to increase the time between postings to get the two elements synched up, but in the end, the users should thank you for it.

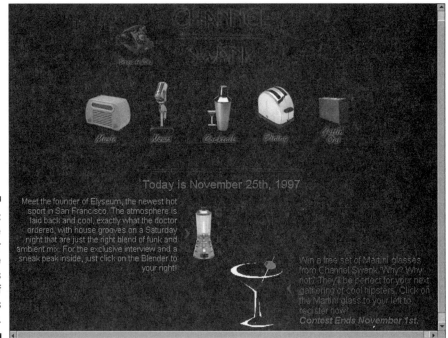

Figure 15-2:
If the banner and the headlines get out of sync, that's bad news.

Don't Spawn Windows

Have you ever seen VCRs that have the picture-in-picture feature? The feature enables you to watch two channels at the same time, although one is inset and over the other. This idea works nicely with VCRs and televisions, but then again, TV and VCR manufacturers have been at this sort of thing a hundred years or thereabouts, so you can figure that they've had some time to get it right.

You can spawn a new window in a web channel as well, however, by using JavaScript. But in my experience, this extra window thing is a bad idea. After either Explorer or Netcaster start up, they take over your screen and eliminate all the standard windows bars. The reason for this action is to enable people to have their channels running in the background while they use other applications.

Spawning a new browser window has two basic effects. One, it looks ugly and breaks the whole channel motif, as shown in Figure 15-3. This effect is perhaps a bit of an aesthetic gripe, but if I were a user and I saw a web browser window pop up after I selected something from the channel, I'd stop believing that a channel was anything different than a web site.

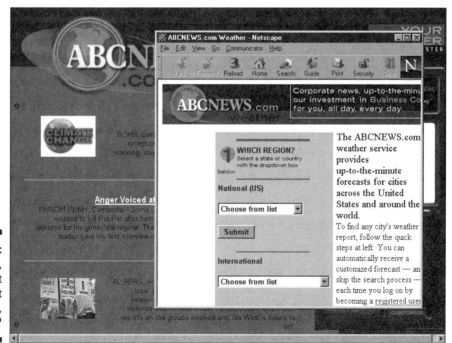

Figure 15-3:
Eck! Man, that just doesn't look right, does it?

The second, and perhaps more prudent, reason for not spawning a new window is that it can crash either browser. Although this effect doesn't occur all the time and may go away in future versions of Explorer and Netcaster, it's a risk that just isn't worth taking.

Note: In the preceding chapter, I talk about doing a remote control for your channel. That activity can involve spawning a window. You can consider that the basic exception to the rule.

Remember the E-Mail Address

I ran into a channel the other day that had a JavaScript problem in it. I thought I'd just drop an e-mail to the person who'd built the channel, letting him know that the error was there. Much to my surprise, I could find no e-mail form anywhere in the channel. I've mentioned this one before, but it bears repeating: No feedback equals a dead channel, from a both a user's and a developer's point of view. From the user's perspective, not having a contact point for problems experienced with the channel is equally frustrating.

Make no mistake, however: You're going to have architecture and content problems with your web channel — problems you may not even know about. An e-mail contact address seems like a little thing, but forgetting to include one could cost you a number of users.

By the way, this tip doesn't mean that you need an e-mail address sitting right there on the front page of the channel. Try creating a specific contact section for the channel. If your ISP okays it, have a series of e-mail addresses for various items, such as *problems* or *feedback*.

Watch Out Up Front!

A number of web channels build really complex front pages with a number of graphics. That's good, because such a channel gives you the opportunity to create an interesting interface for your viewers. Where this course tends to break down, however, is if you're constantly changing the front page. And if you want a truly dynamic channel, you'd want to change the front page pretty often.

So you'd appear to have a conflict in interest between complexity and ease in updating your front page. For a number of channels, the easy way out of this dilemma seems to be to just update the look of the front page, leaving users to suffer a longer wait for the content to come to their desktops. The following list suggests a number of possible solutions to this problem:

✔ Use frames to split up your channel's front page and update only those frames without the big graphics.

✔ Use JavaScript to introduce new layers of content without changing the front page of the channel, as shown in Figure 15-4.

✔ Use Dynamic HTML to show different layers with new content in them without changing the primary front page of the channel.

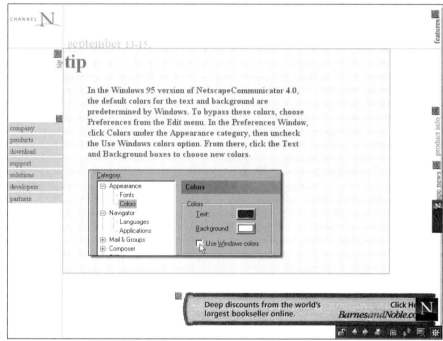

Figure 15-4: You can use JavaScript to show different layers of content that don't affect the graphics-heavy front page of the channel.

Let People Know What They Need

Of course, after you start your first channel, you're going to want a streaming video, RealAudio tracks, and Shockwave animation — not to mention the dancing elves. The natural course of events is that someone subscribes to the channel and then — bang! They don't have the programs they need to view your channel's content.

Most web-channel viewers, including Explorer, PointCast, and Netcaster, enable you to create promotional pages that pop up before a person subscribes to your channel and tells them what add-ons or plug-ins they need to fully view your channel. On more than one occasion, however, I've found web-channel developers who've simply assumed that I already had a number of plug-ins installed.

Although assuming this sufficiency on the part of their viewers makes the developers' jobs easier, for my part as a viewer, knowing about these requirements a bit sooner would have been nice. So, as a courtesy to your users, always try to include each of the following items as you create that first subscription page:

- ✔ A brief synopsis of the style and content of the channel.
- ✔ A clear icon that starts the subscription process.
- ✔ A list of requirements for running the channel, including the viewer type (more for Explorer and PointCast) and any necessary plug-ins.
- ✔ Links to the locations where your users can obtain those plug-ins, even though both Explorer and Netcaster prompt you to download the plug-ins if you don't already have them installed.

Don't Get Too Chunky or Too Thin

Your users expect the perfect balance of content and interaction, combined with a stunning interface. Nothing like grand expectations on the part of users! I've asked some colleagues about this idea, and they say that the biggest complaints they get from their users are that channels either try to push too much content on the front page or they just have one page for the entire channel.

No doubt, cases come up where having a lot of text on the front page is useful, as shown in Figure 15-5. In most cases, however, lots of text turns users off to your channel. The simplest way around this problem is to point to other areas of the channel that contain the content. However, there are consequences associated with this strategy. The more you expect a subscriber to wander around your channel, the closer you come to being a web site. The whole idea of having channels in the first place is to bring content to the subscriber. Building a channel that's several layers deep goes against the basic goal of a web channel.

In addition, most web channel viewers let the user decide how many levels deep into the channel the browser should go in order to bring content back to the desktop. The more levels the browser has to crawl, the larger the download time. Again, this is in contrast to the goal of small downloads.

For balance and perception of depth, your best bet is set up your channel with the following basic structure:

✔ A front page displaying headlines and sections.

✔ Roughly one page for each section listed on the front page.

✔ One or two floating pages that you push on a semi-regular basis to create the impression of new content. These pages should be highlighted from the front page or at least revealed through it.

Figure 15-5:
The Wall Street Journal channel on Explorer. It can get away with lots of text.

Using this simple format should both satisfy the need for designing with ease and still provide users with a channel that seems rich, even if it is only a few items deep.

Keep It Simple

In the section "Let People Know What They Need," earlier in this chapter, I mention dancing elves, along with streaming video, RealAudio, and Shockwave animations. Although these features are all great things to have in your channel, the one thing that you never want to do is overload people with too much information. If you remember the old TV show *Max Headroom*, I liken this situation to something on that show called "Blipverts." Blipverts were ads that ran so fast that they caused viewers' brains to fry. (Makes you wonder about the future of advertising.)

The idea, however, is that, if you've got a lot going on, viewers get distracted and lose focus on whatever your intentions were for the channel. This potential problem is just something you need to remain aware of as you start having the vision of creating a feature-length film for your web channel!

I can think of no better piece of advice for web-channel developers than to simply KISS — Keep It Simple, Sucka.

Chapter 16

Ten JavaScript and Dynamic HTML Resources on the Internet

• •

In This Chapter

▶ The best places online to get good, solid tutorials on adding JavaScript and Dynamic HTML to your web channel.

• •

*J*avaScript and Dynamic HTML (DHTML) are not for the faint of heart. They require a lot of time, not to mention a good dose of trial and error, to work properly. Unfortunately, I don't have the space in this book to cover them completely and thoroughly. However, I've used a lot JavaScript and some Dynamic HTML throughout the course of the book. So, the fairest trade-off that I could think of was to just give you my list of bookmarks, so to speak. Every day, I visit a wide variety of sites looking for easy and effective ways to add JavaScript and Dynamic HTML to the web channels I work on. Why not impart all that searching to you!

I've already included some sites during the course of the book, including the Netscape (`developer.netscape.com`) and the Microsoft site (`www.microsoft.com/ie/ie4/`), as well as the Developer.com and NoContent sites. There are a number of other sites, however, that also provide you with clearly written code and useful samples for creating Dynamic HTML and JavaScript applications. These sites will be your best bet for getting your web channel supercharged with complex and compelling scripts. Hopefully, you'll find this list as useful as I do!

Webcoder.com

www.webcoder.com

I have found Webcoder.com (pictured in Figure 16-1) to be one of the most useful sites for clear scripting tutorials. This excellent site began as a part of www.webreference.com, but the author signed an agreement with Web Review to include his content as part of their site. Webcoder.com is dedicated almost exclusively to Dynamic HTML and JavaScript, and includes several good tutorials that apply to web channels, including:

✔ Cascading Style Sheets

✔ The new browser Object models

✔ Animations

✔ Cookies

✔ Forms and how to use them with the new browsers.

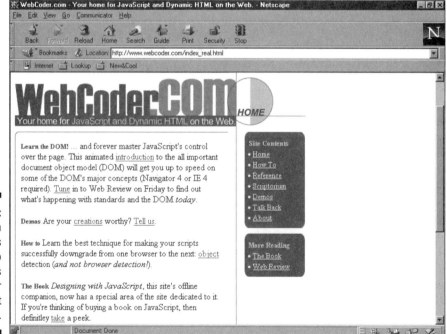

Figure 16-1:
Webcoder.com
provides
step-by-step
instructions
for all their
JavaScript
and DHTML.

Dynamic HTML Zone

www.dhtmlzone.com

Even though the Dynamic HTML Zone (pictured in Figure 16-2) is a relatively new player in the developer site area, it was built by the folks at Macromedia. Macromedia has created a number of well-known multimedia products, including *Director,* and its web extension, *Shockwave.* In other words, they've been doing web development for a while!

With the Dynamic HTML Zone, Macromedia uses a sample company, Superfly Fashions, to show the many different ways in which you can use Dynamic HTML and JavaScript to add life to your web site or web channel. The tutorials take these unwieldy JavaScript applications and break them down into clear, concise steps. The result is a near-perfect tutorial that will, in the end, show you how to build a highly interactive web front page.

In addition to the tutorials, Macromedia is also working on a new Dynamic HTML development tool called Dreamweaver. You can download the beta version free from the Dynamic HTML Zone. Although still beta, this tool can greatly reduce the time needed to create compelling animations and interactivity with DHTML and JavaScript.

Figure 16-2: The Dynamic HTML Zone takes a really complex sample site and dissects it nicely.

Webreference.com

www.webreference.com

Webreference.com (see Figure 16-3) is a "must-have" for web developers. In addition to having a significant archive of JavaScript materials, there's also a bi-weekly column on new Dynamic HTML scripts. These columns cover everything from event handlers to animation and even images that zoom in and out. Although the tutorials can be long and fairly complicated, they are well annotated and come with examples to highlight the various steps of implementation along the way.

In addition to just JavaScript and Dynamic HTML, Webreference.com also provides a number of other services, including design pointers, developer-related news items, and even job postings! Bottom line: Add it to your bookmarks. You'll be happy you did!

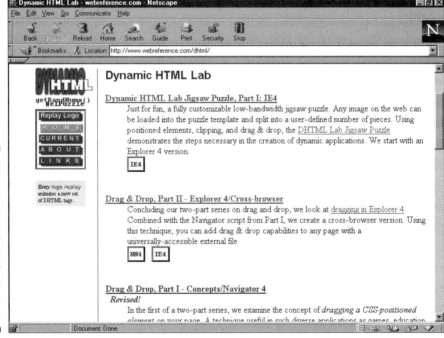

Figure 16-3: The Dynamic HTML Lab provides a number of useful tutorials for experts and even novices.

Builder.com

www.builder.com

Builder.com is part of the CNET family of web sites. Geared to the Web as a whole, Builder.com's coverage of JavaScript and DHTML can sometimes get lost among the increasingly large number of Web-related topics. That small caveat aside, you can still find a large repository of great information on Dynamic HTML and JavaScript. The only hard part is finding it. Take a look into the Builder.com archives and be prepared to go back six or seven months to get the broadest range of tutorials.

Generally speaking, you'll be able to find most everything you need in one of two following sections at Builder.com: Web Authoring and Web Programming & Scripting. However, as figure 16-4 shows, you can also expect to see features that are relevant to web channels!

CNET has a number of other sites which may also prove useful to you in developing web channels. They include Browsers.com (covers the browsers in-depth), ActiveX.com (a Microsoft Active X-specific site) and Download.com (the home of almost every shareware tool you could hope to find).

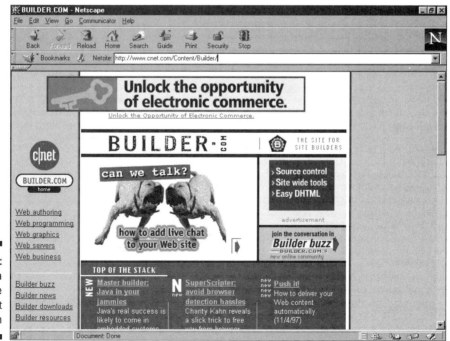

Figure 16-4: Push is a feature today at Builder.com

Web Monkey

www.hotwired.com/webmonkey

After you get past the maddening Hot Wired interface, you'll find Web Monkey (see figure 16-5) to be one of the more useful resources for creating all sorts of web applications. The only problem with this site is that, fundamentally, this is a magazine, so their coverage of JavaScript and Dynamic HTML isn't exactly a constant. They come around to both topics, in one form or another, at least once a month. However, you can never quite be sure what aspect of the topic is going to be covered. You can, though, generally be guaranteed that it will be new and cutting edge.

The only problem with new and cutting edge, as far as web development is concerned, is bugginess. Hot Wired was covering push and web channels long before anyone else, which is good, but a number of the things they wrote about eventually were changed when the final versions of the browsers shipped. While they're good about telling you this, it's easy to forget about something once you've created it, so be careful!

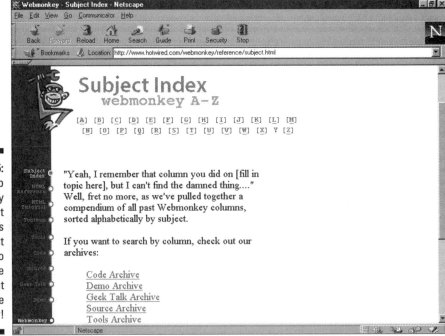

Figure 16-5: The Web Monkey subject index is the best way to find the content you're looking for!

JavaScripts.com

www.javascripts.com/

JavaScripts.com is free, but you still have to pay with a little bit of time up front. To gain access to this site, you need to register, get a password, and then use the password anytime you want to log on. While this registration is mostly a ploy to get your e-mail address, it's worth it, because the site provides a number of really useful JavaScripts that you can put in your web channel.

JavaScripts.com (shown in Figure 16-6) is really more of a no-frills kind of site, with a little bit of an edgy attitude in their presentation. There's not much in the line of tutorials — which happens when twenty-somethings start publishing on the Internet, or worse, start writing *...For Dummies* books! JavaScripts.com has over 75,000 members, and so I wouldn't expect the kind of "personal" attention you may get at some other sites. Still, the scripts are good, and personally, I like their attitude!

Figure 16-6:
You have to register before you can log on to Java-Scripts.com

JavaScript Planet

www.intricate.com/javascript/

JavaScript planet is a repository for a wide variety of simple JavaScripts. Why include it on the list? Well, because sometimes a simple JavaScript may be just what you need. At last check, there were nearly 400 JavaScript applets at this site! When you visit this site, try not to be turned off too much by the design, which is clearly not their strong suit. Also, you'll find a number of strange abbreviations for things. To avoid any confusion, I list in Table 16-1 what the abbreviations really mean.

Table 16-1	Abbreviations for the JavaScript Planet Menu
Abbreviation	**What It Means**
Text	Scripts that somehow involve text (Okay, that one was pretty obvious.)
CCC	Clocks, Calculators, and Calendars
Colors	Scripts that manipulate either the background color or the color of simply colored objects on a page
Images	A lot of the classic image rollover JavasScripts
CCP	Cookies, Counters, and Passwords
Alerts	Scripts that in one way or another tell you that an action has occurred
LBE	Links, Buttons, and E-mail scripts

In addition to a number of JavaScripts, The JavaScript planet also includes some pretty good tutorials. The site is personally maintained, which can be both a good and a bad thing, but having read through the tutorials on the site, I think they provide a good overview of how the JavaScript language is constructed.

The JavaScript Source

www.compfund.com/javascript/

Like the JavaScript planet, the JavaScript Source (see figure 16-7) is a personal web site devoted exclusively to JavaScript. Unlike The JavaScript planet, though, this site is well designed and easy to follow. The JavaScript Source also includes an extensive area for providing feedback and communicating with other like-minded web developers. You have to register to gain access to this area, but in the end, it's worth it. Peruse the chat area or the bulletin boards to find out some good insights on Dynamic HTML and JavaScript specifically, and the web in general.

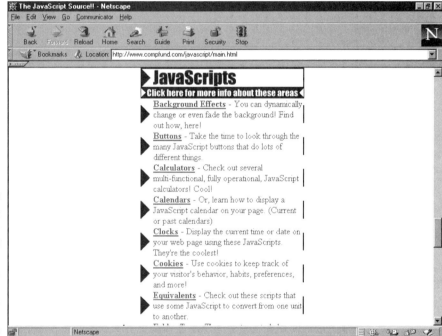

Figure 16-7:
The JavaScript Source is well organized and well thought out.

Web Developers Virtual Library

`wdvl.com`

The Web Developers Virtual Library (see Figure 16-8) provides comprehensive tutorials for a wide range of Web application areas, including JavaScript, Dynamic HTML, CGI, Java, and VRML. The site includes twelve different sections, ranging from the afore-mentioned tutorials to discussion areas and download areas. The site even provides a keyword search tool so that you can search for articles on topics you're interested in!

A lot of developer web sites seem to overlap, and it's true that a number of them include the same basic scripts. However, every developer site has a slightly different look and feel, and some sites may prove easier for you to use, either because the design is better, or because the tutorials are more complete. I list a number of sites in this chapter, with the hope that you may use all of them at different times!

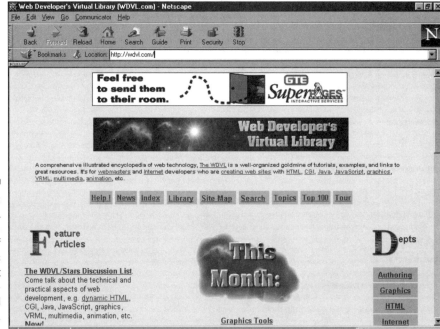

Figure 16-8:
WDVL covers a number of topics pertinent to web-channel developers.

Cut-and-Paste JavaScript

www.infohiway.com/javascript/indexf.htm

At first glance, Cut-and-Paste JavaScript (shown in figure 16-9) may look a little busy, but after your eyes get used to all the overlapping text and various JavaScripts running on the page, you find that the scripts included here are quite good. Every month, there are featured JavaScript selections that can be accessed through a scrolling menu, as well as through a link at the top of the page. In addition, you have a number of scripts in the JavaScript archive to chose from. While they aren't necessarily catalogued all that well, after you find the scripts, they're good to go.

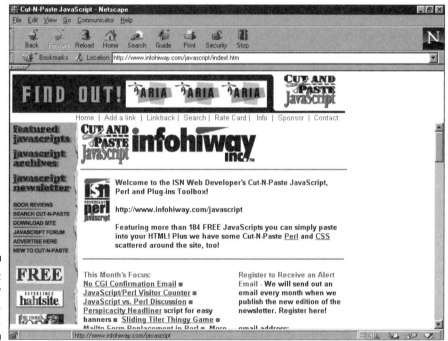

Figure 16-9: It's a busy front page, but it works.

Chapter 17

Ten Quick Steps to Creating a "Dynamic" Dynamic HTML Preview Page

In This Chapter

▶ Creating an animated preview page with Dynamic HTML and JavaScript

*Y*ou can do a lot of things to bring your web channel to life. But, as I mention in several places throughout this book, perhaps the best place to make your first impression on subscribers is with your channel's preview page. So, why not create a preview page that has some life in it? That's exactly what this ten-step process is going to do!

In Chapter 14, I briefly touch on animation using Dynamic HTML and some JavaScript. This chapter goes further by showing you how to animate more than one item — and controlling when the items are shown and animated by using a timeline. It sounds similar, but it's more complicated, and gets pretty deep into Dynamic HTML and JavaScript.

This brings me to my first and only caveat in this chapter. I can't expect to teach you everything about Dynamic HTML and JavaScript in one chapter. Nor, for that matter, should you expect to learn everything about Dynamic HTML and JavaScript in one chapter. There's just too much to cover. Some things in this chapter, unfortunately, you're just going to have to accept on faith.

For more information on Dynamic HTML or JavaScript, I highly recommend checking out *JavaScript For Dummies*, by Emily Vander Veer, and *Dynamic HTML For Dummies*, by Michael Hyman (both from IDG Books Worldwide, Inc.).

That recommendation doesn't mean, however, that I'm just going to print the code and go home. I explain what every little piece of script does, and as always, I am using Channel Swank as an example. Nonetheless, some things may still seem a bit confusing. If this is the case, you may want to check out Chapter 16, which includes a number of JavaScript and Dynamic HTML resources on the Internet.

That caveat aside, let's get down to making the preview page! A couple of notes before I jump into the script. This preview page will be cross-browser compatible, which simply means that you can use it for both Netcaster and Explorer. In addition, in some places in the chapter, I refer to individual snippets of script rather than just showing large script chunks because a number of elements appear in various places — making showing it in one simple place nearly impossible. For your reference, though, the entire script is located in the "Whole Enchilada" section at the end of the chapter.

The entire script is also on the CD-ROM. It's located in the Swank/DHTML directory.

Step One: Set Your Styles

One of the great things about the 4.0 browsers is their use of Cascading Style Sheets (CSS). Using CSS, you can set the properties of any number of objects within an HTML document. Each object can have its own style, which can include everything from the text size to the position of a graphic within on the page.

For the animated preview page for Channel Swank, I have five objects: four graphics that move, and a small bit of text that appears at the very end. All styles are enclosed within a single <STYLE> tag and are included within the <HEAD> of the HTML document. Each individual style includes both a unique name, preceded by a period (.), and followed by the style parameters, enclosed with brackets { }.The parameters for these five objects include the following items:

✔ Position information (for all items)

✔ Object state when the page is loaded (hidden or shown)

✔ Font size (text style only)

✔ Font family (text style only)

✔ Font color (text style only)

✔ Width of the text box (text style only)

Within the styles for the Channel Swank preview page are the initial locations for each of the objects, which will then be moved along a path to create the animation. For your preview page, the names of the styles, as well as their attributes, will no doubt be different. However, the following syntax should get you going:

```
<STYLE type=text/css>
 .swanktext {
position: absolute;
left: 500;
top: 200;
font-family:    arial;
font-size:      11pt;
color: #c0c0c0;
width: 150px;
visibility: hidden;
}

.channelstyle {
position: absolute;
left: 200;
top: 0;
visibility:hidden;
}

.swankstyle {
position: absolute;
left: 200;
top: 400;
visibility:hidden;
}

.barstyle {
position: absolute;
left: 0;
top: 250;
visibility:hidden;
}

.shakerstyle {
position: absolute;
left: 0;
top: 150;
visibility:hidden;
}
</STYLE>
```

A complete listing of the syntax for Cascading Style Sheets can be found at the World Wide Web (W3) Consortium homepage, located at `www.w3.org/TR/REC-CSS1`

Step Two: Make Your Preview Page Browser-Independent

One of the more annoying things about Cascading Style Sheets and Dynamic HTML, at this point, is that they're slightly different, depending upon which browser you're using. That's because there isn't a standardized way of handling CSS and Dynamic HTML that's been implemented by both Microsoft and Netscape. That said, the World Wide Web (W3) Consortium is deciding on a standard, as we speak, so within the next year, this little step will no doubt be moot!

Until, then, however, you're going to need to include some JavaScript that delineates between the two browsers and outputs the right functions for each browser. Yes, it's a hassle, but frankly, you don't have a choice. It's like cough syrup. It tastes nasty, but it works.

The difference between the two browsers lies in the DOM, or Document Object Model, that the two browsers use. I'm oversimplifying a bit, but the syntax for Internet Explorer has a couple more words in its DOM than Netcsape. As a result, if you call an object in Netscape using its DOM, it may not work on Internet Explorer. And if you create syntax for Internet Explorer, Netcsape won't know what to do with the extra words. Nick Heinle provides a nice clear description of the differences in the DOM for both browsers at `www.webcoder.com`

We're concerned about two basic differences in this big script, and they boil down to two words: `all` and `style`. In the Internet Explorer world, when you want to use Dynamic HTML to refer to an object within an HTML document, you use the following syntax:

```
Document.all.insert_object_here
```

In Netscape, because the `all` isn't necessary, the syntax would look like this:

```
Document.insert_object_here
```

The same basic rule of thumb applies when calling the style information of an object. Internet Explorer needs to have a `.style` as part of the call, whereas Netscape allows you to go directly to the object without calling its style.

While, on the surface, these may seem like two very small differences, they tend to mess everything up if they're not handled properly. Of course, this begs a pretty big question. Will I have to call everything twice? The answer is no, because with JavaScript you can replace a set of text with another set of text by using an *if* statement. In this case, the only thing we care about is whether it's Netscape or not. If it is, we output one text string. If it isn't, we output another. Here's the very simple check that we're going to do to see whether or not the browser that's active is Netscape:

```
layerObj = (isNS) ? 'document' : 'document.all';
styleObj = (isNS) ? '' : '.style';
```

What I've done here is take two variables, `layerObj` and `styleObj`, and have them check whether or not the browser is Netscape. This is represented by the `isNS` command contained within the parentheses. I could specify the version of Netscape, but because Dynamic HTML works only in Version 4.0, it's kind of a moot point. If it is a Netscape browser, it will output the first set of variables, either `'document'` or `' '` (which means nothing). If it isn't a Netscape browser, which means it *is* Internet Explorer, it prints out the second set of variables, `'document.all'` and `'.style'`. The same rule about version applies for Explorer as well. Dynamic HTML only works in Internet Explorer 4.0.

Of course, this is just part of the equation. To find out what this little check really does, look at Step Five. Also, you've defined the variables, but you still need to create them. Check out Step Nine for that tidbit.

Step Three: Define the Actor

Every object on the page that is going to be animated needs to (a) have a set of parameters that define it, and (b) a way of handing off those parameters to the JavaScript so that it can execute the animation according to the object's parameters. In this example, the JavaScript function `actor` does exactly that. An actor is an object, like a .gif file, that will eventually do something on the screen.

Each animated object on the page has six parameters:

✔ A unique name (elementName)

✔ A definition of whether the object loops or not (loop)

✔ The object's speed, in milliseconds (speed)

✔ The number of steps it takes per frame (steps)

✔ What the object does when it stops (endRoutines)

✔ The object's animation path (route)

After the parameters are set for the function, those parameters need to be handed off to JavaScript. In addition, though, the function also needs to enable the other functions that it's going to need in the script. In this case, there are four other functions — moveObject, followPath, showObject, and hideObject — that will need to be called in order to get the object to move around on the screen. These functions, by the way, are described in more detail in the next step.

As for the actor function, the script looks like this:

```
function actor(elementName,loop,speed,steps,endRoutines,
route) {
this.elementName = elementName;
this.loop = loop;
this.speed = speed;
this.steps = steps;
this.frameIndex = 0;
this.endRoutines = endRoutines;
this.route = route.split(',');
this.animate = followPath;
this.move = moveObject;
this.show = showObject;
this.hide = hideObject;
```

You may have noticed that the function doesn't contain a closing bracket. That's because the function's not quite done yet. Right now, the function is just a collection of parameters than can't be recognized by any other area of the script. It needs a way to tag each defined object with a unique identifier. The best identifier would appear to be the elementName.

The following script tells the rest of the script functions within the page that when it gets an elementName, it's handling an actor:

```
actors[elementName] = this;
}
```

Step Four: Creating a Timeline

Any timeline has three basic elements. First, you've got to know how long the time interval is. Second, you need to know how to start it. Third, you need to know how to stop it. Because there is no concept of time inherent to the loading of an HTML page (except of course, the excruciatingly long time it takes to load images!), you have a timing mechanism that can handle the showing and animating of objects at given intervals. If, for example, I wanted every object to animate right when the page was loaded, a timing mechanism wouldn't be necessary. However, because I want some objects to come in before others, having a mechanism for controlling time intervals becomes a requirement.

This script requires three functions, `animationStart`, `animationStop`, and `TimeLoop`. As you may suspect `animationStart` starts the animation process, `animationStop` stops it, and the `TimeLoop` manages the time intervals.

The script for `animationStart` is right here:

```
function animationStart(timelineNumber) {
animationTime[timelineNumber] = 0;
TimeLoop(timelineNumber);
}
```

The script for `animationStop` is right here:

```
function animationStop(timelineNumber) {
animationTime[timelineNumber] =
animationTimeline[timelineNumber].length;
}
```

The script that creates the timeline and controls the time loop is right here:

```
function TimeLoop(timelineNumber) {
if (animationTime[timelineNumber] <=
animationTimeline[timelineNumber].length - 1) {
animationTime[timelineNumber]++;
if
(animationTimeline[timelineNumber][animationTime[timelineNumber]]
!= null) {
eval(animationTimeline[timelineNumber][animationTime[timelineNumber]]);
}
setTimeout('TimeLoop(' + timelineNumber + ')', 100);
}
}
```

Step Five: Animating an Object

In Step Two, I briefly mention the Document Object Model (or DOM), and show how you can set up JavaScript to switch text depending on the browser. Here, you'll get to see exactly how that works. Four different functions are covered in this step, and although I gloss over them somewhat quickly, the most important things for you to remember are that they do the following:

- ✔ Hide a shown object
- ✔ Show a hidden object
- ✔ Move an object
- ✔ Allow an object to follow a pre-defined path

There's a command in JavaScript called `eval`. Bascially, `eval` simply allows you to "put things together," though you have to tell `eval` what to put together. In Step Two, I define the question "Is this Netscape or not?" Throughout the following four functions, you're going to see a lot of the `eval` command and the questions that are rooted `layerObj` and `styleObj` elements. By using `eval` with a question element (like `layerObj`) that generates a text string, I can put these strings together to create an argument in Dynamic HTML that, for example, shows an object.

The hide and show functions are the easiest, and provide the best basis for example. The `showObject` function is right here:

```
function showObject() {
eval(layerObj + '["' + this.elementName + '"]' + styleObj +
'.visibility = "visible"');
}
```

The `hideObject` function, similarly, looks like this:

```
function hideObject() {
eval(layerObj + '["' + this.elementName + '"]' + styleObj +
'.visibility = "hidden"');
}
```

All these functions are really doing is generating a string of text, such as this:

```
document.swank.visibility = "visible"
```

The interesting thing, though, is how it's being done. When the showObject function is called, The `eval` command will:

1. Look at `layerObj`, and get the result of it's query
2. Add to it the `elementName` of the current object being handled
3. Look at `styleObj`, and get the result of it's query
4. Add to it `'.visibility = "visible"'`

In the Channel Swank example, I have an `actor` called *swank*. If I was viewing the preview page in Netscape, and the `showObject` function was called, the `eval` would parse together the following string:

1. `document`
2. `.swank`
3. [nothing]
4. `.visibility = "visible"'`

As you may have noticed, when you put all the pieces together, the resulting string is identical to the one noted earlier. That's the essence of how you can use JavaScript to create Dynamic HTML on the fly.

As for the two other functions, they're a bit more complicated. The `moveObject` function, which follows, sets the positions of objects when they are shown, according to the locations set in the Cascading Stye Sheets shown in Step One. That function is right here:

```
function moveObject(left, top) {
eval(layerObj + '["' + this.elementName + '"]' + styleObj +
'.top = top');
eval(layerObj + '["' + this.elementName + '"]' + styleObj +
'.left = left');
}
```

The `followPath` function allows you to set a number of points on the screen to create the animation. The animation can support a number of points, but the thing to keep in mind is how it thinks of pixel locations. The top-left corner of the screen is the 0,0 point. As you move right and down, the numbers get larger in the positive direction. The `followPath` function is described right here:

```
function followPath(){
if (this.route.length > 4 && this.frameIndex <
this.route.length) {
this.move(this.route[this.frameIndex],
this.route[this.frameIndex + 1]); this.frameIndex += 2;
setTimeout('actors["' + this.elementName + '"].animate()',
this.speed); }
else if (this.route.length == 4 && this.frameIndex <=
this.steps) {
this.move(parseInt(this.route[0]) + (this.frameIndex *
((parseInt(this.route[2]) - parseInt(this.route[0])) /
this.steps)), parseInt(this.route[1]) + (this.frameIndex
*((parseInt(this.route[3]) - parseInt(this.route[1])) /
this.steps))); this.frameIndex++;
setTimeout('actors["' + this.elementName + '"].animate()',
this.speed); }
else { eval(this.endRoutines + "");
this.frameIndex = 0; if (this.loop == "yes"){
this.animate(); }
            }
}
```

Step Six: Starting the Animation

Like everything else in JavaScript, you need a function to start the animation process. Too bad you just can't say "Go!" Oh well, maybe it'll happen with the next Internet language! The StartAnimation function, which does exactly that, has a few components, some of which are shown here, and some of which are shown in steps seven and eight. The first part of StartAnimation includes:

- The layerObj and the styleObj elements
- Creating new arrays for the animation
- Creating animation objects

The layerObj and styleObj elements have been pretty well covered by this point, including all the proper syntax, but this is the place in the script where they're actually created. Once again, though, here's the syntax:

```
layerObj = (isNS) ? 'document' : 'document.all';
styleObj = (isNS) ? '' : '.style';
```

Creating new arrays for the animation is a straightforward process. You need two arrays. The first is animationTime, which starts the animation.

The second is `animationTimeline`, which allows you to determine when an object will be shown and start moving. The syntax for creating the arrays looks like this:

```
animationTime = new Array();
animationTimeline = new Array();
```

The third element of the `StartAnimation` function is the creation of the actors. You'll specify the parameters of actors in the next step, but for now, all you need to do is enable those objects to be built, and to do that requires the following script command:

```
actors = new Object();
```

Step Seven: Creating and Cueing Your Actors

An `actor` can be a graphic, HTML, or even a Java applet. The physical content of the object isn't as important as defining its animation parameters. You define the physical content in the `<BODY>` of the HTML document. The attributes for each object are the ones that were laid out in Step Three. Again, an `actor` includes the following parameters:

✔ A unique name (`elementName`)

✔ A definition of whether the object loops or not (`loop`)

✔ The object's speed, in milliseconds (`speed`)

✔ The number of steps it takes per frame (`steps`)

✔ What the object does when it stops (`endRoutines`)

✔ The object's animation path (`route`)

Unlike in Step Three, the syntax for creating an `actor` and setting its attributes is a bit different. To begin with, you give it a name, declare it a new object, and then include the `actor`'s directions as comma separated items within the parentheses. The script for the `swank` actor in the Channel Swank preview page is as follows:

```
swank = new actor( 'swankID', 'no', 25, 25, 'null', '200,
400, 200,275');
```

For every object that you want to animate, there must be a similar declaration of it as an `actor` in the `StartAnimation` function before it can be called within the HTML `<BODY>`.

Step Eight: Animating Your Actors

The last element of the StartAnimation function requires that you now tell your actors when they are to show up and then, subsequently, start following their animation path. You must first consider two basic commands, namely animationTimeline(0) and animationStart(0).

At animationTimeline(0), a new array is created that includes each of the timed elements in the array. Elements of the array are different times, in milliseconds. At each of those points in time, an actor (or multiple actors) is shown and then given the order to animate. The shaker actor, which shows up 10 milliseconds after the Channel Swank preview page is loaded, has the following syntax for starting its animation path:

```
animationTimeline[0][10] = 'shaker.show();
shaker.animate();';
```

The channel and swank actors work similarly, although they show up at the same time, 50 milliseconds after the page is loaded. The script for that is shown right here:

```
animationTimeline[0][50] = 'channel.show(); swank.show();
channel.animate();swank.animate();';
```

The animationStart(0) command follows your actor timeline. All this command does is tell the StartAnimation function to begin right when it's called, which is usually when the page is loaded.

Step Nine: Remember Your Variables

This script has a number of variables, some of which I've covered in depth; others I haven't really touched on. Because there are so many, though, it's best to put them at the end of all the JavaScript in the <HEAD>. The full list of them is right here:

```
var layerObj;
var styleObj;
var animationTime;
var animationTimeline;
var actors;
var isNS = (document.layers);
var isDHTML = (document.layers || document.all);
```

Step Ten: Load Your Body

At this point, you can pretty much start the animation function any way you want. For simplicity's sake, you may just want to do it from the <BODY> tag using onLoad = "startAnimation()". However, you can call it from other places within the body, say from a link using onclick.

When you start the animation, the JavaScript is going to look for the named actor objects specified in the StartAnimation function. To ensure that it finds the right object, you're going to need to assign an ID for each of the actor objects you created in the StartAnimation function in Step Eight. The ID you want to give the object is elementName that you specified when you created the actor. In addition to the ID, don't forget to also use the CLASS command (also shown here) to call the appropriate style of the actor. The syntax for the swank actor graphic follows:

```
<DIV ID = "swankID" CLASS = 'swankstyle' ><IMG SR =
"swank.gif" NAME = "swank_graphic" HEIGHT = "50" WIDTH =
"200"></DIV>
```

The Whole Enchilada

Whew! Talk about moving in a hurry! That was fast. Following, you find the entire script for that page, just as it appears on the CD-ROM. Your best bet is to drag it from the CD-ROM and start fiddling with it. If you need to refer back to the script, or just want it handy, here it is:

```
<HTML>
<HEAD>
<TITLE>Channel Swank Preview</TITLE>
<STYLE type=text/css>

.swanktext {
position: absolute;
left: 500;
top: 200;
font-family:    arial;
font-size:      11pt;
color:  #c0c0c0;
width: 150px;
visibility: hidden;
}
```

(continued)

(continued)

```
.channelstyle {
position: absolute;
left: 200;
top: 0;
visibility:hidden;
}

.swankstyle {
position: absolute;
left: 200;
top: 400;
visibility:hidden;
}

.barstyle {
position: absolute;
left: 0;
top: 250;
visibility:hidden;
}

.shakerstyle {
position: absolute;
left: 0;
top: 150;
visibility:hidden;
}
</STYLE>
<SCRIPT LANGUAGE = "JavaScript">
function actor(elementName,loop,speed,steps,endRoutines,
route) {
this.elementName = elementName;
this.loop = loop;
this.speed = speed;
this.steps = steps;
this.frameIndex = 0;
this.endRoutines = endRoutines;
this.route = route.split(',');
this.animate = followPath;
this.move = moveObject;
this.show = showObject;
this.hide = hideObject;
```

```
actors[elementName] = this;
}

function animationStop(timelineNumber)
{
animationTime[timelineNumber] =
animationTimeline[timelineNumber].length;
}

function animationStart(timelineNumber)
{
animationTime[timelineNumber] = 0;
TimeLoop(timelineNumber);
}

function TimeLoop(timelineNumber) {
if (animationTime[timelineNumber] <=
animationTimeline[timelineNumber].length - 1)
{
animationTime[timelineNumber]++;
if (animationTimeline[timelineNumber][animationTime[timelineNumber]]
!= null)
{
eval(animationTimeline[timelineNumber][animationTime[timelineNumber]]);
}
setTimeout('TimeLoop(' + timelineNumber + ')', 100);
}
}

function showObject()
{
eval(layerObj + '["' + this.elementName + '"]' + styleObj +
'.visibility = "visible"');
}

//hides an object
function hideObject() {
eval(layerObj + '["' + this.elementName + '"]' + styleObj +
'.visibility = "hidden"');
}
```

(continued)

(continued)

```
function moveObject(left, top){
eval(layerObj + '["' + this.elementName + '"]' + styleObj +
'.top = top');
eval(layerObj + '["' + this.elementName + '"]' + styleObj +
'.left = left');
}

function followPath() {
if (this.route.length > 4 && this.frameIndex <
this.route.length) {
this.move(this.route[this.frameIndex],
this.route[this.frameIndex + 1]); this.frameIndex += 2;
setTimeout('actors["' + this.elementName + '"].animate()',
this.speed); }
else if (this.route.length == 4 && this.frameIndex <=
this.steps) {
this.move(parseInt(this.route[0]) + (this.frameIndex *
((parseInt(this.route[2]) - parseInt(this.route[0])) /
this.steps)), parseInt(this.route[1]) + (this.frameIndex
*((parseInt(this.route[3]) - parseInt(this.route[1])) /
this.steps))); this.frameIndex++;
setTimeout('actors["' + this.elementName + '"].animate()',
this.speed); }
else { eval(this.endRoutines + "");
this.frameIndex = 0; if (this.loop == "yes"){
this.animate(); }
        }
}

function StartAnimation() {
layerObj = (isNS) ? 'document' : 'document.all';
styleObj = (isNS) ? '' : '.style';
animationTime = new Array();
animationTimeline = new Array();
actors = new Object();

channel = new actor( 'channelID', 'no', 25, 25, 'null',
'200,0, 200,200');

swank = new actor( 'swankID', 'no', 25, 25, 'null', '200,
400, 200,275');

bars = new actor( 'barsID', 'no', 25, 25, 'null', '0,250,
200,250');
```

```
shaker = new actor( 'shakerID', 'no', 25, 25, 'null',
'0,150, 400,150');

text = new actor( 'textID', 'no', 0, 0, 'null', '500,200,
500,200');


animationTimeline[0] = new Array();
animationTimeline[0][10] = 'shaker.show();
shaker.animate();';
animationTimeline[0][45] = 'bars.show(); bars.animate();';
animationTimeline[0][50] = 'channel.show(); swank.show();
channel.animate();swank.animate();';
animationTimeline[0][60] = 'text.show();';

animationStart(0);
}

var layerObj;
var styleObj;
var animationTime;
var animationTimeline;
var actors;
var isNS = (document.layers);
var isDHTML = (document.layers || document.all);
</SCRIPT>
</HEAD>
<BODY onLoad = "StartAnimation()" BACKGROUND=""
BGCOLOR="#000000" TEXT="#ff8040" LINK="#8080ff"
VLINK="#c0c0c0" ALINK="#800000">


<DIV ID = "channelID" CLASS = 'channelstyle'><IMG SRC =
"channel.gif" NAME = "channel_graphic" HEIGHT = "48" WIDTH
= "199"></DIV>

<DIV ID = "swankID" CLASS = 'swankstyle' ><IMG SRC =
"swank.gif" NAME = "swank_graphic" HEIGHT = "50" WIDTH =
"200"></DIV>

<DIV ID = "barsID" CLASS = 'barstyle'><IMG SRC = "bars.gif"
NAME = "bars_graphic" HEIGHT = "25" WIDTH = "200"></DIV>

<DIV ID = "shakerID" CLASS= 'shakerstyle'><IMG SRC =
"shaker.gif" NAME = "shaker_graphic" HEIGHT = "184" WIDTH =
"75"></DIV>
```

(continued)

(continued)

```
<DIV ID = "textID"  CLASS = 'swanktext'> All the coolest
cats, the loungiest  lizards and history's biggest swingers
all say you should subscribe to Channel Swank. Cheers!
</DIV>
</BODY>
</HTML>
```

Part VI
Appendixes

The 5th Wave   By Rich Tennant

"HOLD YOUR HORSES. IT TAKES TIME TO BUILD
A WEB CHANNEL FOR SOMEONE YOUR SIZE."

In this part . . .

Think of the appendixes as your reference guide to web channels. There's a Glossary, as well as contact information for all of the major software companies that make web channel viewers. And, last but certainly not least, you'll find some tips for using the CD-ROM that comes with the book. Enjoy, and I'll see you on the Internet!

Appendix A

A Glossary of Webcasting Terms

I suppose I could just start with the word in the title: webcasting. Webcasting is the process of publishing content that is distributed via a web channel on the Internet. That should give you a pretty good idea of just how this Appendix is going to look. Every now and then, having a quick reference of terms can be a helpful tool that enables you to describe your work to others.

And now, my rendition of Webster, 14th edition, omitting everything except terms that relate to webcasting. We'll be here performing at the Tonga Room all week long. Please come back and see us again soon!

Active Channels

The Microsoft definition of a web channel, as it appears in Internet Explorer 4.0. Active channels make use of the Microsoft ActiveX technology, which provides an integration of the Windows 95 desktop with the Internet. An example of an Active Channel is shown in Figure A-1.

Active Channel Guide

The Microsoft guide to a number of Active Channels on the Internet. The Active Channel Guide is located at www.microsoft.com/ie/ie40/.

Active Desktop

The Active Desktop is the integration of HTML with the Windows 95 desktop environment. Every item on the desktop becomes HTML-capable, and desktop windows become an extension of Internet Explorer 4.0. Selecting an Internet document, like an HTML file, will automatically spawn Explorer. Web-channel developers can create mini-web channels that are updated from the Internet and reside right on the desktop. The Active Channel Tool Bar, part of the integrated desktop, is shown in Figure A-2.

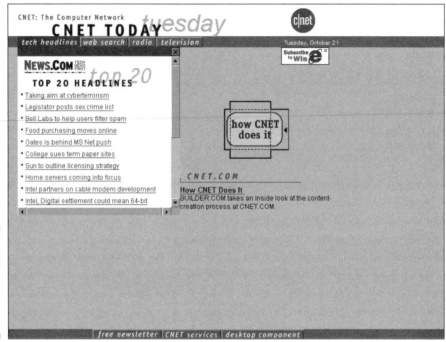

Figure A-1:
A Microsoft Active Channel looks like this.

Figure A-2:
The Active Channel Bar on the Active Desktop.

Active Screen Savers

Active Screen Savers are HTML pages that are updated through the Internet but reside on the desktop in the form of a screen saver. When the screen saver is spawned, it cycles through the available HTML pages, creating a continuously updated slide show.

Bongo

Bongo is the development tool for Castanet web channels. Essentially a graphical interface wrapped around a Java scripting tool, Bongo enables the creation of Java-based web channels without a significant amount of programming.

Castanet Tuner

The Castanet Tuner, shown in Figure A-3, is the Marimba web-channel viewer. Although Castanet is the most versatile web-channel viewer, in that it supports full-blown Java applications, it has not received wide acceptance from developers in the web-channel community.

Castanet Transmitter

The Transmitter works as the server for Castanet channels. All channels need to be housed on a Castanet Transmitter site. Check out the main Castanet Transmitter site at `trans.marimba.com`.

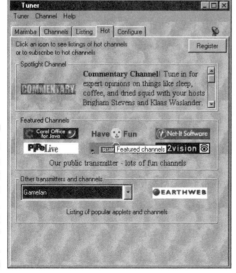

Figure A-3:
The Castanet Tuner uses the Internet, but not necessarily HTML.

Channel Bar

Within Explorer 4.0, the retracting menu that includes all of the Active Channels that you've subscribed to, as well as the channels that automatically come with Explorer. The Channel Bar, inside Explorer 4.0, is shown in Figure A-4.

Channel Definition Format (CDF)

CDF is the new web-channel development standard that Microsoft and PointCast have jointly proposed to the World Wide Web Consortium. CDF controls the definition of a web channel, the location of channel elements and sets a default schedule for the updating of a web channel.

Channel Finder

In Netcaster, the Channel Finder (see Figure A-5) is the Netscape listing of the majority of Netcaster channels available on the Internet. It's just like the Active Channel Guide, except it's in Netcaster instead of Explorer.

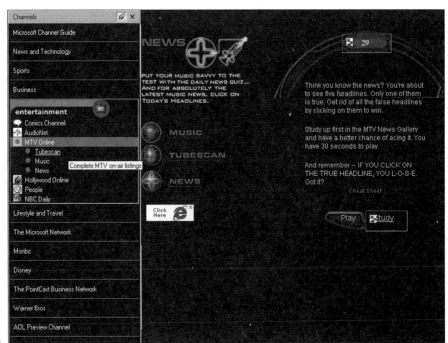

Figure A-4:
The
Channel
Bar inside
Internet
Explorer 4.0.

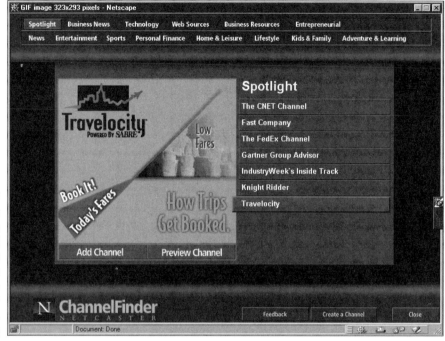

Figure A-5:
The Channel Finder is the home to many Netcaster channels.

Connections Builder

The Connections Builder is the automated CDF file and web-channel tester built into the PointCast Business Network. If you want to build a channel in PointCast, you need to do it by using this tool.

Content

Content is the generic term for anything that exists on a web channel. It can be anything from text to video and even an application. If it gets pushed from the Internet to the desktop, you can pretty well call it content.

Drawer

The Drawer (Figure A-6) is the retractable window in Netcaster where all of your channels, as well as the Channel Finder, are kept. The Drawer floats on the desktop and when it's retracted, all you see is a tab at the side of your screen.

Figure A-6:
The drawer
is home
to your
channels in
Netcaster.

Dynamic HTML

A new and more robust form of HTML that allows you to animate text, specify styles and layers, as well as offers you more control over mouse events. Dynamic HTML needs JavaScript to really make it work well, but you can bet that Dyanmic HTML is going to be one of the next big advancements in Internet technology.

Editorial Calendar

A listing of all the topics you're going to cover on your web channel within a given period of time, say, six months. It's usually a term associated with magazines, but it also works well in describing a long term vision of web channel content.

Interface

The interface is the physical design of your channel. It's what people see when they subscribe to your channel. Designing the interface is one of the most important aspects of good web-channel design. Usually the most important part of your interface is the front page of your channel. An example of a pleasing front page is shown in Figure A-7.

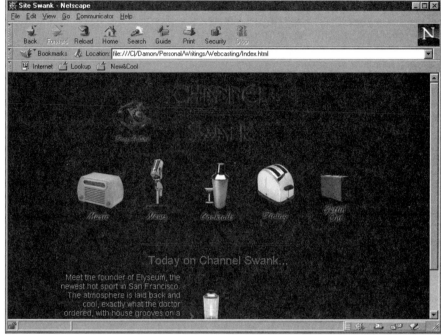

Figure A-7:
The front page of your channel will set the tone of your entire channel interface.

Netcaster

Netcaster is the Netscape web channel viewer. It comes standard with Communicator/Navigator 4.0 professional editions. On the personal editions, you may have to download it separately. Netcaster is not actually another program. It's built on top of Communicator/Navigator, and requires the program to run.

PointCast Business Network

The PointCast Business Network is the PointCast web-channel viewer. The very first push software product on the market, PointCast was also the first push product to capture a million users. PointCast delivers updated content from companies like CNN in the form of a Windows or Macintosh screen saver.

PointCast Studio

The proprietary PointCast tool designed to create animations for screen savers in the PointCast Business Network. PointCast Studio is shown in Figure A-8.

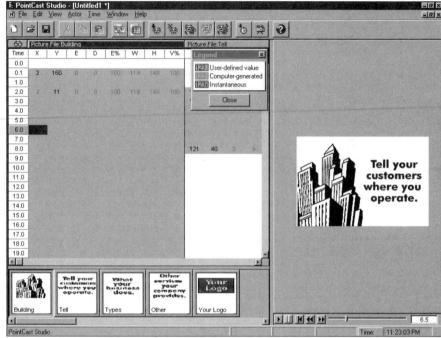

Figure A-8:
Studio
creates
animations
for Smart
Screens
in the
PointCast
Business
Network.

Posting

The process of getting content from the developer's PC to a server on the Internet so that it can be broadcast to subscribers.

Preview Page

A web page that is created to entice potential subscribers. A good Preview Page includes concise but compelling reasons to subscribe to a web channel, and a link that sets up the web channel. An Explorer 4.0 Active Channel preview page is shown in Figure A-9.

Pull

Active Internet browsing. The process of using a web browser to go out onto the Internet, find content, and then download it yourself to your local PC.

Push

Passive Internet viewing. Letting the browser do all the work for you. Instead of you going to look for content, the browser automatically downloads content that you've specified and posts it to your browser so you can view it off-line.

Figure A-9:
Preview
pages such
as this one
allow you to
give users
a taste
of your
channel.

Schedule

For any channel, the dates and times that you specify for that channel to be updated. It can be as short as every few minutes or as long as weeks at a time. By setting a schedule, the browser will know when to go out, get the content for you, and then bring it back and display it on your PC. The Netcaster scheduling window is shown in Figure A-10.

Figure A-10:
You can
set your
channel
update
times
from this
window in
Netcaster.

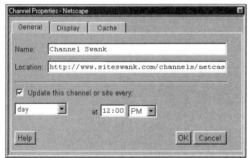

Subscription

The process of selecting a channel and specifying when you want content from that channel to be downloaded to your PC. Subscriptions may be indefinite, or for a very limited period of time.

Web Channel

A web channel is a collection of content that, unlike web site content (which remains on the Internet at all times), is downloaded from the Internet to your PC. You specify when the download is to occur and the web channel viewer retrieves the web-channel content for you.

Web-Channel Viewer

A software product that allows you to both subscribe to web channels, and then view the content of web channels once that content has been downloaded to your PC. Figure A-11 shows Microsoft Explorer 4.0, one of the larger web-channel viewers.

Webtop

The Netcaster-specific term for the front page of a web channel. The Webtop takes over the entire desktop screen and displays content much like a television does. The Webtop also sits in the background, so you can work on other applications while the content on the channel is updated.

XML

Stands for Extensible Markup Language. XML is the base language for Microsoft's CDF format. CDF uses a subset of XML code to specify web channels for Internet Explorer 4.0.

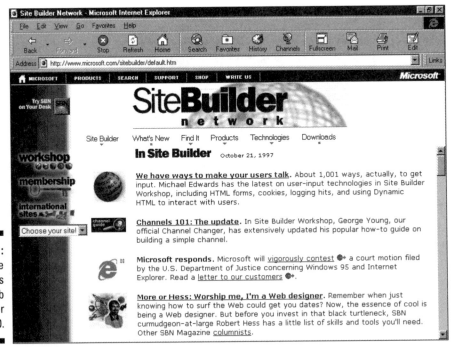

Figure A-11:
There are hundreds of web channels for Explorer 4.0.

Appendix B

Web Channel Companies and How to Contact Them

• •

*T*hroughout this book, I've referred to several companies and their products. If you happened to use any of the products that these companies produce, you may have decided that you need to speak to these companies — either to lay praise or point the finger of blame.

Certainly, I can understand both sides. I've been thoroughly impressed with many of the web-channel products I've seen. Of course, many times, that feeling came after I had to restart my computer, or worse, reformat my hard drive. Like any new software, web-channel viewers can be both astounding and exceptionally frustrating. Just try to remember that these are the companies that are building the technologies of the future. Be gentle.

Microsoft

Good luck trying to find the right person to complain to at Microsoft! The best way to contact Microsoft and make your voice heard is through the Microsoft supported newsgroups, which a number of their engineering and product support staff monitor. You can find those newsgroups at the Microsoft web site. The more general contact information is as follows:

Microsoft Corporation
One Microsoft Way
Redmond, WA 98052-6399
Telephone: 206-882-8080
`register.microsoft.com/regwiz/regwiz.asp`

Netscape

Netscape is really geared towards getting feedback electronically through DevEdge online at `developer.netscape.com`. However, you can also contact the company directly at:

Netscape Corporation
501 E. Middlefield Rd.
Mountain View, CA 94043

415-937-2555: Product and sales information, corporate customers (7 a.m. to 5 p.m. PST)

415-937-3777: Product and sales information, individual consumers (7 a.m. to 5 p.m. PST)

415-937-3678: Government sales (7 a.m. to 5 p.m. PST)

415-254-1900: Executive offices

415-528-4124: Fax

PointCast

To contact PointCast about any of the their products, you can use the following address information:

PointCast Incorporated
501 Macara Ave.
Sunnyvale, CA 94086
Telephone: 408-990-7000
`www.pointcast.com`

Marimba

Marimba has an e-mail address on their web site for just about every person in the company, but I'm guessing you don't really want all that. However, here's the URL, in case you want to find out exactly who to contact: `www.marimba.com/company/`. For more general information, here's the lowdown:

Marimba, Inc.
445 Sherman Ave.
Palo Alto, CA 94306
Telephone: 650-328-5282
Fax: 650-328-5295
E-mail: info@marimba.com
www.marimba.com

Appendix C

What's on the CD?

Here's some of what you can find on the *Web Channel Development For Dummies* CD-ROM:

- ✔ Internet Explorer 4.0, the latest Microsoft web browser that includes support for Active Channels and the Active Desktop.
- ✔ BBEdit Lite, a freeware text editor for Mac OS computers that is useful for HTML editing.
- ✔ Cool Edit, a fantastic sound-editing tool that you can use to add music to your web channel.

System Requirements

Make sure that your computer meets the minimum system requirements. If your computer doesn't match up to most of these requirements, you may have problems in using the contents of the CD.

- ✔ A PC with a 486 or faster processor, or a Mac OS computer with a 68030 or faster processor.
- ✔ Microsoft Windows 3.1 or later, or Mac OS system software 7.5 or later.
- ✔ At least 8MB of total RAM installed on your computer. For best performance, we recommend that Windows 95-equipped PCs and Mac OS computers with PowerPC processors have at least 16MB of RAM installed.
- ✔ At least 60MB of hard drive space available to install all the software from this CD. (You'll need less space if you don't install every program.)
- ✔ A CD-ROM drive — double-speed (2x) or faster.
- ✔ A sound card for PCs. (Mac OS computers have built-in sound support.)
- ✔ A monitor capable of displaying at least 256 colors or grayscale.
- ✔ A modem with a speed of at least 14,400 bps.

If you need more information on the basics, check out *PCs For Dummies,* 5th Edition, by Dan Gookin; *Macs For Dummies,*5th Edition by David Pogue; *Windows 95 For Dummies* by Andy Rathbone; or *Windows 3.11 For Dummies,* 3rd Edition, by Andy Rathbone (all published by IDG Books Worldwide, Inc.).

How to Use the CD with Microsoft Windows

Instructions for Windows 95 and Windows 3.1 users are a bit different. Read on!

If you are running Windows 95, follow these steps to get to the items on the CD

1. **Insert the CD into your computer's CD-ROM drive.**

   Give your computer a moment to take a look at the CD.

2. **When the light on your CD-ROM drive goes out, double-click the My Computer icon. (It's probably in the top-left corner of your desktop.)**

   This action opens the My Computer window, which shows you all the drives attached to your computer, the Control Panel, and a couple other handy things.

3. **Double-click the icon for your CD-ROM drive.**

   Another window opens, showing you all the folders and files on the CD.

If you are running Windows 3.1 (or 3.11), follow these steps to get to the items on the CD

1. **Insert the CD into your computer's CD-ROM drive.**

   Give your computer a moment to take a look at the CD.

2. **When the light on your CD-ROM drive goes out, double-click the Main program group.**

3. **Double-click the File Manager icon.**

   This action opens the File Manager program, which allows you to see the files and folders in any of the drives attached to your computer.

4. **Double-click the icon for your CD-ROM drive. (The drive icons appear under the toolbar buttons. Your CD-ROM drive is probably called the D:\ drive.)**

   Another window opens, showing you all the folders and files on the CD.

Installing the CD Software for Windows

1. **Double-click the file called** License.txt.

   This file contains the end-user license that you agree to by using the CD. When you are done reading the license, close the program (most likely NotePad) that displayed the file.

2. **Double-click the file called** Readme.txt.

   This file contains instructions about installing the software from this CD. It may be helpful to leave this text file open while you are using the CD.

3. **Double-click the folder for the software you are interested in.**

   Be sure to read the descriptions of the programs in this appendix (much of this information also shows up in the Readme file). These descriptions give you more precise information about the programs' folder names — and about finding and running the installer program.

4. **Find the file called** Setup.exe, **or** Install.exe, **or something similar, and double-click that file.**

   The program's installer will walk you through the process of setting up your new software.

 To run some of the programs, you may need to keep the CD inside your CD-ROM drive. This is a Good Thing. Otherwise, the installed program would have required you to install a very large chunk of the program to your hard drive space, which would have kept you from installing other software.

How to use the CD with the Mac OS

To install the items from the CD to your hard drive, follow these steps.

1. **Insert the CD into your computer's CD-ROM drive.**

   In a moment, an icon representing the CD you just inserted appears on your Mac desktop. Chances are, the icon looks like a CD-ROM.

2. **Double-click the CD icon to show the CD's contents**

3. **Double-click the license agreement icon.**

   This text file contains the end user license that you agree to by using the CD.

4. **Double-click the Read Me First icon.**

   This text file contains information about the CD's programs and any last-minute instructions you need to know about installing the programs on the CD that we don't cover in this appendix.

5. **To install most programs, just drag the program's folder from the CD window and drop it on your hard drive icon.**

6. **Some programs come with installer programs — with those you simply open the program's folder on the CD and double-click the icon with the words "Install" or "Installer."**

   After you have installed the programs that you want, you can eject the CD. Carefully place it back in the plastic jacket of the book for safekeeping.

What You'll Find on the CD

BBEdit Lite 4.0

For Mac OS

BBEdit Lite 4.0, from Bare Bones Software, Inc., is a Macintosh freeware text editor with powerful features that make creating HTML scripts for your Web pages easy. (See Figure C-1.)

The commercial version of this program, BBEdit 4.0, has stronger HTML editing features. I've also included a demo version of BBEdit 4.0 on the CD. This demo is fully-featured but cannot save files.

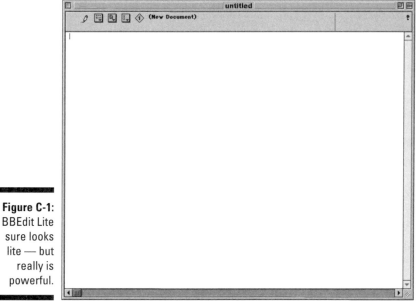

Figure C-1:
BBEdit Lite
sure looks
lite — but
really is
powerful.

Bongo

For Windows 95

`marimba\bongo\bongo1_1.exe`

From Marimba, Bongo is a Java-based development tool for creating Casta-net Channels. Using a traditional drag-and-drop interface, you can build a web channel from the ground up that includes a wide variety of Java func-tionality.

The version of Bongo included on the disk is a fully featured version. For more information on Bongo and how it works with the Castanet Tuner, visit Marimba at `www.marimba.com`

Castanet Tuner

For Windows 95 and Mac OS

```
marimba\tuner\tuner1_1.exe
```

From Marimba, the Castanet Tuner is the application that you need to view Castanet Channels. Castanet Tuner is free, and this is a fully featured version of the product. For setting up and configuring your Tuner, be sure to check out Chapter 10.

Castanet Transmitter

For Windows 95

```
marimba\tuner\transmit.exe
```

Every Castanet Channel is broadcast from a server using the Castanet server software, Transmitter. Although a single copy of Transmitter costs about $1000, you can use this trial version to help you get your channel up and working. The trial version includes five sessions, which should be enough for you to create a mock transmitter and test your Castanet channel. After the fight session, the product turns itself off.

Cool Edit

For Windows 3.1 and Windows 95

```
cooledit\win31\cool153.exe
```

```
cooledit\win95\c96setup.exe
```

From Syntrillium Software, Cool Edit is one of the most powerful shareware sounds editing utilities available on the Internet. You can use Cool Edit (shown in Figure C-2) to create a range of sounds and effects to be used throughout your web channel.

Cool Edit has many distinct feature sets to chose from. In the shareware version, you can only use two of these feature sets at any one time. Just be sure that one of the sets is always the "Save" set so you can save your work (as shown in Figure C-3)!

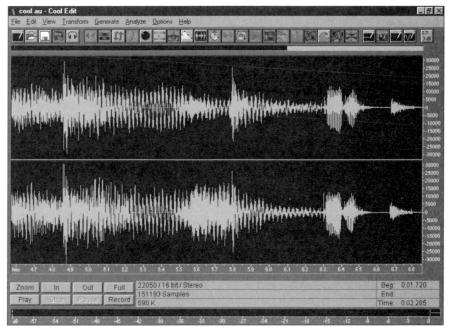

Figure C-2:
The Cool
Edit
interface
invites your
cool editing.

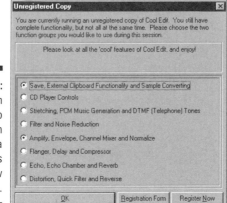

Figure C-3:
You can
choose two
function
groups at a
time in this
preview
version.

HotMetal 3.0 Lite

For Windows 95

```
hotmetal\hm3cv.exe
```

From SoftQuad, HotMetal is one of the more popular HTML editing tools on the Internet. With HotMetal's large tag icons, and drop-down menus, HTML scripting is a snap. (See Figure C-4.) The version of HotMetal included on the disk is a Lite version, meaning not all the features are available. For more information on HotMetal, visit the SoftQuad web site at www.softquad.com

Figure C-4:
HotMetal makes HTML editing easy.

Internet Explorer 4.0

For Windows 95

```
msie4\ie4setup.exe
```

Internet Explorer 4.0, the latest version of the popular web browser from Microsoft, includes support for CDF-based web channels. In addition to Active Channels, Explorer 4.0 includes components that will allow Windows users to use the Active Desktop, as well as Active Screen Savers. For more information on Internet Explorer, visit Microsoft at www.microsoft.com/ie/ie40/

PageMill 2.0

For Windows 95 and the Mac OS

`pagemill\pmwtry5.exe`

A true drag-and-drop HTML editor, PageMill allows you to create powerful HTML documents using the familiar Adobe graphical interface (see Figure C-5). With PageMill, you can create your entire web page with virtually no HTML scripting. Just put your graphics where you want them to appear on the page, and PageMill does all the scripting for you!

This is a tryout version of PageMill 2.0. For more information on this product, including pricing and availability, check out the Adobe web site at `www.adobe.com`

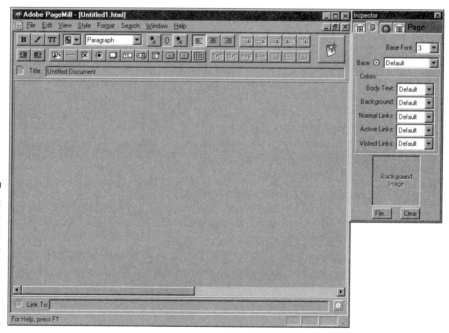

Figure C-5:
The Adobe PageMill HTML editor invites you to drag and drop.

PhotoShop

For Windows95 and the Mac OS

`photoshp\ps4try.exe`

From Adobe, Photoshop is the most powerful image-editing software on the market. From layering to filters to all types of image editing, Photoshop does it all. For any web-channel developer, Photoshop is a must-have.

The version of PhotoShop included on this disk (shown in Figure C-6) is a limited demo version. For more information on PhotoShop, including pricing and availability, visit the Adobe web site at `www.adobe.com`

Figure C-6:
Try your
hand at
PhotoShop.

Sample files on the disk

For reference, I've included a number of the Channel Swank files on the disk. Within the Swank folder, I've included the following items:

✔ The set-up files for Netcaster, as well as CDF files for PointCast and Internet Explorer web channels.

✔ Mock preview pages.

✔ Front pages for both Netcaster and Internet Explorer.

✔ A sample Netcaster Webtop, created from the Webtop Wizard.

✔ Some other sample pages for things such as the billboard, and the drop-down menu.

Although the graphics and the underlying JavaScript for all of these files works, there are a couple things you need to know:

✔ The links on each of the pages are dummy links. They don't actually connect to anything, so clicking them will just give you an error message.

✔ Most of the files work fine on both Explorer and Communicator. However, some of them don't work on Explorer because of the small differences in the way that Explorer handles syntax for JavaScript. This is most noticeable on the Channel Swank front page. It works fine on Communicator, but in Explorer you'll find that the icon animation doesn't quite work properly.

If You've Got Problems (Of the CD Kind)

I tried my best to compile programs that work on most computers with the minimum system requirements. Alas, your computer may differ, and some programs may not work properly for some reason.

The two likeliest problems are that you don't have enough memory (RAM) for the programs you want to use, or you have other programs running that are affecting installation or running of a program. If you get error messages like `Not enough memory` or `Setup cannot continue`, try one or more of these methods and then try using the software again:

✔ Turn off any anti-virus software that you have on your computer. Installers sometimes mimic virus activity and may make your computer incorrectly believe that it is being infected by a virus.

✔ Close all running programs. The more programs you're running, the less memory is available to other programs. Installers also typically update files and programs. So if you keep other programs running, installation may not work properly.

✔ Have your local computer store add more RAM to your computer. This is, admittedly, a drastic and somewhat expensive step. However, if you have a Windows 95 PC or a Mac OS computer with a PowerPC chip, adding more memory can really help the speed of your computer and allow more programs to run at the same time.

If you still have trouble with installing the items from the CD, please call the IDG Books Worldwide Customer Service phone number: 800-762-2974 (outside the U.S.: 317-596-5430).

Index

Notes

Notes

Notes

Notes

Notes

Notes

Notes

IDG Books Worldwide, Inc., End-User License Agreement

READ THIS. You should carefully read these terms and conditions before opening the software packet(s) included with this book ("Book"). This is a license agreement ("Agreement") between you and IDG Books Worldwide, Inc. ("IDGB"). By opening the accompanying software packet(s), you acknowledge that you have read and accept the following terms and conditions. If you do not agree and do not want to be bound by such terms and conditions, promptly return the Book and the unopened software packet(s) to the place you obtained them for a full refund.

1. **License Grant.** IDGB grants to you (either an individual or entity) a nonexclusive license to use one copy of the enclosed software program(s) (collectively, the "Software") solely for your own personal or business purposes on a single computer (whether a standard computer or a workstation component of a multiuser network). The Software is in use on a computer when it is loaded into temporary memory (RAM) or installed into permanent memory (hard disk, CD-ROM, or other storage device). IDGB reserves all rights not expressly granted herein.

2. **Ownership.** IDGB is the owner of all right, title, and interest, including copyright, in and to the compilation of the Software recorded on the CD-ROM ("Software Media"). Copyright to the individual programs recorded on the Software Media is owned by the author or other authorized copyright owner of each program. Ownership of the Software and all proprietary rights relating thereto remain with IDGB and its licensers.

3. **Restrictions on Use and Transfer.**

   (a) You may only (i) make one copy of the Software for backup or archival purposes, or (ii) transfer the Software to a single hard disk, provided that you keep the original for backup or archival purposes. You may not (i) rent or lease the Software, (ii) copy or reproduce the Software through a LAN or other network system or through any computer subscriber system or bulletin-board system, or (iii) modify, adapt, or create derivative works based on the Software.

   (b) You may not reverse engineer, decompile, or disassemble the Software. You may transfer the Software and user documentation on a permanent basis, provided that the transferee agrees to accept the terms and conditions of this Agreement and you retain no copies. If the Software is an update or has been updated, any transfer must include the most recent update and all prior versions.

4. **Restrictions on Use of Individual Programs.** You must follow the individual requirements and restrictions detailed for each individual program in Appendix C of this Book. These limitations are also contained in the individual license agreements recorded on the Software Media. These limitations may include a requirement that after using the program for a specified period of time, the user must pay a registration fee or discontinue use. By opening the Software packet(s), you will be agreeing to abide by the licenses and restrictions for these individual programs that are detailed in Appendix C and on the Software Media. None of the material on this Software Media or listed in this Book may ever be redistributed, in original or modified form, for commercial purposes.

5. **Limited Warranty.**

    (a) IDGB warrants that the Software and Software Media are free from defects in materials and workmanship under normal use for a period of sixty (60) days from the date of purchase of this Book. If IDGB receives notification within the warranty period of defects in materials or workmanship, IDGB will replace the defective Software Media.

    (b) **IDGB AND THE AUTHOR OF THE BOOK DISCLAIM ALL OTHER WARRANTIES, EXPRESS OR IMPLIED, INCLUDING WITHOUT LIMITATION IMPLIED WARRANTIES OF MER-CHANTABILITY AND FITNESS FOR A PARTICULAR PURPOSE, WITH RESPECT TO THE SOFTWARE, THE PROGRAMS, THE SOURCE CODE CONTAINED THEREIN, AND/OR THE TECHNIQUES DESCRIBED IN THIS BOOK. IDGB DOES NOT WARRANT THAT THE FUNCTIONS CONTAINED IN THE SOFTWARE WILL MEET YOUR REQUIREMENTS OR THAT THE OPERATION OF THE SOFTWARE WILL BE ERROR FREE.**

    (c) This limited warranty gives you specific legal rights, and you may have other rights that vary from jurisdiction to jurisdiction.

6. **Remedies.**

    (a) IDGB's entire liability and your exclusive remedy for defects in materials and workmanship shall be limited to replacement of the Software Media, which may be returned to IDGB with a copy of your receipt at the following address: Software Media Fulfillment Department, Attn.: *Web Channel Development For Dummies*, IDG Books Worldwide, Inc., 7260 Shadeland Station, Ste. 100, Indianapolis, IN 46256, or call 800-762-2974. Please allow three to four weeks for delivery. This Limited Warranty is void if failure of the Software Media has resulted from accident, abuse, or misapplication. Any replacement Software Media will be warranted for the remainder of the original warranty period or thirty (30) days, whichever is longer.

    (b) In no event shall IDGB or the author be liable for any damages whatsoever (including without limitation damages for loss of business profits, business interruption, loss of business information, or any other pecuniary loss) arising from the use of or inability to use the Book or the Software, even if IDGB has been advised of the possibility of such damages.

    (c) Because some jurisdictions do not allow the exclusion or limitation of liability for conse-quential or incidental damages, the above limitation or exclusion may not apply to you.

7. **U.S. Government Restricted Rights.** Use, duplication, or disclosure of the Software by the U.S. Government is subject to restrictions stated in paragraph (c)(1)(ii) of the Rights in Technical Data and Computer Software clause of DFARS 252.227-7013, and in subparagraphs (a) through (d) of the Commercial Computer-Restricted Rights clause at FAR 52.227-19, and in similar clauses in the NASA FAR supplement, when applicable.

8. **General.** This Agreement constitutes the entire understanding of the parties and revokes and supersedes all prior agreements, oral or written, between them and may not be modified or amended except in a writing signed by both parties hereto that specifically refers to this Agreement. This Agreement shall take precedence over any other documents that may be in conflict herewith. If any one or more provisions contained in this Agreement are held by any court or tribunal to be invalid, illegal, or otherwise unenforceable, each and every other provision shall remain in full force and effect.

Installation Instructions

How to use the CD with Microsoft Windows

1. Insert the CD into your computer's CD-ROM drive.

2. *Windows 95:* Double-click the My Computer icon (it's probably in the top-left corner of your desktop).

   Windows 3.1: Double-click the File Manager icon.

3. Double-click the icon for your CD-ROM drive.

   Note: In Windows 3.1, the drive icons appear under the toolbar buttons. Your CD-ROM drive is probably called the D:\ drive.

4. Double-click the icon for your CD-ROM drive.

5. Double-click the file called License.txt (which contains the end-user license that you agree to by using the CD) and double-click the file called Readme.txt (which contains instructions about installing the software from this CD).

   It's good to take care of legal stuff first and see if we needed to include any last-minute information!

6. Double-click the folder for the software you are interested in.

7. Find the file called Setup.exe, or Install.exe, or something similar, and double-click that file.

   The program's installer will walk you through the process of setting up your new software.

How to use the CD with the Mac OS

1. Insert the CD into your computer's CD-ROM drive.

2. Double-click the CD icon to show the CD's contents

3. Double-click the license agreement icon and the Read Me First icon in order to take care of legal stuff first and see if we needed to include any last-minute information.

4. To install most programs, just drag the program's folder from the CD window and drop it on your hard drive icon.

5. Some programs come with installer programs — with those you simply open the program's folder on the CD and double-click the icon with the words "Install" or "Installer."

Note: Detailed instructions on how to use the CD as well as system requirements and software descriptions are in the "What's on the CD?" appendix in this book.

IDG BOOKS WORLDWIDE. BOOK REGISTRATION

We want to hear from you!

Register This Book and Win!

Visit **http://my2cents.dummies.com** to register this book and tell us how you liked it!

✔ Get entered in our monthly prize giveaway.

✔ Give us feedback about this book — tell us what you like best, what you like least, or maybe what you'd like to ask the author and us to change!

✔ Let us know any other *...For Dummies* topics that interest you.

Your feedback helps us determine what books to publish, tells us what coverage to add as we revise our books, and lets us know whether we're meeting your needs as a *...For Dummies* reader. You're our most valuable resource, and what you have to say is important to us!

Not on the Web yet? It's easy to get started with *Dummies 101®: The Internet For Windows® 95* or *The Internet For Dummies®,* 4th Edition, at local retailers everywhere.

Or let us know what you think by sending us a letter at the following address:

...For Dummies Book Registration
Dummies Press
7260 Shadeland Station, Suite 100
Indianapolis, IN 46256
Fax 317-596-5498

BUSINESS AND GENERAL REFERENCE BOOK SERIES FROM IDG

COMPUTER BOOK SERIES FROM IDG